ALTERNATIVE ACTION THEORY

THEORY AND DECISION LIBRARY

General Editors: W. Leinfellner (*Vienna*) and G. Eberlein (*Munich*)

Series A: Philosophy and Methodology of the Social Sciences

Series B: Mathematical and Statistical Methods

Series C: Game Theory, Mathematical Programming and Operations Research

SERIES A: PHILOSOPHY AND METHODOLOGY OF THE SOCIAL SCIENCES

VOLUME 26

Scope: This series deals with the foundations, the general methodology and the criteria, goals and purpose of the social sciences. The emphasis in the Series A will be on well-argued, thoroughly analytical rather than advanced mathematical treatments. In this context, particular attention will be paid to game and decision theory and general philosophical topics from mathematics, psychology and economics, such as game theory, voting and welfare theory, with applications to political science, sociology, law and ethics.

The titles published in this series are listed at the end of this volume.

ALTERNATIVE ACTION THEORY

Simultaneously a Critique of Georg Henrik von Wright's Practical Philosophy

by

OTA WEINBERGER

Karl-Franzens-Universität, Institut für Rechtsphilosophie, Rechtssoziologie und Rechtsinformatik, Graz, Austria

KLUWER ACADEMIC PUBLISHERS

DORDRECHT / BOSTON / LONDON

A C.I.P. Catalogue record for this book is available from the Library of Congress.

Published by Kluwer Academic Publishers,
P.O. Box 17, 3300 AA Dordrecht, The Netherlands.

Sold and distributed in North, Central and South America,
by Kluwer Academic Publishers,
101 Philip Drive, Norwell, MA 02061, U.S.A.

In all other countries, sold and distributed
by Kluwer Academic Publishers,
P.O. Box 322, 3300 AH Dordrecht, The Netherlands.

Printed on acid-free paper

English translation of Ota Weinberger, *Alternative Handlungstheorie: gleichzeitig eine Auseinandersetzung mit Georg Henrik von Wrights praktischen Philosophie*,
Böhlau Verlag, Wien-Köln-Weimar, Austria, 1996. 310 S.
Translator: Jacques Zwart

Published with the support of the Austrian Federal Ministry for
Science and Traffic and of the Alfred Schachner Memorial Foundation.

Contents

Foreword

This book has both a short and a long 'case history'. It was directly occasioned, first, by the recent appearance in the German language of two books by G. H. von Wright: "Normen, Werte und Handlungen" (Norms, Values and Actions), Frankfurt (Main) 1994, and "Erkenntnis als Lebensform. Zeitgenössische Wanderungen eines philosophischen Logikers" (Knowledge as a Mode of Life. Contemporary wanderings of a philosophical logician), Vienna/Cologne/Weimar 1995; and, second, by the decision of his friends, professors Meggle, Krawietz and Valdés, to stage a two-day discussion in April 1996 at the Bielefeld, Germany, Center for Interdisciplinary Research ("Zentrum für interdisziplinäre Forschung", or ZiF) on von Wright's book, "Normen, Werte und Handlungen" (Norms, Values and Actions) with its author. I had the very special honor and pleasure of being invited to this symposium. In anticipation of that discussion I prepared a small compendium of theses, which eventually took the form of this book.

My more fundamental motive for writing this book has, on the other hand, a long 'case history'. In my life and thinking, G. H. von Wright has played a very important part, even though I can neither count myself among his pupils, nor among his scholarly companions on life's path. Like probably anyone interested in logical analysis as an instrument of practical philosophy, I am indebted to von Wright for a great many suggestions and stimulations, but it was not primarily by him that my path was determined.

Rather, it was my famous teacher František (Franz) Weyr – a close friend and Czech collaborator of Hans Kelsen – who, through a remark in a lecture on legal philosophy, opened my eyes to the problem field of the logic of norms. He pointed out that the question whether a norm is a judgment (a proposition in the logical sense) had not been settled, hence was open. The problem he addressed in this form was later to become the subject of investigations by his friend, the Czech economist and logician Karel Engliš, under whose influence[1] it eventually led to the skepticism displayed with regard to the logic of norms by Hans Kelsen in his later period. I immediately realized that we were confronted here with the fundamental question whether there is such a thing as a logic of norms at all, rather than merely with the question whether norm-sentences can be regarded as a kind of descriptive propositions. For many years I pondered this problem from various angles, fairly unburdened by the tradition of logic and guided instead by my conviction that the logical analysis of norms and a theory of deduction according to the logic of norms are indispensable prerequisites for a structure theory of law and for the theory of legal dynamics.[2]

Thus my answer to Weyr's question went in a direction exactly opposed to Engliš's and Kelsen's skepticism.[3]

My first contact with G. H. von Wright arose from my critique of his 1951 publication on deontic logic and particularly of his opinion

---

[1]I am aware, having been so informed personally, that Kelsen was familiar with Engliš's arguments against the possibility of a logic of norms (unfamiliar though he was with the Czech language). Kelsen moreover knew my book "Die Sollsatzproblematik in der modernen Logik" (The Problems of Imperative Sentences in Modern Logic), Rozpravy ČSAV, 1957, which comments in detail on Engliš's theory. Kelsen's arguments are so closely related to Engliš's presentation that there can be no doubt as to Kelsen's research in his later period having been influenced by his Czech friend.

[2]It was only later that I made a thorough study of logic and even qualified for lecturing on this subject in Prague.

[3]After the 1947 appearance of Engliš's Malá logika [Kleine Logik] (Short Logic), Melantrich, Prague, I criticized his skepticism within academic circles, but, aware as I was that Engliš was among the political and ideological persecutees after the 1948 Communist revolution, it was only in 1957 that I published my critique – then already available in the form of an article in Czech – in the book mentioned in Footnote 1 above.

that a sentence of the form '$O(p \to q)$' can present the structure of the conditional norm-sentence. What impressed me was the fact that von Wright soon already took a very critical view of his own 1951 system, concluding his pertinent considerations in a 1958 letter to me with the remark: "I hope to be able to do fresh work on the subject in future."

Great was my gratitude when Prof. von Wright invited me to the 1962 Helsinki congress on logic. While the Czechoslovak authorities did not permit me to attend this congress, they took note of the fact that my work was finding attention abroad, a circumstance which for me, a non-party member working in a field where party membership was a sine qua non for any appointment, was existentially of great importance at the time.

While my interests, views and research intentions are in very essential respects in agreement with those of G. H. von Wright, there are also very essential differences in our respective approaches and attitudes towards life.

It was always with great respect that I observed the famous author's vast erudition and universal view of things, both undoubtedly resulting in part from his expressly declared interest in history, including the history of ideas. I myself have never had any particular predilection for the historical sciences, profoundly doubting as I do the objectivity and persuasive strength of any interpretations of the great events in history. Nor has the history of ideas ever commanded my primary interest. Rather, my philosophical reflections have always sprung from an urge to clarify scientific questions, first and foremost problems of structure and proof.

What we have in common is our joint conviction of the semantic and logical peculiarity of practical philosophy (in a broad sense) as well as the endeavor to carry structure theory and logical analysis as far as possible into the realm of action-related thinking. However, the paths by which we try to reach this goal are wholly different: While Prof. von Wright makes use of everything which the tradition of logic and of philosophical analysis is able to offer, erecting his investigations – usually in a most original fashion – on that foundation, I prefer instead to keep myself largely unburdened by previous relevant knowledge and the history of ideas, proceeding, as it were, as a reflective amateur.

Agreement prevails among us in the question of non-cognitivism, with both of us clearly recognizing that non-cognitivism and relativism of values by no means exclude rational argumentation. I also perceive a fair similarity in our respective stands on the determinism vs. indeterminism dispute.

In a methodological respect there seems to be a substantial difference between von Wright's and my own understanding of the relationship between language and philosophy. Von Wright, probably influenced here by Wittgenstein, tends to equate philosophical analyses with linguistic ones, evidently recognizing that non-conformity to linguistic customs is a valid argument to be given consideration. I, for my part, reject such manners of argumentation: "People don't talk that way" is not a philosophical argument to me. Argumentations on the basis of ordinary language are doomed to failure because of the important discovery of the difference between the superficial and the in-depth structure of statements. Though able to function satisfactorily in communication, ordinary language may nevertheless distort structures in trying to represent them. To me, the linguistic turnabout in philosophy does not mean the recognition of language as the yardstick for argumentation, but merely the important reminder that any philosophical problem field needs to be examined with a view to the possibility and structure of its linguistic representation.

Unlike Wittgenstein, I am furthermore of the opinion that there are true philosophical problems that cannot be reduced to linguistic ones.

Philosophical analysis is not linguistic analysis, but rather the analysis of problem situations, in which, admittedly, language is always involved as well. This means an essential difference from the linguo-analytical approach and in particular from Ordinary Language Philosophy; the goal is the structural analysis of the given concrete situation, whose linguistic representation is only one of the necessary means toward this end. Wittgenstein's analyses are in essence analyses of problem situations. Philosophizing, however, he characterizes as mere linguistic analysis, thus subjecting philosophical thinking to the critique by ordinary language, although actually it is the other way around: ordinary language is subject to the critique by in-depth structural analyses.[4]

Von Wright considers norm logic (deontic logic) as an offspring of modal logic, whereas to me it is a product of the problem situation and of the requirements imposed by the relevant practical disciplines. I therefore regard it as impermissible to apply logical relationships valid in some other system to the logic of norms, merely because certain structural similarities are perceived.

Both in von Wright's writings and in the development of my own reflections on the logic of norms the concept of action has acquired a more and more significant role, be it in wholly different ways: to von Wright, actions are contents of the norms, thus necessitating a theory on the structure of these contents, whereas in my case the theory of action becomes a philosophical framework, and it is only within this framework that norms and their function can be understood and explained. This information-theoretical action concept provides a philosophical basis and motivation for the caesura between Ought and Is, for the semantic dualism of descriptive-cognitive and practical statements, since the determination of the action through information processing requires two categorially different – namely: descriptive and practical – types of information.

[4]Cf. *O. Weinberger*, Tiefengrammatik und Problemsituation. Eine Untersuchung über den Charakter der philosophischen Analyse (In-depth Grammar and Problem Situation. An investigation into the nature of philosophical analysis), in: *Wittgenstein and his Impact on Contemporary Thought. Proceedings of the 2nd International Wittgenstein Symposium, Kirchberg 1977*, Hölder–Pichler–Tempski, Vienna 1978, p.290–297. In this paper I tried to show that Wittgenstein always performs his analyses within the situational context and within the framework of pragmatic relationships, thus engaging in problem situation analysis, whereas in his theory of philosophy he characterizes philosophizing as mere linguistic analysis and language critique. (See Appendix).

The explication of the action concept by means of the transformation concept as von Wright sees it appears to me to be insufficient for a definition of the action concept. Nor does von Wright's thesis that for any given action a corresponding contrafactual assertion will always apply ("If the subject of the action had not behaved in this or that fashion, the result of the action would not have come to pass") suffice, in my opinion, to delimit the given action from other modes of behavior of the subject.

In entitling this book "Alternative Action Theory", I wanted to give expression to the fact that I am neither an adherent of a behavioristic-causalistic approach to action theory, nor a champion of an intentionalist and transformation-logical view as propagated by G. H. von Wright. In my view of things, action theory acquires its central position in practical philosophy together with the conception of institutions as frameworks of social action.

The action theory concept presented by me in this book is based on the one hand on anthropological insights, while being on the other hand a theoretical construction by which the structure of the action is explained by means of the information-processing fundamental for the action. That man in general is capable of action, able to realize intentional behavior as a function of information is something we know from experience. It is likewise in agreement with our experience when we attribute this capacity to act not only to individual human beings, but also to collectives and institutions. And finally, the relationship between the action and institutions as the established and relatively fixed framework of the action is likewise verifiable by experience. For all that, however, the theory itself is not a summarization of this experiential basis, but rather a theoretical construction which makes the core of the action concept explicit, namely through the structures and operations of the information processes that determine the action.

This theoretical construction must prove its worth. To this end, use must be made of methodological principles. It is essential in this connection that the analyses of the action comprise two fundamentally different approaches as application fields of the formalism determining the action: 1. the reflections of the agent, the acting person, on how he should act, and 2. the interpretative effort of the observer who, by interpretatively reconstructing the intentional characteristics of the action, tries to understand the observed behavior of the acting person as an action.

In the introduction to his book "Erkenntnis als Lebensform" (Knowledge as a Mode of Life) von Wright writes: "As a young man I was hardly bothered by political and social questions; (...) worries about 'the state of the world' did not particularly oppress me in my younger years" (p.8). Although I myself have never – except for the time of the Prague Spring – been politically active, or even wished to be, the social question has always been an urgent problem for me, as have questions of democratic life, particularly in the face of discriminations and persecutions.[5]

The translation of the original German book into English was obligingly performed with great care by Mr. Jacques Zwart, Dipl.-Met. I am indebted to the Austrian Ministry for Science and Traffic and to the Alfred Schachner Memorial Foundation for their financial support of the publication of the English version of the book. I likewise owe thanks to Messrs. Kluwer academic publishers for having included this book into their edition program and having published it in an attractive form. I thank Mr. PhDr. Karel Hlavoň for his exact preparation of the manuscript for publication.

Ota Weinberger

December 1997

[5]I never was a Marxist, however, nor a member of any political party. During the Prague Spring I was active on the executive board of the Club of Non-Party Members (KAN).

Chapter 1

The Nature of Logic and the Concept of the Logic of Norms

In a passage of the introduction to his book "Logical Studies" (1957) von Wright writes: "Deontic logic gets part of its philosophical significance from the fact that norms and valuations, though removed from the realm of truth, yet are subjected to logical law. This shows that logic, so to speak, has a wider reach than truth." (p.III)

A noteworthy if not quite convincing statement, for deontic logic regards deontic sentences as arguments of truth-functional junctors, while passing over the actual basic philosophical problems inherent in the nature and possibility of deduction in the field of norm-sentences. Moreover, the existence of deductions according to the logic of norms was called into doubt for some time by von Wright himself.[1]

[1]G. H. von Wright, Bedingungsnormen – ein Prüfstein für die Normenlogik (Conditional Norms – A Touchstone for the Logic of Norms), in: W. Krawietz et al.(eds.), *Theorie der Normen. Festgabe für Ota Weinberger zum 65. Geburtstag* (Theory of Norms. Presented to Ota Weinberger as a tribute on his 65th birthday), Duncker & Humblot, Berlin 1984, p.449, where we read: "In the end I arrived at the view that between norms there exist no logical relationships at all. Even the 'subsumption inference according to the logic of norms' is not a logical conclusion."

The above quotation from the year 1957 presupposes that a logic of norms (deontic logic) has a right to exist and says implicitly that deontic logic works with objects of thought that cannot be characterized as true or false, namely norms, from which conclusions are then drawn on the nature of logic. Given the fact that deontic logic actually remains entirely within the framework of truth relationships, the probandum is not conclusively proven; and the possibility of a genuine logic of norms, as the study of logical relationships between objects of thought incapable of being true, is not discussed and examined on its merits at all.

Inasmuch as prominent thinkers, J. Jörgensen, K. Engliš, Hans Kelsen and to some extent even von Wright himself have raised skeptical objections to the possibility of a logic of norms I deem it expedient to ask the general philosophical and methodological question what preconditions must be fulfilled so that a logical theory may be built up. Next, the question will have to be discussed whether an envisioned logic of norms can fulfill these conditions. In addition it will be meaningful to discuss the various arguments of the skeptics, and finally to analyze, from the opposite direction, the reasons why practical philosophy does need a genuine logic of norms.

1.1. Take Jörgen Jörgensen seriously!

The question as to the possibility of a logic of norms can, in my opinion, be understood in a twofold way: 1. Can, on the basis of the historically handed-down concept of logic and the established concept apparatus of this discipline (comprising e.g. the customary concepts of contradiction, of deduction), a logic of norms be called into being? 2. Is it meaningful, expedient or maybe even necessary to recognize a theory of structure and deduction as logic in an expanded sense,

---

Furthermore: *id.*, Is and Ought, in: E. Bulygin et al.(eds.), *Man, Law and Modern Forms of Life*, Kluwer, Dordrecht 1985, p.263–281 (translated as "Sein und Sollen", in: G. H. von Wright, *Normen, Werte und Handlungen*, Suhrkamp, Frankfurt/M 1994, p.19–43).

namely with a generalized concept apparatus, and to introduce this expanded conception of logic into philosophy?

If we keep the difference between these two types of questions clearly before our eyes, we cannot only understand those remarks of J. Jörgensen from the years 1937/38[2] which express the basic thoughts of all skeptics with respect to a logic of norms, we can also gain clear insights into the question of the possibility of a (genuine) logic of norms.

Although Jörgensen's work was widely known, hardly anyone subjected his skeptical objections to a philosophical critique.[3]

The development of deontic logic proceeded on its course unburdened by this entire problem complex. If one had stopped to reflect on Jörgensen's dilemma, and remained stuck there, many interesting insights on the deontic logics might never have come about, but one would also have avoided wrong paths and misunderstandings about these systems.

It is undisputed that logic deals traditionally with the structure of and the relationships between descriptive sentences (thoughts) and that the attendant concept apparatus of logical methodology is mainly defined with the aid of truth relations. Contradiction, consistency, deduction (inference), the extensional functors and other basic concepts that one works with in logic have been coined for working with statements (propositions), and ex definitione are not applicable to norm-sentences (insofar as one regards these as incapable of being true, which one as a rule – and rightly – does).

Hence it can hardly be disputed that the question as to the possibility of a logic of norms on a conservative conceptual basis (question 1) must be answered in the negative: If one sticks to the traditional concept apparatus, there is no such thing as a logic of

[2] J. Jörgensen, Imperatives and Logic, in: *Erkenntnis*, Vol.7, 1937/38, p.288–296.

[3] An exception was my book "*Die Sollsatzproblematik in der modernen Logik*" (The Problems of Ought-Sentences in Modern Logic), Rozpravy ČSAV, Prague 1958.

norms (or, put more precisely, such a discipline can then only be based on a purely formalistic conception, with any interpretative explanation being dispensed with and logic being regarded only as a formal game).

If one now focuses on the second question, arguments from tradition will then be out of place; one can then, from the perspective of the history of ideas, only point out that analogous conceptual expansions have been and still are wholly customary in the history of the sciences. And then two points of view will be decisive as to whether a logic of norms is possible:

(a) What preconditions must be present so that a logic-like doctrine can be constituted, and are these present in the case of norms (or of norm-sentences)?

(b) Is there in the field of the practical disciplines (especially of jurisprudence and ethics) a need for a logic of norms?

The second question can, in my opinion, be unequivocally answered in the positive with the aid of two arguments. For one thing, the fact that – as far as I know – all skeptics on the logic of norms (from Jörgensen to Engliš, Kelsen and von Wright) offer in the same breath "substitute theories" so as to avoid the absurdities that would follow from a denial of logical relationships between norms, or of conclusions with normative elements, proves that a logic of norms is necessary. Second, it is just as little possible to get along without the concept of the inconsistency of a system of norms in the sense of a logical defect as without some sort of logical conclusions with normative elements[4]: What sense would a general norm make if no individualizing conclusion from it would follow (on the basis of some sort of regula de omni et nullo)? After all, the universal quantificator is defined by precisely such a rule. And what pragmatic rule would a general norm play if nothing would follow from it for the individual case, considering that in reality only individual cases exist? How could a theory of law dynamics be drawn up if there were no such

[4] Here the concepts "inconsistency", "contradiction", "conclusion" naturally are not to be understood in a truth-functional sense, but in a specific one still to be defined.

thing as deduction from norms? How could one define the concept of material derogation if there were no logical contradiction between norms? How could one even so much as articulate the problem of conflicts of duties if there were no incompatibility between norms? How could one speak of inconsistency of a system of norms if there existed no logical relationships between norm-sentences? The list of problems that would be unsolvable without a logic of norms might still be considerably expanded.

The skeptics with respect to a logic of norms – beginning with Dubislav and Jörgensen – did not base their doubts on a claim that in the disciplines of the logic of norms no logical relationships can be ascertained, or that the practice of thinking in these fields knows of no deductions with normative conclusions; on the contrary, they claim that the thinking and argumentation practice of these fields speaks unconcernedly of contradictions between norms and draws conclusions with the persuasive power of evidence, while noting simultaneously, however, that in accordance with the concepts, introduced into logic, of logical contradiction and inference (deduction) it is inexplicable how the argumentations of the thinking practice in the normative disciplines can be grasped and explained on the basis of the traditional concept apparatus. The spiritus rector of the skeptics on a logic of norms, Jörgen Jörgensen, has presented his doubts in a reflection which in the philosophical literature has received the name "Jörgensen's dilemma". The dilemma comes about precisely because of the plausibility, even the apparent indisputability, of the following theses:

(a) Norm-sentences (in Jörgensen's terminology 'imperatives') cannot be assigned the attributes 'true'/'false'.

(b) The concept 'inference' (logical entailment) is defined in logic as a truth relationship and is therefore applicable only to sentences to which truth values can be ascribed.

(c) There are deductions in which norm-sentences (imperatives) occur as elements (premises, conclusions) and which in the thinking practice of the normative disciplines are attributed the same evidential force as the indicative deductions.

Hence the source of the dilemma is not the denial of normative conclusions, but, on the contrary, rather their universally recognized evidential power.

I find it amazing that the evident answer, i.e. the solution to the dilemma, was not sought in a revision and generalization of the basic concepts of logic, but that, instead, skepticism came about as to the very idea of a logic of norms and that every effort was made to arrive at a conservative satisfaction – i.e. one not changing the traditional concept apparatus of logic – of the logical-analytical needs of the normative disciplines. Substitute theories were proposed which were not, nor could be, successful. (I will revert to this question later.)

1.2. *General preconditions of logical theories*

Let us determine the field of possible logical systems by discussing the preconditions which objects of logical systems must fulfill.

Objects of logical systems are ideal entities, not psychical acts or thoughts in the psychological sense, i.e. mental contents experienced by a specific person. Today – since Edmund Husserl[5] – it is communis opinio that it is not thoughts in the sense of psychical acts (mental contents of such acts) that constitute the object of logic, but thoughts in the logical sense, i.e. thoughts as ideal entities, which may, to be sure, be contents of psychical acts, but which, independently of what actually occurs on the mental plane, can be understood as ideal entities. For it is evident that consequences from presupposed thoughts may follow logically, regardless of whether a thinking subject realizes or perceives these consequences. Psychologically, in a suitable sequence of acts, sentences can occur as "conclusions" which are not valid consequences from the premises. On the other hand it is likewise possible that a subject conceives of a class of sentences (as premises), but does not, nor is able to, draw the consequences derivable from

[5]E. Husserl, *Logische Untersuchungen* (Logical Studies), 2 vols., Max Niemeyer, Halle/Saale 1900/1901.

them. The determination of consequences is a logical question, not a matter of the sequence of psychical acts or contents of acts, nor a matter of the subjective capability of insight of subjects. *Logic and logical analysis must, as a matter of principle, be conceived of anti-psychologistically.*

Thoughts as objects of logical analysis or of logical theories are linguistically formulizable. This postulate accounts for the fact that in a given linguistic system it is possible to distinguish between form and content. It is possible to draw up a constitutive system which determines the structure of the language, with the individual sentence of the language then coming into existence by assigning to the elements of the sentence structure (representable by formulae) values of the corresponding semiotic category.

Through the constitutive system (the formation rules of the language) the field of the forms is determined which constitute the object of the logical discipline, and the possibility is created to carry out formal operations, i.e. operations determined only by structure rather than by meaning.

The validity of logical relationships is determined by the structures of and the connections and links between sentences of the language, not by objective relationships of the objects of this world. (Logic is not a generalized image of the world or of the subjects spoken about by the sentences, as e.g. some Marxists believe.) In descriptive language, too, structural and consequential relationships do not owe their validity to a corresponding structure of reality. This manifests itself also in the fact that these relationships and the logical rules are valid also for possible worlds (including contrafactual ones). Furthermore, the validity of entailments is independent of the factual truth of the premises hence is not affected by the factual untruthfulness of the premises. Yet untrue premises obviously do not portray any reality.

Logical research concentrates on two aspects between which a certain internal kinship exists: on the compatibility of sentences, and on the determination of consequences from premises. From the structure of sentences – regardless of what they speak of – it may be determined whether two presented sentences are mutually compatible or incompatible. Co-existence of sentences (the fact of their being simultaneously asserted) can be proven to be impermissible, purely from the structure of the sentences, without paying any attention to facts. From premises, conclusions may be arrived at on the basis of the structural relationships between premises and conclusions. This determination of the conclusions from premises is form-determined and independent of the relationship of the sentences to reality (of their truth).

The presentation of logic, i.e. the formal determination of compatibility (incompatibility) and derivability, can be realized differently: through a system of axioms and transformation rules, through a system of deduction rules, or through truth rules (the so-called semantic presentation of logic).

When logic is pursued as a purely formal game, the concept of truth does not enter into the picture at all: the possibility in the sentences being true is not a precondition of this "game". On this platform the possibility of a logic of norms cannot be excluded. Philosophical analysis is not concerned, however, with a purely formal possibility, but with an explanation of the meaningfulness and justification of such operations.

1.3. Can norms (norm-sentences) be regarded as objects of logic?

We will now have to examine whether norm-sentences meet the preconditions of logic and whether the fundamental relationships and operations can be meaningfully introduced for them.

Norms can be regarded as thoughts in themselves that are linguistically formularizable. Hence a logicistic (anti-psychologistic) view of norms is evidently possible and on many grounds reasonable. It is possible to construct a constitutive system of language that determines the form of the norm-sentences in which form normative contents may then be represented.

To me it seems evident that there exists incompatibility between norms, e.g. between 'p shall be' and 'non-p shall be'. The reason is neither conditioned by experience, nor by volition, but rather decreed by the constitutive system of the normative language, though not as a truth relationship between these two norm-sentences, hence not by the definition that these two sentences cannot be simultaneously true. One might define - without attributing to norm-sentences the true/false characteristic – that the norm-sentences N_1 and N_2 will precisely then be incompatible when the contents (the states of affairs) decreed to be prescribed) of N_1 and N_2 are incompatible from the point of view of descriptive logic.

The testing of ought-sentences for logical incompatibility is based on a test whether the contents of these sentences are compatible from the point of view of descriptive logic; but the compatibility or incompatibility of the norm-sentences does not depend on this finding alone. It depends also on the normative operator; if this operator is a prescriptive one, then there will be incompatibility between the sentences, whereas there will be no incompatibility when the norm-sentences are permissive ones. ['Pp' and '$P\neg p$' are compatible.)

The epistemological and methodological consequences of the logical incompatibility of norm-sentences differ to a not unimportant extent from those of a contradiction between descriptive sentences. *But there is no doubt that the incompatibility of norm-sentences is of a purely logical nature:* it is determined by the structural relationship between the expressions used, thus being independent of the experience and practical orientations of the subjects concerned (the law-giver or the addressee of the norm).

No model can conform to inherently contradictory systems of propositions. Norm systems containing incompatible norms can exist in social reality, where, although marred by a logical shortcoming, they do not lose their function or social importance.[6]

The process of deduction confers upon the conclusion thereby reached a hereditary property if the starting propositions (premises) possess this property. That, so to speak, is the pragmatic achievement of deduction. In the deduction theory of the descriptive language it is the truth value "true" which constitutes this hereditary property. For deduction according to the logic of norms a different hereditary property must be introduced, e.g. the concept of validity (in a norm system under current consideration).

The generalized theory of deduction can be readily represented, but with respect to deduction according to the logic of norms attention must be paid to the following particularities:

1. The validity of norms is always to be understood relative to a specific system ("Norm N is valid" always means: "N is a component of a norm system under consideration").

2. Objects of the logic of norms are two semantically different categories of sentences: descriptive sentences and norm-sentences. Both types of sentences may be elements (premises, conclusions) of deductive relationships.

3. With respect to the hereditary property transmitted by the deduction there are, for a system with two disjunctive categories of sentences – such as the logic of norms – two construction possibilities: (a) The two sentence categories of the logic of norms are attributed different hereditary properties (truth for descriptive sentences, validity for norm-sentences), and as a result of the transmission precisely that hereditary property of the conclusion will then come about which conforms to the semantic character of the conclusion: In the case of descriptive conclusions their truth will be inferred, in the case of norm conclusions their validity. (b) A superordinate concept superordinated to the hereditary properties of the sentence categories is introduced

[6] Cf. O. Weinberger, Ex falso quodlibet in der deskriptiven und in der präskriptiven Sprache (Ex Falso Quodlibet in Descriptive and in Prescriptive Language), in: *Rechtstheorie* 6/1975, p.17–32.

(e.g. "ranking") with which the hereditary operation is carried out and which thereupon will assume the meaning of truth when acting as an attribute of statements, and the meaning of validity when attributed to norm-sentences.

That it is possible to introduce the deduction concept regardless of the nature of the hereditary property (and especially regardless of the truth concept in this function) has been shown by Alchourrón and Martino in their essay "Logic Without Truth".[7]

In their paper "Logic Without Truth", Alchourrón and Martino expound a consequentialistic view of logic, regarding as they do the consequence concept as basic and defining it formally, without recourse to the truth concept, by the following three postulates:

1. $A \subset Cn(A)$ – this inclusion expresses the fact that every proposition is contained in the set of its consequences.

2. $Cn(A) = Cn(Cn(A))$ – the set of consequences of the set of consequences of A is identical with the set of consequences of A.

3. If $A \subset B$, then $Cn(A) \subset Cn(B)$ – if A is a subset of B, then the set of consequences of A is likewise a subset of the set of consequences of B.

This definition is evidently independent of any semantic interpretation, in particular of an interpretation by means of the truth concept. Therefore it is also applicable to non-descriptive sentences such as norm-sentences.

1.4. Main types of substitute theories

It is not possible to draw up a complete list of all arguments against the possibility of a (genuine) logic of norms and to discuss the substitute theories connected therewith. The possibility will always remain open that new arguments can be found and that new methods for substitute theories will be proposed. The field of possible theoretical

[7] C. E. Alchourrón, A. A. Martino, Logic Without Truth, in: *Ratio Juris*, 1990, p.46–67.

conceptions is never a priori overseeable. Nevertheless I find it meaningful to present a cursory overview of the basic approaches to substitute theories, for the fundamental ideas repeat themselves in various modifications.

We are indebted here first of all to *Jörgensen*, who as far back as in 1937/38 presented two proposals for arriving at substitute theories.

1. Jörgensen speaks of the splitting-up of the imperative into an imperative and an indicative component (in *Hare's* terminology one would speak of neustic and phrastic) and expounds the view that the logical relationships and logical operations pertain only to the indicative component, so that a specific logic of norms is unnecessary, these relationships and operations being based on descriptive logic.[8] The most important continuation of this approach – marked by a conceptual expansion in that it no longer concerns only norms, but also e.g. questions – is *Alchourrón's* and *Bulygin's* doctrine, based on a general semiotic theory specifically designed to this end, of the expressive conception of norms.

It can be shown that the limitation of the logical character to the propositional content will not work and that the construction, according to this recipe, of a logic of norms, or more precisely: of a substitute theory for the logic of norms, is not possible. I will not enter here into a discussion of all attempts of this nature and will deal briefly instead with the Alchourrón-Bulygin variant.[9]

[8] J. Jörgensen, *Imperatives and Logic*, op. cit.; furthermore my detailed critique in: Die Sollsatzproblematik in der modernen Logik (The Problems of Ought Sentences in Modern Logic), op.cit. (reprinted in: id., *Studien zur Normenlogik und Rechtsinformatik* (Studies on the Logic of Norms and Legal Informatics), J. Schweitzer, Berlin 1974, p.59–186). The possibility of such a substitute theory was suggested as far back as in 1935 by W. Dubislav. Cf. W. Dubislav, Zur Unbegründbarkeit von Forderungssätzen (On the Non-Justifiability of Postulating Sentences), in: *Theoria* 1935, p.330–342.

[9] C. Alchourrón, E. Bulygin, The Expressive Conception of Norms. In: R. Hilpinen (Ed.), *New Studies in Deontic Logic*. Reidel, Dordrecht 1981, p.95–124; O. Weinberger, The Expressive Conception of Norms – an Impasse for the Logic of Norms, in: *Law and Philosophy* 4(1985), p.165–198.

The semantics developed by Alchourrón and Bulygin rests in essence on the following theses:

(a) Propositions are the sole bearers of meaning, they alone have meaning in a semantic sense.

(b) The propositions are to be understood in a non-psychologistic sense, hence as ideal entities between which logical relationships may exist and which in any given case are to be so understood that a class of propositions implies a class of consequences of these propositions that explicitly expresses the meaning of the presupposed propositions.

(c) Propositions can be used in speech acts in various ways, e.g. in an assertive, commanding, questioning or still other way. This gives rise to different, mutually separated classes of propositions.

(d) The propositions posited in pragmatically different ways can be designated by special symbols, e.g. the assertion symbol '⊢' or the command symbol '!'. These symbols do not create any differences on the semantic level; they merely express what the speaker does when placing the propositions in a speech act. It is expressly emphasized by the authors that these indicators contribute nothing to the meaning of the propositions uttered.

It is a mistake to assume that the indication of the pragmatic indicator is semantically irrelevant. The thesis claiming that the logical relationships of the different types of sentence – assertions, norms (imperatives), questions, etc. – are determined solely by the propositional contents and not by the pragmatic indicator is wrong and can be readily and convincingly disproved.

The users of language undoubtedly must always be aware whether a content (a proposition) is placed in this or that pragmatic role. Hence disjunctive and, in their nature, different classes of propositions are formed, with the characteristic of the type of class establishing different categories of meaning, so that it is absurd to claim that the knowledge whether a communication acts as a question, norm or as a thesis describing facts is semantically irrelevant.

A confrontation of the use of propositions in different pragmatic functions in accordance with the Alchourrón-Bulygin theory clearly shows the absurdity and untenability of the thesis that the logical relationships pertain only to the substantial, propositional component of the sentences. It may be readily shown that the logical relationships are not exclusively determined by the propositional content of the speech acts. In my opinion it must be assumed that speech acts can be expressions of semantically different sentences. If the Alchourrón-Bulygin conception of the speech acts and of the logical relationships of the speech act contents were correct, then, given the contradiction between the propositions 'p', '$\neg p$', one would, as a result, also have to regard 'Pp'/'$P\neg p$' as a contradiction between permissions and '$?p$'/'$?\neg p$' as a contradiction between questions. However, these evidently are compatible pairs of sentences.

Not devoid of importance as an objection to the Alchourrón-Bulygin semantics is the fact that certain important types of sentences cannot be built up in this system at all. What I have in mind here are the questions of the type 'What time is it?' and the hypothetical norm-sentences, whose importance for the prescriptive discourse is beyond dispute. Through classes of conditioning and conditioned propositions, conditional norm-sentences can as little be constituted as the relationships deduced therefrom, namely the modus-ponens and subsumptive conclusions.

Despite their explicit rejection of the possibility of a logic of norms, the authors manage to bring about some sort of logical entailment for the field of norms by introducing the concept of a normative system, which they define as follows: If A is the class of the propositions posited through command acts, then the normative system is the class of consequences from A: $Cn(A)$.[10] The purpose and function of the introduction of this concept evidently is the fact that with the aid of the set of consequences implicit commands can be deduced. When commands are given whose contents are A_1, A_2 ... $A_n(\equiv A)$, then every contents A_j for which $A_j \in Cn(A)$ holds is likewise regarded

[10] "We can now define the concept of a normative system as the set of all propositions that are consequences of the explicitly commanded propositions" op.cit., p.101.

as a command. Though not explicitly expressed by the authors, this rule undoubtedly lies at the basis of their system; instead, they only speak of the analogous relationships of the normative sentences, which they define as assertion on the fact of p being comprised and hence commanded in the set of commanded propositions (respectively in the normative system). De facto they hence present some sort of logical deduction with normative sentences. This is an unavoidable consequence of the non-psychologistic interpretation of the sentences (respectively the speech act contents), as well as of the introduction of the concept of the normative system as the set of consequences of the norm contents. Thus the authors abandon – without being fully aware of it – the skepticism which, with respect to the logic of norms, they expressly advocate.

I am of the opinion, however, that the deduction system derived from the Alchourrón-Bulygin semantics and based on the thesis that these conclusions are consequences of the propositional contents of the commands is inadequate. According to the deduction theory conforming to the Alchourrón-Bulygin concept, both the Ross paradox (from '$!p$' follows '$!(p \vee q)$') and the problematical splitting-up of the conjunction as content of a prescriptive norm (from '$!(p \wedge q)$' follows '$!p$'; '$!q$') are provable.[11] A further argument against the deduction theory propagated by the authors is the fact that the conclusions most important for the practice, namely the normative modus-ponens conclusion and the subsumptive conclusion from a normative rule, cannot be justified within the framework of this theory.

The second development phase of the expressive approach to the problem field is characterized above all by the fact that the two authors now recognize the relevance of the pragmatic indicator for the logical relationships, thus taking a major step towards my conception of the logic of norms. I will refrain here from going into the further

[11] On these forms of conclusions I have commented critically before. Cf. O. Weinberger, The Concept of Non-Satisfaction and Deontic Logic, in: *Ratio* 1972, p.16–35; cf. also below.

development of Alchourrón's and Bulygin's expressive conception of norms.[12]

2. The second recipe proposed by Jörgensen for obtaining the substitute theory is based on replacing the imperative "This action is to be executed" by a statement of the form "There exists a person X who commands this action to be executed". Operations with such descriptive sentences, which contain the imperative (the norm) in indirect speech and with a reference to the norm-establishing act, evidently do not permit the execution of logical transformations within the field of the indirect speech. A substitute theory thus does not come about.

This manner of proceeding as proposed by Jörgensen is related, on the one hand, to the substitution theory by means of a statement on a norm-sentence, while on the other hand there exists a certain kinship with Kelsen's act-related definition of the norm in his last work and with his concomitant denial of the possibility of logical relations and operations with norms.

The "descriptive sentences about a norm" may be conceived differently; their use as a basis for substitute theories does not lead to the desired success.

Karel Engliš advocates a two-side theory of the norm: What is a postulate (demand, purpose-determined volition content) on the part of the commanding person is a norm for the addressee. But it is only from the mouth of the law-giver (or other creator of norms) that the norm comes forth; all other persons – e.g. the duty-bound subjects – think judgments about norms. This certainly is not an unproblematical conception, for perfect communication presupposes that sender and receiver associate the same thought contents with a given series of characters or other signs.

[12]I refer the reader here instead to my analysis in the book *Moral und Vernunft. Beiträge zu Ethik, Gerechtigkeitstheorie und Normenlogic* (Morality and Reason. Contributions to Ethics, Theory of Justice, and the Logic of Norms), Böhlau, Vienna/Cologne/Weimar 1992, p.463–482.

The transformation of the conclusion according to the logic of norms into the form of a conclusion with descriptive sentences (judgments) about norms can evidently only then be regarded as a substitute theory when a valid deduction rule of the logic of the descriptive language is presented according to which the proposed conclusion form is valid: This is not the case here. Engliš's example reads[13]:

(1) All males aged 20 to 65 are obligated to work
N is a 35-year old male
N is obligated to work

This conclusion is replaced by the indicative conclusion:

(2) The norm holds that all males aged 20 to 65 are obligated to work
N is a 35-year old male
The norm holds that N is obligated to work

A formalization of this conclusion should introduce a functor forming a descriptive sentence and having a normative argument, e.g. 'G' with the meaning: 'The norm exists that...'. Then (2) has the form:

(3) $G(p)$
q
———
$G(r)$

Hoever, (3), could only be valid by virtue of a specific inference rule which takes into account the relationship existing both as to structure and to contents between 'p', 'q', and 'r'. This rule – hence the conclusion rule according to the logic of norms – would be the reason why one might regard (3) (and therefore also (2)) as valid, but not an inference rule according to descriptive logic.

---

[13] K. Engliš, Postulát a norma nejsou soudy (Postulate and Norm are not Judgments), *Časopis pro právní a státní vědu*, p.104.

The "substitute theory" proposed by Engliš is a deception, not a reduction of the deduction with norms to inferences in the descriptive language.

With Kelsen, the differentiation between legal norm and legal proposition plays a part analogous to the contrastation of norm and descriptive statement about the norm. Legal propositions are defined by the author as "hypothetical judgments which assert that within the framework of a – national or international – legal order presented to the recognition of law, certain consequences determined by this legal order should, under certain conditions laid down by this legal order, occur."[14] In his book "Reine Rechtslehre" (Pure Theory of Law) Kelsen tries, on the one hand, by means of the legal propositions (i.e. descriptive sentences about norms) to introduce the concept of logical contradiction between norms (while in his later period denying any logical relationships between norms) and, on the other hand, seeks a possibility, by means of the assertions about norms, to find a substitute theory for the logic of norms. In his later period he regards the existence of a logic of norms as an utter impossibility, whereas formerly he took pride in his Pure Theory of Law having stimulated the development of such a very logic.[15]

In the 2nd edition of his Pure Theory of Law (p.209) Kelsen rightly contend that between norm-sentences there exists no logical contradiction in the sense defined for descriptive sentences. He believes, however, that the contradiction theorem, valid as it is for sentences describing legal norms, can indirectly also be applied to

[14] H. Kelsen, *Reine Rechtslehre* (Pure Theory of Law), 2nd ed., Deuticke, Vienna 1969, p.73.

[15] "The logic which, so to speak, discovered the Pure Theory of Law in the first place is a general logic of norms, that is: a logic of Ought or of prescriptive sentences, the logic of a knowledge directed at norms, rather than at natural reality." (H. Kelsen, Was ist Reine Rechtslehre? (What is Pure Theory of Law?), in: *Demokratie und Rechtsstaat* (Democracy and the Law-Abiding State), Festschrift for Zaccharia Giacometti, Zürich 1953, cited after: H. Klecatsky, R. Marcic, H. Schambeck (eds.), *Die Wiener rechtstheoretische Schule* (The Vienna School of Legal Theory), Manz, Wien 1968, p.617.

legal norms (p.210). This is wrong for the following reasons: Let us assume a norm system NS which contains the mutually incompatible norms 'p ought to be' and 'non-p ought to be'. Then the two legal propositions on the legal norm 'It is valid in NS that p ought to be' and 'It is valid in NS that non-p ought to be' are both true. Hence there is no logical contradiction between them. Evidently, of course, one cannot base an incompatibility existing between legal norms on a non-existent logical contradiction between the corresponding legal propositions.

The opinion – as advocated e.g. by Kelsen – that inferences in the field of norms do not exist, whereas valid inferences between the respective descriptive sentences, about norms do exist, is inacceptable. Let a norm system contain the norm-sentence 'N_1', but not 'N_2'. According to the premise, 'N_2' cannot be deduced from 'N_1', for it is claimed that there are no norm-logical inferences at all. If it is now claimed that from the descriptive sentence on the norm 'In the norm system SN, N_1 holds' follows the descriptive sentence on the norm 'In the norm system NS, N_2 holds', then we claim that a deductive relationship with a true premise and a false consequence holds, which contradicts the very definition of the inference relationship.

In his later period Kelsen bases himself on his act-related definition of the norm: A norm is the meaning of the volitional act of a subject over the behavior prescribed thereby of another subject. When one defines the norm psychologistically and as meaning of an actual volitional act one thereby excludes a limine the possibility of a logic of norms.[16]

---

[16]H. Kelsen, *Allgemeine Theorie der Normen* (A General Theory of Norms) posthumously published by K. Ringhofer, R. Walter), Manz, Wien 1979; furthermore O. Weinberger, *Normentheorie als Grundlage der Jurisprudenz und Ethik. Eine Auseinandersetzung mit Hans Kelsens Theorie der Normen* (A Theory of Norms as a Foundation for Jurisprudence and Ethics. A Critique of Hans Kelsen's Theory of Norms), Duncker & Humblot, Berlin 1981; *id.*, Kelsens These von der Unanwendbarkeit logischer Regeln auf Normen (Kelsen's Thesis of the Inapplicability of Logical Rules to Norms), in: *Die Reine Rechtslehre in wissenschaftlicher Diskussion.* Referate und Diskussion des Internationalen Symposiums zum 100.

The conceptional linking of the norm to the generating act excludes logical deduction with normative elements. In his "General Theory of Norms" Kelsen writes: "Just as the existence of a fact cannot logically follow from the existence of another fact – the paths of thinking are not the paths of being – , so the existence of a norm, i.e. its validity, cannot logically follow from the existence of another norm, i.e. from the validity of another norm" (p.186).

"Since between the validity of the general norm and the validity of the individual norm corresponding to it a volitional act must insert itself whose meaning is the individual norm, the validity of the individual norm cannot logically – i.e. by way of a thinking operation – follow like the truth of an individual assertion follows from the truth of the general assertion corresponding to the individual one. Between the general norm and the individual one corresponding to it there exists no direct relationship at all, but only an indirect one, mediated by the volitional act whose meaning is the individual norm. For that reason alone there can, basically, be no question at all of a possibility to arrive at a validity of the individual norm by way of a logical deduction from the validity of the general norm" (p.186 et seq.). Although knowing and citing Husserl's antipsychologistic remarks, Kelsen applies them only to propositions. Evidently he thinks that in the field of propositions there exists an objective basis permitting abstraction from the act of thinking, whereas in the case of norms no such basis exists. He thus failed to see (a) that in the case of propositions, too, it is not the objective reality which is the basis of the validity of logical relationships, but the constitutive system of the language, and (b) that the preconditions for a logicistic conception are fulfilled in the case of norms, too.[17]

Geburtstag von Hans Kelsen (The Pure Doctrine of Law in Scientific Discussion. Papers presented and discussion held at the International Symposium on the Occasion of Hans Kelsen's 100th birthday), (Vienna 1981), Manz, Wien 1982, p.108–121.

[17]Interestingly, Kelsen recognizes an exception in his later period as well, i.e. a case in which a logical norm inference is possible, namely in the case of norms of different generality (p.201 et seq.). As an example of a pair of general norms of

As substitute theories, various constructions occur in Kelsen's writings:

(a) Relations of statements about the validity of norms;

(b) His dark theory of the relations between the subjective and the objective meaning of the norm.

Ad (a):

"Nevertheless there is a syllogism in which a general norm and an individual one corresponding to it have a place. Under the condition,

---

different degrees of abstractness Kelsen mentions:
(1) People should not harm one another.
(2) People should not calumniate one another.
The concept 'calumniate' is contained in the concept 'harm'. Therefore the norm (2) did not establish anything not already established by norm (1).
"The relationship between norm (1) and norm (2) can be represented in the form of a conclusion:
1. People should not harm one another.
I: When a person calumniates another person, he or she harms him or her.
Hence a person should not calumniate another person." ...
"But this conclusion does not lead to the validity of a new norm. The norm presented as conclusion is already valid when the norm presented as major premise is valid, implied as it is in the latter" (p.202).

The analysis of the relationship presented between general norms and the comparison of the results of the analysis with the relationship between individual and general norm shows that in reality a precisely analogous – namely a logical – relationship is valid for the relation between a general norm and the corresponding individual one.

It is not correct that the less abstract general norm can be made explicit from the more abstract one through interpretation (i.e. through explanation of the meaning) of the more abstract norm. In our example, (2) cannot be arrived at through explanation of the meaning of (1). To arrive at (2), it is necessary to include as a premise (or as recognition) the second sentence of I "When a person calumniates another person, he/she harms him/her". Then, however, I is a valid conclusion according to the logic of norms.

In exactly the same sense, the individual norm, too, is contained in the general one, namely so that a second premise must be added which ascertains the existence of an element of the quantification universe (or the subsumability of the concrete facts of an individual case under the factual criteria of the general norm). Then and only then will this conclusion according to the logic of norms be valid.

namely, that a general norm is valid and that the individual meaning, corresponding to it, of a volitional act is present. Also, it must be a matter here of assertions on the validity of the general norm and of the already valid individual one corresponding to it. E.g.:

1. The general norm holds: 'All persons should keep the promises they give to other persons'.

2. A volitional act is present whose meaning is: 'A should keep the promise he gave to B to marry her.'

3. Hence the individual meaning cited in the minor premise is a norm which corresponds to the general norm cited in the major premise" (p.203).

In the descriptive language there is no rule on which such a inference could be based.

Ad (b):

"The subjective meaning of a volitional act directed at the behavior of someone else will also be its objective meaning, namely: a valid, binding norm, if this act has been authorized by the valid norm of a positive moral or legal order. If this proposition forms the major premise (1) and if the following propositions function as minor premises: (2) It is a valid general moral norm that 'All persons should keep their promises', (3) 'Jones promised Smith to pay him 1000', and (4) 'Jones or some other member of the community posited a volitional act whose subjective meaning is that Jones shall pay Smith 1000', then the conclusion (5) reads: 'The subjective meaning of the volitional act mentioned sub (4) is also its objective meaning, i.e. a valid, binding norm.' By way of this syllogism the validity of the individual norm: Jones should keep his promise to Smith to pay him 1000, is justified with the validity of the general norm: When a person gives a promise to another person he or she should keep it" (p.204).

While this is, of course, very unclear, "becoming justifiable through a syllogism" hardly means anything else but "being justified through logical deduction".

I. Tammelo and *H. Schreiner* try to solve the problems to which the logic of norms gives rise by means of a "protological calculus" in which they give this calculus – which has exactly the structure of the descriptive calculus – two interpretations alongside one another: an indicative and a normative one. This conception of an isomorphism between descriptive logic and the logic of norms is, for at least two reasons, not a practicable approach: The logic of norms is a system of two semantic categories of sentences (of norm-sentences and descriptive sentences), and such a system cannot be isomorphous with a system comprising only one semantic category: in the logic of norms there are molecular sentences which consist of elements of both categories, first and foremost the conditional norm-sentences. Such structures and their "logic" cannot be adequately represented in the protologic.[18]

With a number of widely varying viewpoints on the logic of norms we are confronted by the great master of research in this field, *G. H. von Wright*. His first attempts – they had a decisive influence on the research on logic in this field – were wholly marked by the analogy of different groups of linguistic expressions, each characterized by an operator and a description of a state of affairs and by the possibility to place negations before the operator and/or the description of the state of affairs. At that time von Wright's analyses were entirely based on linguistic considerations; with regard to the philosophical problems involved as to how the essence of deduction in the field of the norms is to be conceived of the theory was naive: it neither perceived nor articulated a problem here. The logic of norms was understood as a kind of modal logic.[19] The first doubts arose when for the representation of the hypothetical norm-sentences neither the form '$O(p \rightarrow q)$', nor the form '$p \rightarrow Oq$' appeared to be suitable. The

[18] I. Tammelo, H. Schreiner, *Grundzüge und Grundverfahren der Rechtslogik* (Fundamentals and Basic Procedures of the Logic of Law), Vol.1, Verlag Dokumentation K. G. Saur, Munich 1974 (UTB).

[19] G. H. von Wright, Deontic Logic, in: *Mind* 60, 1951, p.1–25; *id. An Essay in Modal Logic*, Amsterdam 1951.

answer was von Wright's dyadic deontic logic in which a conditional norm-sentence was introduced as a primitive term and the apodictic norm-sentence was defined as a conditional norm-sentence with a tautological antecedent.[20] While this is, admittedly, correct, it is not quite simple: This property of the conditioning part of the sentence need not always be recognizable at first glance. And these sentences are always equivalent with any sentence of this structure whose condition is factually true. A modus-ponens rule is replaced by the rule that the ascertainment of the truth of the condition leads to the conclusion in the form of a tautologically conditioned sentence corresponding to the apodictic norm-sentence. The problems inherent in the use of truth-functional junctors with normative arguments and the conceptual explication of the norm-logical deduction were not clarified thereby. Next, doubts arose concerning the interpretation of the permission concept, particularly when a disjunction occurred as argument. Fresh light was cast by von Wrights's famous book "Norm and Action. A Logical Enquiry" (1968). From the point of view of our reflections on "Norm and Truth" as well as on the solution of the problems inherent in the logic of norms it is particularly the chapter "Norms, Language, and Truth" which is important. To Frege's conception of the truth value being the referent (designatum) of the proposition von Wright prefers the view that the fact which makes the sentence true is to be regarded as the referent of the sentence. Then only true sentences will have a referent, but not untrue ones (although they, too, have meaning).

Von Wright contrasts 'norm-formulations' with 'normative statements'. The former are linguistic instruments of norm-giving and as such neither true nor false, while the latter constitute (true or false) information on an Ought (or May). The logic of norms is expressly identified by the author with deontic logic: "The Logic of Norms we call Deontic Logic." (p.130). Posing himself the question at

[20]G. H. von Wright, An Essay in Deontic Logic and the General Theory of Action, *Acta Philosophica Fennica*, Fasc. XXI, North Holland Publ. Co., Amsterdam 1968.

this point whether deontic logic is to be interpreted in terms of norm-formulations or of normative statements, he opts for the descriptive interpretation, since only normative statements can be posited as arguments of truth-functional functors. Deontic logic thus is turned into a theory of the sentences about norms (to remain within my terminology). The laws of this logic portray the logical properties of the norms themselves; the logic of norms is mirrored in the logical properties of the normative statements (p.134). Deontic logic thus, so to speak, indirectly assumes the part of a (true) logic of norms. This is where, in my opinion, the philosophical problem is rooted: is this a valid path toward a descriptive substitute theory? How do we know that the descriptively interpreted deontic logic portrays the logic of norms correctly? The genuine logic of norms is the yardstick and foundation of truth for the logic of the norm-describing sentences, not the other way around. When one starts out primarily from the logic of the normative statements, then the analogies to other systems of modal logic will be more likely to come into play than the logical properties of the norms (of the norm-formulations).

The difficulties of adequately interpreting deontic logic and above all the suggestive influence of Kelsen's writings from his later period led von Wright back to the conviction that the traditional deduction concept should be maintained unchanged and that logical relations are ex definitione truth relations. He opted for this conception probably for two reasons: (a) because it conforms to the long-standing tradition of logic, and (b) because it permits a relatively clear definition of what 'logical' means. However, he has never – as far as I know – presented any proof for the impossibility of an expanded deduction concept. He now believes, standing entirely on the ground of the truth-functional tradition, to have found satisfactory recipes for dealing with norms. He now interprets his structural analysis of the normative realm not as logic of norms, nor as deontic logic (insofar as it had been conceived of as a logical system), but as "rules of rational law-giving", as a "theory of the principles of the rational law-giver"; on the concept of 'practical necessity' he bases a theory which one may regard as a substitute theory for norm-logical deduction. To the extent that he keeps abiding by deontic logic he interprets its laws as principles which "any norm-giving must obey if it wants to be regarded as reasonable".[21]

Von Wright's skepticism concerning the logic of norms, as it finds expression in this paper, can be summarized in the following theses:

(I) There is no logic of norms, for norms are the content of expressions of volition; they cannot claim any truth values, and it is the essence of logic to discover logical, i.e. necessary truths.

(II) There are no logical relations between norms, but only such relations as consistency and/or inconsistency; these, however, are not logical relations in the strict sense, but only relations resulting from the requirements one imposes on a rational norm-giver.

(III) There are no deductions according to the logic of norms, no logically valid conclusions with normative elements; there are only practical necessities that exist when one wants to be rational, or that indicate how one must behave to fulfill given norms.

(IV) The so-called deontic logic admittedly has validity, but neither as a representation of the logical relations between norms, nor as a logical system of descriptive sentences about norms, but only as rules or principles of the rationality of the law-giver.

The idea of the rational law-giver as a mainstay of normative rationality calls for closer study. The author writes: "If there existed no source, *like* a will, for the unity of a set of norms there would be no reason, it seems, why the contents of norms should be mutually consistent rather than contradict each other."[22] Hence he justifies the consistency postulate for norm systems with a really existing entity as the source of these norms. Apart from the fact that this entity, the

---

[21]G. H. von Wright, Is and Ought, opening address at the 11th IVR World Congress at Helsinki 1983, in: E. Bulygin et al.(eds.), *Man, Law, and Modern Forms of Life*, D. Reidel, Dordrecht 1985, p.263–281, German translation by Peter Philipp, in: G. H. von Wright, *Normen, Werte und Handlungen* (Norms, Values and Actions), Suhrkamp, Frankfurt/M. 1994, p.19–43. See also O. Weinberger, *'Is' and 'Ought' Reconsidered*, in: *ARSP* 1984 no.4, p.454–474.

[22]G. H. von Wright, Norm, Truth, and Logic, in G. H. von Wright, *Practical Reason (Philosophical Papers, Vol.I)*. Basel Blackwell Inc., Oxford 1983, p.149.

law-giver's will, is a mental construction and hardly a reality,[23] this justification strikes me as extremely problematical.

Is there not also a consistency question with respect to a moral codex, where the assumption of such a will would be entirely fictitious? Whether a norm is logically (as I put it) compatible with another one does not depend at all on whether both belong to *one and the same* system.[24] Hence neither the concept of the incompatibility of norms, nor the consistency postulate can be based on a will-like entity as source of the norms.

There are various reasons for a law-giver to be called rational: (a) if he takes measures that serve his aims and preferences; (b) if he sets socially acceptable goals; (c) if he provides adequate motivation for the fulfillment of his norms; (d) if he posits no linguistic-logical incompatibilities, thinks consistently and draws only logically valid conclusions. – Only the property mentioned last comes into play in von Wright's appraisal of the law-giver (and indirectly of his norm system). And precisely here one would expect that it should be logic, and particularly the logic of norms, which must place criteria at our disposal for judging whether the law-giver (or applier of the norm) is proceeding rationally (consistently), and not, conversely, that the rationality of the law-giver decides on the logic, on logical compatibility and consistency of the norms.

The author treats the question of the incompatibility between norm-sentences and the consistency postulate for norm systems as a problem of the criteria of rational law-giving. This I do not regard as correct. As Hans Kelsen most correctly notes, the incompatibility of norm-sentences (the conflict between them, as he puts it) is independent of whether they belong to one or to different norm systems. The

[23] A parliament has no will in the psychological sense; when one speaks of 'the legislator's will' this is meant figuratively and constitutes a meaningful construction only for the reason that the norm system concerned is seen as an ideal complex that can be understood as the "will" of a hypostatized subject, hence as a rational unity.

[24] H. Kelsen, *Allgemeine Theorie der Normen* (A General Theory of Norms), op.cit., p.169.

conflict (the incompatibility) between norms of different systems can, in any event, not be explained by a reference to rationality requirements imposed on the law-giver. The rationality of different law-givers can, after all, not be judged on the basis of whether the contents of the volitions of different law-givers are in conflict with one another or not.

Von Wright defines satisfiability – and satisfiability is to him the decisive criterion for the rationality (the consistency) of a corpus of norms – both for prescriptive norms and for permissive norms.

"I shall say that a permissive norm is satisfiable if, and only if, it is possible that the permitted state of affairs obtains at some time in the history of the norm. And it is satisfied if, and only if, at some time in its history that which it permits actually is also the case."[25] This determination is justified by the author with the fact that otherwise there would only be a "mock-permission". I consider such a determination inexpedient. In my opinion it simply makes no sense to speak of the satisfaction – nor, hence of the satisfiability – of permissive norms. Such a norm evidently cannot be violated, for failure to make use of a permission does not violate the corresponding permissive norm. Since permissive norms hence cannot be violated it strikes me as senseless to speak of their satisfaction. In reality it is not a matter at all here of the alternative "satisfaction/violation of a norm", but of the requirement that only what is logically possible (perhaps also only empirically possible) shall be permitted. The question whether the permitted situation will ever exist, i.e. whether use will be made of the permission or whether there will in fact be an opportunity to make use of it, is irrelevant for the rationality of the permitting act.

Man (including the law-giver or issuer of commands) not being omniscient, one can – without doing so for fun or mockery – permit something without knowing whether there will be an opportunity to make use of the permission. The law-giver (or other norm-setter) can

[25]G. H. von Wright, The Foundation of Norms and Normative Statements, in: *id., Practical Reason (Philosophical Papers, Vol.1).* Basil Blackwell, Oxford 1983, p.139).

be rational without asking any such question at all when giving his permission. The father who permits this son to marry does not act irrationally, even though he does not know at all and does not examine whether the son can find a bride.

I think that the author fell victim to an error in the following presentation of satisfiability as a criterion for the rationality of a corpus of norms: "A corpus of norms is satisfiable if, and only if, it is possible that all states which the norms of the corpus make obligatory obtain throughout the history of the corpus and all states which the norms permit obtain at some time in this history." ... "A law-giver may be said to envisage an ideal state which agrees with his wish or will, and in which everything obligatory is the case as long as the obligations exist and everything permitted *is the case* (emphasis mine, O. W.) at some time or other in the history of the permissions."[26]

The satisfiability of the permissive norm had earlier been defined by von Wright in the following way: "I shall say that a permissive norm is satisfiable if, and only if, *it is possible that* (emphasis mine, O. W.) the permitted state of affairs obtains at some time in the history of the norm."[27] This 'it is possible that' must not be omitted here, for it is undoubtedly justified to require that the thing permitted must be possible – as it is said in the definition of the satisfiability of permissive norms –, but it is erroneous to declare a corpus of norms only then rationally admissible if the permissive norms contained in it are made use of at least once. Furthermore, in the definition proposed of the consistency of norm systems the possible incompatibility between prescriptive and permissive norm is not taken into account.

In his skeptical phase, G. H. von Wright made even a second attempt to deny the possibility of a logic of norms and – with the aid of a substitute theory – to get along without it.[28] "In the end I arrived at

[26]G. H. von Wright, op.cit., p.140.

[27]G. H. von Wright, op cit., p.139.

[28]G. H. von Wright, Bedingungsnormen – ein Prüfstein für die Normenlogik (Conditional Norms – A Touchstone for the Logic of Norms), in: W. Krawietz et al.(eds.), *Theorie der Normen. Festschrift für Ota Weinberger zu seinem 65.*

the opinion that between norms there exist no logical relations at all. Even the 'subsumptive inference' is not a logical inference." (p.449)

With every right von Wright terms the explication of the conditional norm the touchstone for the logic of norms. A second, equally important touchstone is, in my opinion, the ability of the theory to express the general norms and to explain the relation between the general norm-sentence[29] and the corresponding individual norm-sentences (usually regarded as consequences of the general one). Thus the question presents itself how the author seeks to master these two problems by means of his substitute theory.

As passage dealing with the relation between general norm and individual norm I understand the following one: "Does the norm, together with the fact that a promise has been given, create a *new* obligation? I would say definitely: No. The only obligation existing here is the obligation to keep promises given. Now a man has given a promise. To be able to fulfill this obligation of his he *must* do now what he has promised. That he must do it is not a 'new' obligation that has 'arisen' from his promise – rather it is a practical necessity to which, through his promise, he has subjected himself in order to be able to fulfill his duty never to promise anything without keeping the promise" (p.454). The norm that promises should be kept evidently is a general norm. Whether a new duty arises from the fact that in a certain situation S_1 a person P_1 has promised a person Q_1 to do p_1 needs to be examined more closely. This fact (or its ascertainment) insofar does not create a *typically new obligation* as it has been pre-established by the general norm that there exists an obligation here arising from a promise; *but there does exist a new obligation of the person* P_1. *And from a conditional obligation there arose an*

Geburtstag (A Theory of Norms, festschrift for Ota Weinberger on the occasion of his 65th birthday), Duncker & Humblot, Berlin 1984, p.447–456.

[29]Perhaps it would – at least for the purpose of legal theory – be more appropriate here to speak of general norm-sentences. From the logical point of view it is a question here of the universal normative proposition and a rule of the type of a conclusion "de omni et nullo". The universal proposition assumes a general character when type-forming criteria are applied.

unconditional one. That an obligation can be specified (perhaps individualized) by – among other things – indicating the person so obligated is certainly indisputable, and just as little can it be doubted that there was no such specification before. Von Wright evidently thinks that no individual norm arises at all, since everyone has already been conditionally obligated by the general norm to fulfill a promise if he has given one. There would then not exist any unconditional obligations at all; the subject of the duty P_1 is subjected only to the practical necessity of fulfilling the general conditional norm by keeping his promise.

Undoubtedly one should also take unconditional universal norm-sentences into consideration, e.g. 'Everyone should love his neighbor'. Here it is evidently valid for every subject who is an element of the quantification universe that he should love his neighbor. To say instead that he must love his neighbor – as a practical necessity – strikes me as problematical for two reasons: (a) The universal norm-sentence can hardly be defined otherwise than by the individualization rule, and (b) it strikes me as absurd to say that this subject has no obligation; rather, he must love his neighbor then and only then if he wants to fulfill the norm. The practical necessity can hardly be regarded here as a descriptive relation; rather, it is a normative category, for evidently it is not a question here of a Must as dictated by a causality of nature.

The fulfillment of an Ought-norm can be defined in the following way: 'Op' is fulfilled if, and only if, when p is a fact. This means that an individual subject cannot fulfill a general norm; he can fulfill only the individual norm that follows from the general norm-sentence because of a normative individualization rule. Now one might of course introduce a terminology of such a nature that the phrase 'The subject fulfills the general norm' would be permissible. This sentence, however, would be true if, and only if, the subject fulfills the derived individual norm (in the usual sense). Thus there is no way around deriving the individual norm from the general one; while one may veil this terminologically, critical analysis will always bring to light that an inference of individualization is needed.

If, on the basis of the adequacy of the theory of the conditional norm-sentence, one wishes to examine whether a proposed method for the analysis of norms is adequate, one must achieve clarity from the start as to what properties a conditional norm-sentence has that are to be portrayed through the formal presentation. I believe that such a theory can be recognized as adequate only if it is capable of the following:

(I) It permits a clear differentiation between an indicative conditional sentence, which can be adequately defined in a truth-functional way, and a conditional norm-sentence, which evidently must be defined in some other fashion.

(II) The conditional norm-sentence as a whole must be a norm-sentence. (This is shown also by the fact that it can be the content of a norm-setting act.)

(III) It must be so structured that it is recognizable both in the case of the antecedent and of the consequent sentence whether the partial sentence has normative or indicative meaning.

(IV) The conditional norm-sentence must express a conditional Ought (or conditional May), which means: As long as the condition is not fulfilled there is no (actual) Ought or May, but with the condition fulfilled an unconditional Ought (May) is derivable.

Within the framework of the deontic logics, particularly the following three forms of the structural scheme of the conditional Ought sentence have been proposed:

1. $O(p \rightarrow q)$
2. $p \rightarrow Oq$
3. $O(q/p)$

The first form does not permit the detachment of the fulfilled condition so as to arrive at an unconditional Ought. Because of the possibility of a transposition of the implication in the content of the prescriptive sentence, no clear distinction of the epistemological characteristics of the partial sentence comes about here either.

The second proposed form does not constitute a norm-sentence, since the main functor is a proposition-forming one.

The third form might perhaps be so interpreted that the entire sentence is understood as a prescriptive one, with the argument 'p' being assigned normative and the argument 'q' descriptive character. The possibility also exists that the system lays down an adequate detachment rule; the significance of this form in the dyadic deontic logics does not, however, have these properties, for the entire sentence is interpreted as a truth-functional relation. Since the unconditional norm is defined as a norm with a tautological condition there are certain problems with the detachment rule, since merely factually true conditions should likewise express an unconditional Ought (this problem does not strike me as insurmountable, however). If the dyadic deontic sentence is interpreted as a true norm-sentence, then one will thereby alone have introduced a specific functor of the conditional norm-sentence, which von Wright rejects with a view to Occam's razor. From a methodological point of view the following objection can be raised here: Occam's demand must envisage not only the expressions of the language; rather, it must assess the complexities of the stipulations of a theory also from the point of view of the operation rules and the terms occurring in them. And von Wright's theory requires instead of the functor for the formation of conditional norm-sentences the introduction of the – anything but simple – concept of the technical Ought (or of the practical necessity), hence is by no means less complicated and does not get along with fewer basic concepts than a theory which introduces a normative conditional-sentence functor.

When we designate a sentence as conditional sentence this means, in my opinion, nothing else but that this is a sentence which describes as conditional something (be it a state of affairs, an obligation, a permission or some other thing) which will be valid unconditionally when the condition is fulfilled; this means, however, that together with every conditional sentence some sort of detachment rule (with the effect of cancelling the fulfilled conditions) holds *ex definitione*.

Now the author thinks that '$O(p \rightarrow q)$' is the basic form of a conditional norm. This formula he reads as follows: "It ought to be thus that either it is not the case that p, or it is the case that q". "For example: The obligation to keep promises given means that it ought to be thus that either a promise has not been given or, if given, will be kept. Put differently: it is forbidden to make a promise without fulfilling it. ($O(p \rightarrow q) = O \sim (p \,\&\, \sim q)$.)" (p.451). Von Wright also perceives, however, possible objections to this conception, particularly that with this form no detachment rule is valid through which 'Oq' might be obtained. "The 'tautologies' of deontic logic present criteria for intelligent (rational) norm-giving." (p.453).

There are other reasons, too, why I doubt the adequacy of the reconstruction of the conditional norm-sentence through the formula '$O(p \rightarrow q)$'. There evidently are two types of conditions: (1) external ones, and (2) action-dependent ones. 'When it rains, open your umbrella' is conditioned by an external state of affairs independent of the addressee. To say that the addressee should either see to it that it does not rain, or he should open his umbrella, appears rather queer. But the result remaining is only that, unable as he is to effect non-raining, he must open his umbrella. So far, so good: But in what does this Must differ from Ought? Is it a technical insight (a technical norm) that he can fulfill the hypothetical norm only by opening his umbrella? To understand what is prescribed (what ought to be done) always means: to know what must be the case so that the 'Ought' norm is fulfilled. The decisive thing, however, is that the addressee ought to do this (not that he ought to do it if he wishes to fulfill the norm). Likewise, in the case of action-dependent conditions it is, in my opinion, not thus that the order is given either to prevent the occurrence of the condition or to effect the conditioned. 'If you have a corresponding income you shall pay income tax' cannot, with unchanged meaning, be transformed into 'See that you have no income, or pay income tax'.

Since the proposed theory constitutes neither a semantically adequate formalization of the conditional norm-sentence, nor arrives, by means of the concept of technical 'Ought' or of practical necessity, at a substitute for norm-logical deduction, I do not deem this skepticistic approach acceptable.

I doubt whether the remarks on the normative contradiction by means of the auxiliary concept of the negation norm and on the definition when a norm "normatively" implies another one, are compatible with the strictly skeptical point of view.[30] They rather represent the end of von Wright's skeptical period and his transition to the conception expressed in the essay "Is there a logic of norms?"[31]

The article in the festschrift for W. Krawietz marks von Wright's return to belief in the logic of norms. He wishes to make up for the "sin" that consisted in deontic logic positing norm-sentences as arguments of truth-functional functors. He reflects on a (genuine) logic of norms and pleads against those conservative logicians who reject logical contradictions and logical consequences because they stick to their traditional narrow conceptual apparatus, applicable only to sentences that can be true or false. "Refusing to consent that from a command there follows logically a corresponding permission is simply pigheadedness." (p.72) Important is that von Wright is now

[30] "By the negation norm of an O-norm I understand the P-norm with the (contradictorily) opposite content – and by the negation norm of a P-norm an O-norm with opposite content. E.g.: the negation norm of 'it ought to be thus that p' is 'it may be thus that non-p'; and the negation norm of 'it may be thus that p' is 'it ought to be thus that non-p' (or 'it is forbidden that p'). Two O-norms, as well as an O-norm and a P-norm, contradict each other 'normatively' when their contents, i.e. that which ought to be (or may be), contradict each other *logically*. On the basis of these stipulations it can now be said when a norm implies another one 'normatively'. This is the case when the first norm and the negation norm of the second one contradict each other normatively." (G. H. von Wright, *Bedingungsnorm – ein Prüfstein für die Normenlogik* (Conditional Norm – A Touchstone for the Logic of Norms), op.cit., p.452 et seq.)

[31] G. H. von Wright, Gibt es eine Logik der Normen? (Is There a Logic of Norms?), in D. Wydukel et al.(eds.), *Rechtsnorm und Rechtswirklichkeit*, Festschrift für Prof. Dr. Dr. Werner Krawietz on the occasion of his 60th birthday on 14 December 1993 (Legal Norm and in Legal Reality), Duncker & Humblot, Berlin 1993. (Also in G. H. von Wright, *Normen, Werte und Handlungen* (Norms, Values and Actions), op.cit., p.56–83. The page references refer to this book.)

convinced "that there is something which can be called a genuine logic of norms" (p.82). The deductions according to the logic of norms he justifies by means of the negation norm: A deduction according to the logic of norms will be valid if, and only if, the negation norm of the conclusion renders the (formerly contradiction-free) set of premises inconsistent. Whether this is sufficient is, in my opinion, not wholly unproblematical. The following questions would have to be asked: 1. The definition of the negation norm is dependent on the relations between the deontic operators, whose mutual definability is not undisputed. 2. The validity of the laws of deontic logic is implicitly assumed (e.g. '$Op \rightarrow O(p \vee q)$'; '$O(p \,\&\, q) \equiv (Op \,\&\, Oq)$'). 3. How is deduction from hypothetical norm-sentences defined (detachment rule)? 4. Should not deduction from inconsistent premises be taken into consideration as well? – But these are only minor problems in comparison with the recognition, in principle, of the genuine logic of norms as a scientific task.

Chapter 2

Once more: Is and Ought

The action-theoretical approach

2.1. Dichotomous semantics as basis of practical philosophy

There is little point in again and again discussing basic questions and repeating or summarizing long familiar arguments. If of anything, this is true of the problem field indicated in the title of this chapter. But this problem field appears in a new light when it is viewed from an action-theoretical perspective, or more precisely put: on the basis of an information-theoretically founded action theory. Point of departure is then the anthropological thesis of man's capability of action, together with the following corollaries (as prerequisites for the possibility of conceiving of the action concept):

1. Man has a scope of behavior (i.e. possible behavior alternatives) at his disposal within which he can determine his behavior on the basis of information processes.

2. The structure of the behavior-determining information processes defines the action concept.

3. These information processes have two sides: (a) They are cognitive ones, based on knowledge of situations, of causal (including

causal-stochastic) relationships and of possible behavior alternatives all the way to the invention of procedures, technologies and action programs with feedback, (b) they are processes of the selection of alternatives from the field of possibilities, with this selection, in principle, not being accidental (arbitrary, uncontrolled, devoid of express justification), but rather determined by information acquired.[1] Cognitive information, descriptions of facts and the ascertainment of relationships between them as well as of chains of causal consequences constitute frameworks for selection decisions, but never in themselves a justification for the selection. For the latter, pieces of position-taking (or, as one might put it: practical) information is indispensable. According to customary usage they include: ends (objectives), values, preferences and norms.

The new perspective in which, to me, the Is/Ought problem and the caesura between Is and Ought expresses itself, and the logical-methodological postulate of the mutual non-derivability of Is and Ought (and conversely of Ought from Is, which postulate corresponds to the so-called prohibition of the naturalistic fallacy), are characterized by the following theses:

(I) Philosophically they are primarily founded on our ability to perform actions and on the structure of the action as information-determined behavior. Asking whether this semantic duality results from the constitution of our mind and our thinking or from the structure of language falls short of furnishing its basic justification and explanation, but is rather a prerequisite for the possibility of acting. The caesura need not be sharp and clearly marked, not even in linguistic practice or linguistic awareness. Seen philosophically, the dichotomous semantics, which corresponds to the opposition and separation of descriptive and practical sentences and constitutes an indispensable prerequisite for the information-determined conception of action, is the actual reason for the separation of Is and Ought and of

[1]The place to be accorded to random selection needs special discussion. See p.99 seq.

the non-derivability postulates that characterize the logics of practical (action-related) thinking.

The caesura in the language and to the analysis of our thinking is not the primary reason for regarding dichotomous semantics as the basis of all practical philosophy, but rather a secondary symptom of the prerequisites for the possibility of action and of the rational-reconstructive construction of an action theory.[2]

(II) The caesura is now localized one step higher (more general): It is not only a matter of a separation of Is and Ought, but of the detachment of practical (selection-justifying) sentences from cognitive-descriptive ones. The Ought-sentence is a special case of a practical sentence.

Evaluating and preferential sentences are in this semantic classification practical sentences; they express positions taken by the subject (by the practical system). The corresponding predication "*a* is good (beautiful, ...)" and "with respect to *a* specific criterion (or globally) *a* is preferred to *b*" – although seemingly a descriptive sentence – is de facto not purely descriptive, since it contains non-descriptive predicates. "Good", "better", ... are not descriptive predicates and not ascertainable by pure observation alone.[3]

---

[2]Cf. O. Weinberger, Eine Semantik für die praktische Philosophie (A Semantics for Practical Philosophy), in: R. Haller (ed.), *Beiträge zur Philosophie von Stephan Körner* (Contributions to Stephan Körner's Philosophy), *Grazer Philosophische Studien* 20 (1983), p.219–239; reprinted in: O. Weinberger, *Moral und Vernunft. Beiträge zu Ethik, Gerechtigkeitstheorie und Normenlogik* (Morality and Reason. Contributions to Ethics, Theory of Justice, and Logic of Norms), Böhlau, Vienna/Cologne/Weimar 1992, p.412–430. For the concept of dichotomous semantics I use in this article the somewhat unwieldy expression "erkenntnismäßig differenzierte Semantik" (cognitively differentiated semantics).

[3]That evaluating and preferential sentences are often treated as descriptive ones is well known. This can be regarded as superficial grammar of the language, which in the case of a critical analysis in the light of in-depth grammar requires a correction by which the position-taking, not purely descriptive, character of the so-called evaluating and preferential sentence parts is brought to light. It is equally revealed by the in-depth analysis that the evaluating and preferential judgments are, as a matter of principle, relative to the system under consideration.

(III) The definition of the so-called naturalistic fallacy is corrected: Not every deduction of normative consequences form non-normative premises is invalid. From knowledge gained and ends envisaged (these are position-taking premises) normative conclusions may under certain circumstances be obtained.[4] If one defines non-derivability postulates on the basis of the dichotomous semantics one obtains a more precise antinaturalistic deduction theory than when proceeding from the Is/Ought dichotomy.

(IV) The action-theoretical approach leading to the justification of the dichotomous semantics as a basis for practical philosophy also has the consequence that not only a logic of norms (frequently under the name "deontic logic", "imperative logic" and the like) is to be introduced as an analysis of the forms of thinking and argumentation – hence as a logical discipline –, but that also the formal structure of other elements of the action-related thinking become the object of logical analyses: teleology, formal axiology, logic of preferences.

This also has important implications for the philosophical analysis: The formal relations are separated from the determination of the content, namely the actual ends, preferences, etc. When speaking e.g. of teleological rationality one must distinguish between (a) the fact that a justification through ends is presented, according to which justification means are determined on the basis of suitable causal relationships and are made use of for action-determination, and (b) the stipulation of the actual ends; the teleological determination of the action (decision) becomes possible only through this stipulation.

To speak of teleological rationality is deceptive. It would falsely suggest the existence of an objectively given utility; but in fact there is only a rational structure of the teleological argumentation. How-

[4]If it has been formulated as an end to provide a precise overview of the status of one's capital and of the capital movements occurring, and if it is realized that proper bookkeeping in these fields is the only means to obtain exact capital information, then the norm may be derived from this that orderly bookkeeping is obligatory. This manner of deduction does not violate the correctly understood prohibition of the naturalistic fallacy, for among the premises there is a practical sentence expressing the intended end.

ever, a teleological justification is always dependent on the selection (stipulation) of the actual ends and preferences which enable one to make a justified choice between possible means.

2.2. Two remarks on the traditional contrasting of Is and Ought

1. Widespread is the view that Is and Ought are two different and separated ontic domains (the world of the existent, of things, and the world of norms). The background of this conception is the opinion, originating from criticist thinking, that man is a partaker of two ontic spheres, the world of objects, which he grasps in principle through sensual experience, and the sphere of Ought, of ends and values. From the disjunctive duality of these spheres in which man lives there follows also the fact that elements from the one sphere cannot be founded on the elements from the other sphere. In the light of the ontic duality of Is and Ought the non-derivability theses – brief formulation: "Ought does not follow from Is", "Is does not follow from Ought" – appear plausible. Their exact formulation does not follow from this division into ontic fields, however.

To this ontic conception, i.e. the claim of the existence of two worlds, there are a number of objections:

(a) The genesis and function of the Ought phenomena as well as the relations between objective reality and Ought can hardly be explained on this basis.

(b) The Ought is not a world (in the sense that possible worlds are spoken of in modal logic). There is not just *one* consistent system of Ought. Various systems of Ought are conceivable alongside one another which among one another are by no means consistent – in fact, in social reality such mutually incompatible systems of Ought do indeed exist.

(c) The logical non-derivability of Ought from Is does not mean that Ought conclusions are derivable only – and solely – from Ought premises. The thoroughly common subsumption conclusion has normative and cognitive-descriptive premises. Norm-logical deduction is thus by no means merely a matter of operating in the "world of Ought".

(d) From the ontic two-domain conception the difficulty arises how to understand the factual – real – existence of norm systems, hence, pointedly formulated, "the Is of Ought". Here a philosophical problem is generated which by and for itself does not exist at all, but merely results from the problematical dual ontology. If, on the other hand, one views the Is/Ought problem as a semantic differentiation and proceeds from a dichotomous semantics, the real existence of norm systems becomes intelligible – without suspicion of a paradox of "the Is of Ought".

2. The concept of Is is burdened by a categorial ambiguity: (I) 'Is' is regarded as a global designation of all things and objective relationships between states of affairs. 'Is' is the world, or in an expanded sense a class of possible worlds. 'Is' is either something objectively existing or something imagined as existing. 'Is' in this sense has the character of a name, of a very broad (the broadest) designation of an object. (II) 'Is' ('To exist') has linguistically the role of an attribute. E.g. "God is (is not)." "Graz (the capital of Styria) exists." "There exists no golden mountain." The 'Is' (Existence) means the ascertainment that an object mentioned by a name or by a uniquely identifying description is a component of the world. The attribution of non-being is categorially of the same nature. These two categorially different meanings of Is usually are not clearly kept apart. As a result the existence of Ought systems is ascribed the character of the paradoxical. When speaking of the 'Is' (the existence) of an object one recalls *Kant's* assertion, important of and for itself and playing a central part in disproving the ontological proof of God, that – according to Kant – existence (being) is not a predicate. What a thing is, the totality of its properties, is – so we can say – determined by descriptors. 'Is' (Being, existence) is not one of these descriptors. When I say that the object A, which is determined by a class of

descriptors, exists, I do not supply an additional factual description of the object, but rather claim that the object determined by the descriptors exists, i.e. forms part of the world experienced.

Regardless of whether in the sentence form of the language 'exist' ('is', 'being') occurs as a grammatical predicate, Kant is right in saying that the attribution of existence does not constitute a description of the object, i.e. does not change the conceptual substratum characterizing the object. The existence of an object can therefore never be inferred from its characteristics, but rather always rests on empirical processes through which proof is furnished for the existence (or non-existence).[5]

2.3. Differentiation of Ought

In the conception originally advocated by *Hume*, *Kant* and the legal philosophers, particularly by the classical Pure Theory of Law (*H. Kelsen*, *F. Weyr*), Ought (the imperative) occurs as a uniform concept contrasted to Is (the descriptive sentence). The first differentiation between various kinds of Ought was stimulated by the contrasting analysis of the deontic operators. Several authors have noted structural analogies between the fundamental sentences of various fields:

---

[5]This seems to be contradicted by the case where the object is determined by logically or analytically determined characteristics. When a tautological characteristic has been stipulated (e.g. "to be red or not to be red"), then no differentiating designation comes about. But when a designation function is expressed by a contradiction ("to be circular and be non-circular") or by an analytically non-satisfiable characteristic (e.g. "to be circular and quadratic"), then a statement on the non-existence (e.g. of the circular square) is justifiable without experience from the structure of the analytical meaning of the designating function. (Cf. in this connection Ch. Weinberger, *Zur Logik der Annahmen* (On the Logic of Assumptions), Vienna 1976, p.34 et seq). These considerations, which call to mind earlier work by A. *Meinong*, have their place on a different level from that of *Kant*'s dictum on existence.

Leibniz[6], *A. Höfler*[7], *G. H. von Wright*[8]. The latter author contrasted here with one another the alethic, the epistemic, the deontic and the existence modes. The modal conception of the logic of norms as realized by the deontic systems has influenced the research in the field of logic, but also the juridical theory of Ought. In logic the mutual definability of the deontic (normative operators was presupposed as unproblematical – so much so that von Wright used permission (P) as a primitive concept of his system from 1951[9] – and deductions were accepted which in the problem field of the norm systems are not self-evident.[10] The fact that classical deontic logic did not provide an adequate structural theory of the conditional norm-sentence (although

---

[6]Cf. G. Kalinowski, J.-L. Gardies, Un logicien déontic avant la lettre: Gottfried Wilhelm Leibniz, *ARSP*, 60(1974), p.79–112. The title of the article shows that it was not with Leibniz that the priming of deontic logic originated. But it is interesting that these analogies were already perceived by him.

[7]A. Höfler, Abhängigkeitsbeziehungen zwischen Abhängigkeitsbeziehungen (Dependency Relationships between Dependency Relationships). *Proceedings of the Imperial Academy of Sciences in Vienna*, Vienna 1917, Vol.181, Section 4, p.41.

[8]G. H. von Wright, An Essay in Modal Logic, North-Holland Publishing Co, Amsterdam 1951. It was particularly by this book that the foundation was laid for the modal conception of the logic of norms, for deontic logic as an offspring of modal logic, and that research work in the field of the logic of norms was shaped. In the same year von Wright's article "Deontic Logic" in *Mind* 1951 (p.1–15) appeared.

[9]If one had proceeded from an analysis of the norms and the problem situation of their application and pragmatic role itself rather than from logico-systematic analogies, one could never have accepted permission as a basic concept of the field of norms. Permissions alone cannot have a regulating function, for they do not exclude any mode of behavior. Nor, by any means, does the interdefinition of normative operators appear unproblematical to us today (since their validity depends on additional characteristics of the norm system).

[10]I am thinking here first and foremost of "From '$O(p)$' follows '$O(p \vee q)$'" and "From '$O(p \wedge q)$' follow '$O(p)$' and '$O(q)$'".

this is the fundamental structure for legal thinking) was likewise soon realized[11], but did not lead to the disqualification of deontic logic.

The influence of the modal-logical approach to the logic of norms has influenced also the concept of Ought in jurisprudence. *Kelsen* introduces various types of Ought: first commanding, forbidding, permissing, then also derogating and empowering. The problems are still very much under discussion, but this is not the proper place for going into them. On the other hand, I wish to discuss in somewhat greater detail the contrastating of descriptive and prescriptive Ought as well as the distinction between three types of Ought: prescriptive, descriptive, and technical Ought.

2.4. Two types of Ought?

The duality of descriptive and prescriptive Ought occurs in the analytically oriented practical philosophy not only as an interpretation problem of the term 'Ought', but as a problem whose roots go deeper. It appears in different terminological variations:

(a) as interpretatio duplex of 'Ought',

(b) as a prescriptive and descriptive interpretation of O- and P-sentences of deontic logic (*von Wright*)[12],

(c) as a contrastating of 'norm-formulation' and 'normative statement' (*von Wright*),[13]

(d) as distinction between 'legal norm' and 'legal sentence' with *Kelsen*[14], or

[11]The dyadic systems of deontic logic were to provide recourse here. See G. H. von Wright, A Note on Deontic Logic and Derived Obligation, *Mind* 1956, p.507–509.

[12]Cf. G. H. von Wright, *Norm and Action. A Logical Enquiry*, Routledge & Kegan Paul, London 1963, p.132.

[13]G. H. von Wright, op.cit., p.101 et seq.

[14]H. Kelsen, *Reine Rechtslehre* (Pure Theory of Law), 2nd edition, Deuticke, Vienna 1960, p.57 et seq, 73 et seq.

(e) as 'norm' and 'judgment about the norm' with *K. Engliš*[15].

These conceptual contrastings are interrelated, but not identical. They are not only, and maybe not even primarily, intended to shed light on the relevant linguistic usage, but also play an essential part in ontological, communication-theoretical and logical analyses of norms.

It is undisputed that the German word for Ought, "sollen", expresses various things, and that sentences containing the verb 'sollen' have various pragmatic functions, depending on the circumstances.

Prescriptive 'Ought' is a pleonasm. 'Ought' always has prescriptive meaning. The mental contents presented through norm-producing acts – commands, legislation, origination of Customary Law, legal decisions – always, and particularly when decreeing an Ought, have prescriptive meaning. What is to be explained are the concepts of the descriptive Ought and the attempts to arrive, with the aid of these concepts, at a method for treating these norm-logical problems within the framework of a descriptive language.

A descriptive Ought must not be regarded as a type of Ought. That a descriptive Ought (as well as the introduction of analogous concepts such as 'legal sentence', 'judgment about the norm') is spoken about results from the fact that the question as to an Ought can be understood (and hence also answered) in different ways. Apart from being interpreted as a question as to the contents of a normative order (in that case the fitting answer is a norm- or Ought-sentence) it can be understood in two other ways: (a) as a question as to what should, correctly, be valid in the normative order considered (the answer will, as to its contents, be a norm-justification of the type of a *de lege ferenda* argumentation); (b) as a question as to the existence (the validity) of the norm under consideration as a component of the given normative order. Here the answer will be an ascertaining sentence, a sentence which can be true or false: a descriptive sentence about the norm (or the norm system concerned),

[15] K. Engliš, Malá logika (Brief Logic), Melantrich, Prague 1947; id., Postulát a norma nejsou soudy (The Postulate and the Norm are not Judgments), in: Časopis pro právní a státní vědu, Brno 1947, p.103.

or about an ontic relationship between both. This answer expresses an insight gained; it is an empirical, existential statement about the institutional existence of norms, and as such it can be true or false. But it has two peculiarities which distinguish it from other empirical statements about observations made. It is individualized by its normative content, which must be grasped, i.e. understood so that the statement about the existence of the norm will be meaningful and determined as to its contents. Here, therefore, it is necessary to understand the Ought (the norm-sentence concerned), and only then can the statement about the existence of the norm-sentence (the norm) be meaningfully made. Regardless of whether this existential statement is formulated as a statement on the validity of the norm N (of the Ought) or as a statement on N's belonging to the order of norms under consideration, in any event it will be a *meta*-statement about a linguistic entity: a norm-sentence N, or about its meaning (the norm, the Ought).

Hence to speak of a cognitive Ought is deceptive, for there is no such thing; instead, there are only descriptive statements about norm-sentences or about norms. This applies analogously to the thesis that Ought-sentences (norm-sentences) can be interpreted prescriptively or descriptively.[16] They can be grasped only as sentences that have a prescriptive meaning. Once they have been so grasped, one can make meta-linguistic statements about them (or about their meaning), i.e. say that they are valid or not valid, or that they are, or are not, components of an envisioned order of norms.

When statements on norm-sentences (norms) are taken into consideration, it will be necessary to give attention to a few ontological, gnoseological and logical questions.

How are the truth conditions of these meta-sentences determined? An ontology which regards the existence of norms as a social fact – and this is indispensable when we are speaking of the validity of norms – must include in the universe of the existent also ideal objects

[16]This seems to be the point of view of G. H. von Wright in *Norm and Action*. Cf. op.cit., chapter VI, also p.169.

which as such are not observable but only understandable. This real existence of the norm as a specific entity of thought must not be tied to the psychical or psychosocial process of the norm-setting act, as it is suggested to be necessary by several formulations of *Karel Engliš*, who says that it is only from the mouth of the norm creator that a norm (better probably: a norm-sentence, O.W.) will come forth, whereas all other people only pronounce judgments about norms.[17] The definition of the norm by Kelsen in his later period likewise ties the norm to the generating act. Kelsen's act-related definition, according to which the norm is the meaning of an act of will directed at the behavior of others, should – taken literally – imply that the existence of the norm so defined is tied to the norm-setting volitional act, thus existing only at the moment of its accomplishment. But Kelsen himself rejects this emphatically, so that he, too, arrives at a certain act-transcendent existence of the norm.[18]

If one recognizes that rules of common law, too, exist, come into being and are subject to change, then there are not only norms which outlast the point in time of the norm-setting act, but there is also a genesis of normative rules that are not generated by acts of will of this content.[19]

If one does not accept the idealization of the norm – its existence as ideal entity – but rather strictly ties it to the norm-generating act, then, however, *Engliš's* point of view is the only consistent one: namely that norm-sentences come only from the law-giver's mouth, with all others having knowledge about norms. The continued existence of the content of the norm-setting act, as a valid norm, remains unexplained.

In any event a statement about the norm or about the norm-sentence is dependent on a communication process between the norm-

[17]K. Engliš, Postulát a normy nejsou soudy, op.cit., p.103.

[18]H. Kelsen, *Allgemeine Theorie der Normen* (A General Theory of Norms), (posthumously edited by K. Ringhofer, R. Walter), Manz, Vienna 1979, p.22.

[19]Customary law consists of general rules, its generating basis is formed by individual cases; a general act of will is nowhere discernible here.

giver and the person making statements about the norm (or the norm-sentence). It must be presupposed here that the recipient understands the communication in the sense in which it was sent off. Only then will there be perfect communication. If a norm-sentence was sent off, the recipient must understand the communication as a norm-sentence, otherwise there will be no understanding – or only misunderstanding – between sender and receiver.

The consequences logically derivable from the sentence sent off must be the same as those from the sentence received by the recipient, otherwise the recipient will understand something different from what the sender intended.

Divergence of the consequences of a sentence (or of a thought) proves divergence of meaning. Believing that the sender interprets his sentence differently from the receiver – namely: the former normatively, the latter cognitively – makes for confusion of the analysis. To understand means: to comply with the communication, not to say something about it or to assess it. One may, of course, say something about the communicated message, but only after first having understood it, otherwise one would not know at all what one is talking about.

The truth criteria of the validity statement evidently can only then be applied if the norm-sentence has been understood. Then one can start working with principles of norm dynamics, with recognition rules and/or with the criteria of norm institutionalization.[20]

Here one cannot pass over the question whether logical consequences of the valid norms (e.g. according to the rule *de omni et nullo*) also have co-validity, and whether norm-logical consequences of valid norms and descriptive facts (e.g. according to the norm-logical detachment rule "From 'If p, then q ought to be' and 'p' follows 'q ought to be'") have co-validity if the premises have been set.

Hence the problem of the logic of norms is non-detachable from the theory of two kinds of Ought. I have the impression that these

[20]This question is answered differently be different analytical law theories. Cf. the theories of Kelsen, Merkl, Hart and MacCormick-Weinberger.

theories were developed for the very purpose of mastering the norm-logical problem by means of the logic of descriptive language.

The attempt to develop a logic of Ought-sentences in descriptive interpretation and then to arrive at a logic of norms through prescriptive interpretation[21] I regard as futile. This method is in fundamental conflict with the principles of the methodology of logical analysis (namely the postulate of the unambiguity of the premises), and there is no reason whatsoever to regard this trick of interpreting sentences doubly as a justification of a conclusion in the other (i.e. here: normative) interpretation.

2.5. A third kind of Ought: the technical Ought?

Von Wright also discusses the concept of a technical norm. "By a 'technical' norm one might mean a statement saying that a certain measure (action) or a certain state of affairs is necessary to ensure or to avoid something."[22]

The reflections about a technical Ought (or Must) and about anancastic sentences lead only to unclarities and not at all to a usable substitute theory.

As an example of a technical norm or technical rule the author mentions: "If you want the roof to be safely supported, you ought to make the beams thus and thus thick." He contrasts it on the one hand to the 'anancastic sentences' and on the other hand to the action norms. The anancastic sentence corresponding to the technical norm cited reads: "In order to support the roof (safely) the beams ought to be thus and thus thick. Instead of 'ought to be' we could here also say

[21]Cf. G. H. von Wright in Chapter *IV Deontic Logic: Hypothetical Norms* of the book *Norm and Action*, op.cit.

[22]G. H. von Wright, Bedingungsnormen – ein Prüfstein für die Normenlogik (Conditional Norms – A Touchstone for the Logic of Norms), W. Krawiec at al (eds.) *Theorie der Normen. Festgabe für Ota Weinberger zum 65. Geburtstag*, Duncker & Humblot, Berlin 1984, p. 455.

'must be' or 'have to be'."[23] Anancastic sentences express what must be done (what must be) so that a given goal may be reached.

The difference between anancastic sentences and technical norms is not wholly clear to me. Both sentences are of purely indicative nature. In the technical norms an Ought or Must in a prescriptive sense is just as little contained as in the anancastic sentences. Although containing the phrase 'You ought to', the technical sentences do not, in my opinion, express any Ought at all. An Ought that is valid under the condition that the addressee wishes to attain something is not an Ought (not a command, not a prohibition); all that is expressed is a causal relationship, a possible action program that may be opted for when the goal concerned is pursued. The technical norm is a guide for the case of need, a piece of 'know-how', but not a prescription; it has nothing whatsoever to do with a normative Ought.

[23]G. H. von Wright, The Foundation of Norms and Normative Statements; op.cit., p.73.

Chapter 3

Practical Rationality

If one stands on the ground of a dichotomous semantics which distinguishes and separates from one another two semantic spheres: position-taking mental contents and descriptive ones, one must also confront the question whether in practical (action-related) thinking, too, rational structures can be identified and whether in the practical field, too, proof and justification exist. And precisely this, in my opinion, is the problem of practical rationality.

The analyses are rendered highly complicated by two circumstances: (a) by the confusing ambiguity of the terms "rational" and "rationality", both in everyday and in scientific linguistic practice; and (b) by the tradition, rather deeply entrenched in philosophy and logic, to regard rational thinking as an operating procedure exclusively serving the purposes of cognition and knowledge-processing.

On the other hand, however, it is evident that the point of view recognizing the epistemological primacy of the practice corresponds to the conception that rational operations are not limited to processes of the gathering and processing of knowledge, hence not limited to the cognitive field, but that the processing of information in the field of practical mental contents likewise plays its part and that here, too, proof and justification do exist.

3.1. The relationship between thought, knowledge and action

The traditional conceptions, too, of course pay due attention to the fact that mental operations are relevant for action. Nevertheless, with the epistemological primacy of the practice being presupposed, and with the world being viewed in the light of information-theoretically founded practical philosophy, the interaction of thinking, knowledge-gathering and action is, as a matter of principle, constituted differently from what is customary in philosophical tradition.

Thinking is traditionally regarded as an instrument of cognition and processing of the knowledge system. It takes part in the cognition of truths: factual truths or rational truths, to speak with Leibniz. The knowledge system forms the basis of action. In the traditional view the determination of action is not regarded as a thinking process. Volition is contrasted to thinking. This conception can be graphically indicated by the following scheme (T = Thinking, C = Cognition, A = Action):

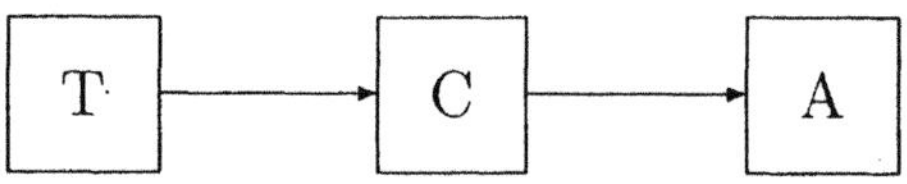

[Thinking influences action (including volition) through cognition. Action-determining volition (the operations conducted with information and leading to decisions) does (do) not form part of (rational) thinking.]

In a wholly different light does the relationship between thinking, cognition and action (willing, deciding) appear if one stands on the ground of a world-view of acting beings. Thinking results from a biologically given activity of every living being and constitutes information-processing both in the field of the pursuit and acquisition of knowledge and in the application of the knowledge system to individual cases and to the prosessing of information, namely of descriptive and practical information, in action-determining operations.

Willing and deciding is in that case not the categorial opposite of thinking (as the instrument of cognition). Highly simplified this leads to the following functional scheme of the relations between thinking and acting:

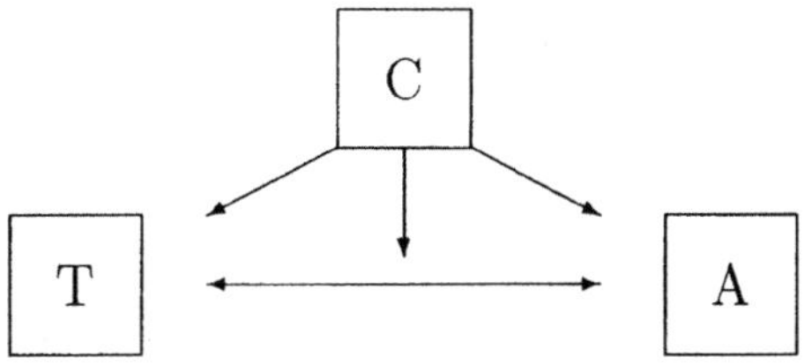

[Thinking is one of the instruments of the stream of life; it serves for the processing of information in the field of cognition and of the acquisition of knowledge, but also for the determination and guidance of actions. The functions of Willing are specific information-processing operations, which, however, are based not only on cognitive, but also on practical information.]

Earlier – see Chapter 1 – I have tried to show that the field of practice, too, i.e. the field of action-related thinking, may be the object of specific logical systems and that such systems – particularly the logic of norms – have succeeded in securing themselves a place in modern logic. This, however, still falls far short of clarifying the philosophical and methodological problem of the relation between action and rationality. A major part of the still open problems springs from the fact that widely varying philosophical explications of the rationality concept are given.

Before entering more deeply into these problems I must analyze the polysemy of "rational" and "rationality" so that it will be clear what I am talking about when using these terms.

"Rational" has acquired a positive emotional tone and is therefore often used in a recommendatory sense, metaphorically, as it were.

These manners of speaking, where something is simply termed reasonable or rational just to make it appear in a favorable light, can be left out of consideration here.

3.2. The ambiguity of "rational"

The most important ambiguity of the concept "rationality" may be characterized by the contrasting of (I) logical-operational rationality, and (II) methodological rationality postulates.

(I) Logical-operational rationality pertains to the structure of thoughts and of their expressions. It strives for structural precision, clarity and adequacy of the forms of expression as well as for forms of thinking and argumentation that will – in conformity with the operating rules – be consistent and logical. We are concerned here with the proving of practical theses and with formally correct arguing.

(II) In various problem fields, certain methods for considering, examining, or justifying matters are postulated as adequate foundations and procedures and recommended as rational or the sole reasonable methods.

It is demanded e.g. that statements of fact and laws of nature be acquired and proven by experience and specific research procedures. Only then will they be considered rational, or rationally justified.[1]

Rationality in a methodological sense is not only to be effective, but must also ensure convincing and useful results of the research carried out and the effort expended. In the field of the practice the methodological rationality postulates run in two directions: they strive for maximum utility of the action and/or for interpersonal (democratic, as it were) optimization through consensual acceptance.

[1] Probably the best known example of a methodologically conceived rationality is *Popper's* doctrine of critical rationalism and of the several variations of rational methodology that can be traced back to this conception. Research methodology not being the subject of this book, I will neither go here into the merits, nor into the problems of this science-theoretical approach.

It is understandable why such mixing-up of the various types of rationality, essentially different though they are in themselves, occurs, notwithstanding the great harm done thereby to the clarity of the philosophical analyses. Logical-operational rationality, which – in my eyes – is the fundamental type, does not suffice for proving and justifying informative (as opposed to logical-tautological) theses. It is therefore believed (though generally not explicitly mentioned) that the rationality of the structural conceptions and of the operations needs to be supplemented by methodological postulates that are concerned with contents and guarantee success. I believe, however, that question (I) embodies the true rationality problems and that methodological principles and recipes should not sail under the flag of rationality. They must prove their worth in practice in a different way than is expected of logical-rational principles.

3.3. The ratio is not a reservoir of material-aprioristic truths

A further difficulty encountered at the threshold of our reflections on practical rationality is the fact that in the history of philosophy rationalistic systems or concepts have often been spoken of in a sense which is incompatible with what philosophical analysis means by logical-operational rationality.

The doctrines that are termed rationalistic in the history of philosophy justify their views chiefly by depicting them as immanent characteristics of reason. Ratio (reason) is thus viewed as a certain reservoir of theses about the field concerned, and the rationalistic philosophers try in different ways to demonstrate the presence of these structures and the validity of these theses, both anchored in reason itself, and thus to arrive at a theory about the contents of the given field.

In practical philosophy, interest centers first and foremost on so-called practical reason, which functions as source of the theory of morality and justice, while in argumentation the conceptions of practical reason vacillate between formal criteria (such as *Kant's* doctrine of the categorical imperative or *Hare's* universalizability principle) and intuitionist assumptions of phenomenological analyses. Somehow, however, the idea always remains present in the background that reason constitutes the decisive immanent reservoir of the principles of morality and justice.[2]

But the idea of reason as a reservoir of conceptions of contents is the very opposite of the basic philosophical-analytical point of view of logical-operational rationality. Only forms are elements (or constructs) of the ratio, and the operations are transformations that are well-founded within the framework of constitutional systems. But neither the structures, nor the operations are themselves theses of contents, but rather tautological, i.e. empty.[3]

Reason and rational analysis are operations that are determinative of structure and equipped with formal certainty, but without premises of contents they cannot establish a conception. Whoever tries to accomplish this is in error, thinks erroneously. This, at bottom, is the basic conviction of modern logical analysis, which is based on the

---

[2] *Kant's* categorical imperative in the formulation "Act only according to the maxim which you can wish at the same time to become a general law" has been determined as a rule for autonomous considerations of morality. It will, however, only then lead to unambiguous determinations of moral Ought if one makes the metaphysical assumption that there is an immanent realm of ends through which this wishing is rendered uniform and conceived of as universally valid. *Hare's* universalization principle, too, is far removed from being an objective deciding instrument of moral analysis, devoid of decisionist moments. It is a matter of decision in what directions the generalization is carried out and how the universe of reference persons is determined. (Cf. O. Weinberger, *Recht, Institution und Rechtspolitik* (Law, Institution, and Policy of Law), Steiner, Stuttgart 1987, p.252 et seq.).

[3] "Tautological" need not be truth-functionally understood here as "true for every possible assignment of values". In the practical field, too, this "being empty", "being non-informative", as opposed to (informative) theses of contents applies. Here, too, logical operating is non-creative inasmuch as no substantial results can be obtained without premises of contents.

separation of form and content. From the logic of descriptive language alone – i.e. without empirical premises – no physics or other science can be derived. Just as little does a substantially determined morality or conception of justice follow from the logics of practical thinking alone. The justification of practical theses will always require practical premises. The consequence of this for practical philosophy in a broad sense is: There is no purely cognitive and decision-free justification of values, ends and norms. This thesis is termed non-cognitivism in practical philosophy.

3.4. Philosophy of the sources of logical rationality

The philosophical justification of rationality as a necessity of structures and strict logical binding force is of highly varying nature, with every approach and epistemological construction employed supplying its own view. Here, in a rough overview, I merely wish to mention a few schools of thought.

The forms of the thought may be regarded as immanently given matters which, while possibly obscure from the beginning, have nevertheless absolute validity as platonic ideas and structures of thought – immanent structures of our mind which can be understood and analytically grasped. This view corresponds first and foremost to a criticistic or neo-criticistic philosophy.

The phenomenological approach is related to platonic immanentism to the extent that objectively existing structures are presupposed. However, in this approach chief weight is attached to the manner of analysis. The essentialities are elaborated from a consideration of the investigated phenomena through a special manner of analyzing, namely through phenomenological reduction. The result is an objectively conceived survey of the basic structures and basic elements (e.g. values) of the field.

Exponents of ethology (especially Konrad Lorenz) try to explicate the aprioristic elements of cognition and thinking as results of independent tribal evolution, in contrast, as it were, to the usual acquisition of knowledge through individual experience[4].

The modern form of logicism does not emphasize the immanent structures of thought, but rather the explicit and constructive structure of the system, with the binding element being the strict observance of the operational rules – this being, according to this conception, the core of the fundamental postulate of every logic "Logique oblige" –, while the possibility of laying down various principles is kept open. Modern logicism is "tolerant" in that it, as a matter of principle, regards every consistent system as admissible, and it is constructivistically oriented in that it regards various systems as equally acceptable from the logical point of view, regardless of whether or not they conform to everyday linguistic and thinking practice. The tolerance principle and free constructivistic approach have, however, the following important corollaries:

1. It must be explained and proven why and that the system proposed is adequate. For the consistency of this system alone does not warrant its adequacy for the given field or analytical task. (We may e.g. present a logically faultless system which, as deontic logic, aspires to offer a theory of norm-logical deduction; but whether the system does in fact accomplish this must be the object of an adequacy test.[5])

2. The system is non-creative as far as contents are concerned: From the proposed structures and operations alone – without empirical

[4]K. Lorenz, *Kants Lehre vom Apriorischen im Lichte gegenwärtiger Biologie* (Kant's Doctrine of the A priori in the Light of Present-day Biology, 1941), Blätter für deutsche Philosophie 15, p94–125, *id., Vergleichende Verhaltensforschung, Grundlagen der Ethologie* (Comparative Research of Behavior, Fundamentals of Ethology), Springer, Vienna, New York 1978; furthermore: Ch. Weinberger, *Evolution und Ethologie. Wissenschaftstheoretische Analysen* (Evolution and Ethology, Science-Theoretical Analyses), Springer, Vienna, New York 1983, p.206 et seq.

[5]Cf. chapter 7 of this book.

or practical premises (preconditions, inputs) no ascertainment of a state of affairs or practical information can be obtained.

3.5. Excursion on discursive rationality

A peculiar approach to our problem field is supplied by the philosophy of discourse (*J. Habermas, K.-O. Apel, R. Alexy*, et al.). This conception has come to influence practical philosophy to a not inconsiderable extent – particularly in the German-speaking part of the world. Therefore, although considering this theory to be out of place, I must devote some reflections to this so-called discursive rationality here. The philosophical basis for this conception of rationality is furnished by the *Habermas* variety of discursive philosophy.

While discursive rationality is more of a theory of rationality in a methodological sense than a theory of operational reason, it does contain certain elements that are relevant for the view of an existing logical-operational rationality: namely the consensus theory of truth, and the constrasting of thinking by the individual subject to argumentation in interpersonal discursive processes. The essence of rationality is conceived of here as being founded precisely in the interpersonal manner of proceeding.

Discursive philosophy is based on a "collectivization of the ratio". This philosophical conception adhered to by *Jürgen Habermas*, *Karl-Otto Apel* and others advocates above all the following theses:

1. The rationality of discourse: Rational is what produces consensus in (an ideal) discourse. The reasonable is sociologized by the presentation of an interpersonal process, as opposed to individual thinking, as a characteristic of the rational.

2. The processes of dispute occurring in real life are contrasted to an *ex definitione* unreal, so-called "ideal discourse", which is defined as free from domination, accessible to all, and of unlimited duration. It is used as a means for the defining of truth and correctness and is held out as a standard which real discourses should approximate.

3. The traditional concept of truth is contrasted to the concept of truth by consensus: True is what brings about a universal consensus in the ideal discourse.

4. Both in the cognitive and in the practical sphere, consensus is regarded as the goal and the sole decisive criterion.

5. Sound reasons in argumentation are precisely those which convince the audience: the quality of the arguments is judged by their persuasiveness.

6. Certain preconditions for communication are posited as universally necessary, namely: veracity and the preparedness to defend theses (any communication) in open discourse.

7. From the immanent principles of communication – those presupposed all along – necessary valid principles of morality are derived.

Ad 1:

Processes of rational argumentation – proofs and justifications – are neither individual, nor collectivistic. They are to be understood, not as pragmatic operations between people, but as justifications that are based on good arguments. It is a fundamental characteristic of them that they are understood objectively. They are judged to be either valid or invalid. The rational relation on which any rational argumentation is based must be clearly distinguished from the pragmatic processes of interpersonal persuasion. (One can persuade somebody with rational arguments, but sometimes also with false or deceptive theses. And it may even happen that a strict, mathematical proof does not convince a listener at all, e.g. because he fails to understand it, or because it runs against thoroughly entrenched prejudices.)

Ad 2:

The concept of an ideal discourse is a bad idealization: it neither grasps the essence of a clash of opinions, nor the conditions of progress-promoting discussion. Freedom from domination is unrealistic under any circumstances under which people live. Furthermore, despite oppression, courage of conviction can make people speak the truth and fight for progress. (Consider the actions of dissidents, or the struggle of free spirits against ecclesiastical prejudices.) Even if we could imagine a domination-free discourse (in which not even the authority of great thinkers would be allowed special influence), this does not ensure yet by any means that the participants in the discourse will have good ideas and/or think up research methods and procedures of proof that will bring things ahead. While freedom from domination does indeed obviate the need for courage to criticize, this woould not ensure that the critique will analytically hit the mark. Nor do universal and free participation or unlimited time guarantee that the ideal discourses will take a fruitful course and lead to a consensus. It cannot even be safely said that a later stage of the opinion prevailing in the discourse will always be closer to true cognition than an earlier one. *Habermas's* criteria for an ideal discourse guarantee neither optimization of the argumentations, nor a universal convergence of the opinions. The ideal discourse is therefore not a usable yardstick for real discourses. The practice of real discourses is often disturbed by circumstances which *Habermas's* theory does not visualize at all: eristic moments, prejudices of various kinds, an inadequate apparatus of concepts, insufficient conceptual analysis, and the like.

Ad 3:

The consensus theory of truth is inacceptable for at least two reasons: (a) Every participant in the discourse advocates a subjective opinion. Even if all are of the same opinion, it remains exactly that: an opinion – which may well be wrong, for all may err. (b) Truth by consensus has the character of a limit which should be approximated in an ideal discourse. Since it has not been proven and is not provable that (I) discourse, as it progresses, will necessarily approach its limit, namely truth, and that (II) every ideal discourse approximates one single value, the existence of this limit has not been proven. To speak of consensual truth as meant by *Habermas* is, therefore, logically inadmissible, since the existence of the entity defined as limit has not been proven.

Ad 4:

Even in the case of a universal consensus of opinion – and all the more so in that of mere majority opinions – the objective validity of the thesis will remain open and the possibility of critique and revision will always continue to exist.

As a matter of principle it is necessary to distinguish between a consensus in discourses that have actually taken place, and a presupposed consensus[6] in an ideal (and hence unreal and merely figurative) discourse. In favor of the former alternative speaks the (disprovable) presumption of the currently prevailing opinion and, if the issue is one of practical political matters, the democratic vote. In the case of the ideal discourse, which is always non-realistic, a reversal of the justification path comes about: The consensus is not an ascertained fact from which the justification might start out; rather, a thesis is considered so plausible (so well justified of and for itself) that one presupposes that it ought to find general recognition. Consensus in the ideal discourse is, therefore, not a means of proof or justification, but only a suggestive manner of presentation.

Consensus is not a criterion for truth or correctness, but only a rhetorically effective suggestion of where they are to be found. The orientation of efforts to a social consensus detracts from the true basic tasks of the sciences and of philosophical analysis, namely the invention of methods of research, of proof, and of justification.

From the philosophy of discourse there does not result an adequate view of the disputes in society in which the critical analysis of the argumentations plays a decisive part – vitally important especially in an era in which more and more marketing methods are penetrating into political life.

Democratic practice should not concentrate on the finding of a consensus, but should also put up with differences of opinion and with

---

[6]In an ideal (hence non-realistic) discourse, an actual consensus of course cannot come about.

dissent.[7] Democracy is an "open society", a toleration of differences of forms of life and of critical dissent, not a standstill in the spirit of the opinion on which consensus reigns. The dynamics of spiritual and political progress is an interaction of a search for consensus and processes of critical dissent.

Ad 5:

A consequence of the view that argumentation is a pragmatic process between speaker and audience is the evaluation of good reasons according to the persuasive power they exert on the audience. Here the erratic nature of discourse philosophy manifests itself quite markedly: The problem of the objectively good reasons, which depend on the methodology of the various fields under discussion, is misinterpreted as a pragmatic relationship of convincing (or persuasion). Justification and objective plausibility are mixed up with the ways and means of persuasive communication. The absurdity of *Habermas's* conception of the "good reasons" leaps to the eye when one considers that objectively wholly false reasons – "The earth cannot be spherical, for otherwise our antipodes would fall into space." "The downfall of Stalinism disproves the possibility of socialist systems." – would have to be recognized as good reasons because they have been factually accepted and have produced convictions.[8]

Ad 6:

In and for itself it is correct that the carrying-out of interpersonal communication presupposes certain pragmatic principles which the users of language presuppose implicitly as their basis for mutual understanding. However, the postulates which discourse philosophy regards here as having existed all along, as necessary and obligatory, are something quite different from the preconditions for communica-

[7]Cf. N. Rescher, *Pluralism. Against the Demand of Consensus*, Oxford Univ. Press, Oxford 1993.

[8]Vide O. Weinberger, Zur Theorie der politischen Argumentation (On the Theory of Political Argumentation), in: *Rechtstheorie* 2/1995, Vol.26, p.163–182.

tion according to my conception. In my opinion, when making factual communications one presupposes that the communicated descriptions of states of affairs are presented as communications conforming to the truth, a principle which I have called Assertion Convention.[9] (This is not a logical necessity; under certain circumstances people can also talk with one another on the basis of an opposite stipulation. In ironical parlance a state of affairs is described which is communicated as not being true.) This postulate does not exclude lies: it is, on the contrary, also the basis of the lie. A communication falling under the Assertion Convention will become a lie precisely if and only if something is presented as true by a speaker who knows that the assertion is in fact not true.

Habermas believes that the requirement always to speak the truth constitutes an indispensable prerequisite for communication. Now while this view of *Habermas* is up to a point backed up by correct considerations, it is wrong nevertheless. Were one to know, when receiving information, that there is only a 50% chance of the information being true, one would not, by this communication, receive any information at all. Communications will only then have any informative value if there is a far better than 50% chance of the communication being true. This does not mean, however, that communication is possible only under the duty of telling the truth. The statements of a defendant in court are understood – even though he is not obligated to tell the truth. Even lies do not destroy the communication system, for the Assertion Convention remains in existence, being as it is, as already mentioned, the very basis of the possibility to lie.

Of course there are relationships – e.g. interpersonal discourse in search of knowledge – where veracity is the precondition of effectiveness. Yet veracity, i.e. the strict endeavor of the speakers to say exactly that which they believe to be true, is not a necessary prerequisite of communication.

---

[9] O. Weinberger, *Rechtslogik* (The Logic of Law), 2nd ed., Duncker & Humblot, Berlin 1989, p.54.

And wholly misplaced is the view that every speaker, in making an assertion, implicitly commits himself to justifying it in discourses. If I were only allowed to say what I can prove, I would have to keep my mouth shut far more often.

Ad 7:

The attempt to derive an *a priori* ethics, as it were, from those principles of communication "that were always presupposed" is misplaced. The principles of communication as presupposed by *Habermas* and *Apel* do not, in my opinion, apply; and it is inacceptable, conflicting as it does with the ideas of ethical autonomy, to regard as morally binding that which the living and communicating community universally recognizes as such and heteronomously imposes on me in this fashion.

Of the basic positions of the discourse philosophy hardly anything remains valid; but what appears to me to be the worst is that it diverts the methodology of science away from objectivity and from reflecting on problems of researching and proving methods to the pragmatics of gaining acclaim. Nor does it offer a good starting position for the critical study of argumentation, for without distinguishing between objective validity and persuasive effect no practicable analysis of argumentation is possible: The currently virulent problems of political indoctrination and marketing propaganda hardly come into the field of vision of this doctrine, although these are the very problems which constitute the most important difficulties of present-day political life in the democratic systems. The massive employment of propaganda material – from giant posters to the exertion of influence on the manner of presenting matters or issues in the mass media (as effected by economic and/or ideological-eristic means) – not only provides the politicians concerned and their programmatic theses with publicity, without – or practically without – any objective arguments needing to be put up. The poster as a public opinion formation agent and a determinant of electoral behavior flies in the face of the opinion that social discourse is a means of rational dispute, and that the effectiveness of the means employed in the dispute defines their quality. To assume that the rationality of a dispute is assured by the collectivity of the discourse processes themselves is, given the political reality of propaganda – even in the democracies –, simply naive.

A special variety of discourse rationality is *R. Alexy's* attempt to define the rationality of the discourses through rules of discourse.[10] This does not make discourse philosophy any clearer. What, in the final instance, is decisive for the rationality of a thesis: the consensus as presented in an ideal discourse, or the observance of the rules of discourse? The two need not amount to the same thing. Critical remarks on Alexy's rules of discourse have been presented by me elsewhere.[11]

Alexy's theory is oriented primarily to the practical field – ethics and jurisprudence. Nevertheless it has the setback that Alexy does not explicitly take a stand on certain basic questions of discourse philosophy, such as, in particular, the consensus theory of truth, or on the question "whether by and for itself the justification of one's views is, by its nature, a monologic or a communicative undertaking".[12]

---

[10]R. Alexy, *Theorie der juristischen Argumentation. Die Theorie des rationalen Diskurses als Theorie der juristischen Begründung*), Suhrkamp, Frankfurt am Main, 1st ed. 1978, 2nd ed. 1983. English version: A Theory of Legal Argumentation. The theory of Rational Discourse as Theory of Legal Justification, Clarendon Press, Oxford 1989.

[11]O. Weinberger, Grundlagen des Institutionalistischen Rechtspositivismus (Fundamentals of Institutionalist Legal Positivism), in: P. Koller et al.(eds.), *Institution und Recht* (Institution and Law), International Symposium in Graz, Austria, in Honor of Ota Weinberger, *Rechtstheorie*, Beiheft (Special Issue) 14, 1994, Chapter "Theorie der Argumentation: Was heisst rational begründen?" (Theory of Argumentation: What does rational justification mean?), p.253–266; *id.*, Streit um die praktische Vernunft. Gegen Scheinargumente in der praktischen Philosophie (Practical rationality in dispute. Against fallacious arguments in practical philosophy), in *ARSP*, Beiheft (Special Issue) 51, R. Alexy, R. Dreier (eds.), *Rechtssytem und praktische Vernunft* (Legal System and Practical Rationality), 1993, p.30–46.

[12]Cf. in this connection R. Alexy, Ota Weinbergers Kritik der diskurstheoretischen Deutung juristischer Rationalität (Ota Weinberger's Critique of the Interpretation of Juridical Rationality According to the Theory of Discourse), in P. Koller et al.(eds.), *Institution und Recht* (Institution and Law), op.cit., p.143–157.

I feel united with Robert Alexy not only in collegial friendship, but also by two moments of scientific orientation: 1. our joint endeavor to make the field of practical philosophy as accessible as possible to rational analysis and argumentation, and 2. the conviction that argumentation must be logically consistent ("Logique oblige"). Therefore our dispute can be fruitful, despite differences of opinion on fundamental questions.

Alexy's doctrine proceeds in essence from *Habermas's* discourse philosophy: it is chiefly directed at the field of practical philosophy. The particularity of Alexy's point of view is, in my opinion, to be seen first and foremost in the following moments: Ideal discourses play only a less important part in his writings; he works with the concept of relative correctness and tries to formulate rules of discourse whose observance is to define the rationality of the discourses. His controversial special-case thesis and four-step model of the legal system are intended to provide a foundation for a discourse-theoretical theory. Regrettably, however, he did not occupy himself in an analytical-critical way with the foundations of discourse philosophy: consensual truth, the problematical postulate of the communication of argumentation, the problem of consensus in an ideal discourse, and the like. One cannot go only so far as to say: "I wish to leave open whether by and for itself the justification of one's views is, by its nature, a monologic or a communicative undertaking"[13] – and leave things at that.

Alexy is always prepared to meet objections by more or less convincing counter-arguments and modifications of his theory – and he does so with great skill and ingenuity, but he shows little preparedness to abandon problematical preconditions of discourse philosophy.

[13]It is not without interest – for it casts light on part of the motivation for discourse theory – that Apel concedes humanitarian-emancipatory Neo-Marxism an ethically-founded function. "For it is clear that the task of realizing the ideal communication community also implies the elimination of the class society, or, as formulated in terms of the communication theory: the removal of all socially conditioned asymmetries from interpersonal dialog", says Apel (op.cit., p.432).

Alexy concedes that discourse theory is not decision-definitive. (If he applies this also – as he actually should – to the theoretical sphere, the consensus theory of truth will collapse.)

The author introduces the concept of relative correctness, corresponding to the finding that it cannot be assumed that exactly one answer will be possible to every practical question. Such a correctness concept is undoubtedly problematical, not so much because it runs contrary to the customary understanding of correctness, but rather because of its inevitable consequence: Correctness will then not tell us how we should act ethically, but will rather make ethical decisions dependent on the taking of positions, at least insofar as it is a question of deciding between correctness alternatives.

When the correctness of a norm or evaluation is conceived of as a procedural possibility, we will end up with so weak a concept of validity as will hardly be of any use for an argumentation that will determine our action.[14]

If different solutions are termed equally correct, this is apt to raise linguistic eyebrows. It would be better to speak of "justifiable solutions" – as lawyers usually put it –, for when different things are all recognized as correct, further discussion is cut short, which I, although a relativist, would hate to do and which would be even less fitting for Alexy, operating as he does with the concept of practical rationality.

It is unacceptable in this situation nevertheless to claim: "Basic to the theory of discourse is ... an *absolute procedural* concept of correctness." The absolute character of the correctness striven for is justified by the author by stipulating, as regulative idea, the goal of finding one single correct answer to practical questions. For one thing, such a demand does not help us when we know it to be non-satisfiable (it was presupposed that there is no single correct answer), and for another, even every relativist – if in search of justification at all –

[14] R. Alexy, op.cit. in footnote 12.

strives to determine – if possible – in an unambiguous fashion just what is correct.[15]

Discourse theory as a theory of practical rationality in the sense of a cognitivist method for grasping the objectively correct in the realm of values and of Ought is by no means a well-founded conception.

The rationality of practical discourse is perceived by Alexy not only in the observance of the moments defining the ideal discourses (in the case of real discourses this obviously can come to pass only approximately), but also in the observance of the rules of discourse. If one determines the rationality of a discourse according to whether the pre-set rules are observed, the persons lose the role of deciding authorities and are reduced to producers of discussion remarks.

I consider it problematical to stipulate simultaneously the criterion of consensus and that of the observance of the rules of discourse as conditions of rationality. What happens if a universal discourse comes about without the rules of discourse being observed? They can never be perfectly satisfied. Will e.g. the result of the discourse already become irrational for the sole reason that some participant in the discourse has failed to make use of his right to raise objections, propose solutions or claim specific interests? One probably would then have to declare practically everything irrational that is produced in real discourses. If one, with Alexy, regards correctness as a set of alternatives, then anything which can be brought to pass without violation of the rules might be considered rational. Then, however, the dispute itself and a possible result by consensus become relatively unimportant for the determination of what is rational.

The rules of discourse are in many a respect problematical; in any event they have the following shortcomings:

---

[15] "A normative statement N is correct if and only if it can be the result of the procedure P." [R. Alexy, Die Idee einer prozeduralen Theorie der juristischen Argumentation (The Idea of a Procedural Theory of Juridical Argumentation), in: A. Aarnio et al.(eds.), Methodologie und Erkenntnistheorie der juristischen Argumentation (Methodology and Epistemology of Juridical Argumentation)], *Rechtstheorie* 1981, Beiheft (Special Issue) 2, p.178.

They do not determine what reasons are to be considered good, nor what interest is to be preferred among conflicting ones. Hence in the most vital respects they let one down as decision aids.

They are culture-dependent, or more precisely: marked by the ideals of *our* culture. They render many a stand on contents immune to change.

No matter whether one defines, in accordance with *Habermas'* conception, truth and correctness as the result of discourse or, with Alexy, proceeds from procedureal possibilities and several "correct"[16] answers to practical questions, discourse philosophy appears to me to be in both cases an extremely problematical doctrine:

1. From the opinion of the participants in the discourse there is no way leading to objective truth or to correctness. From the field of opinions there leads no valid path to the objectivity of knowledge.

2. There is the danger that the discourse theoreticians will, through their rules of discourse, introduce certain conceptions of contents as indisputably correct, this *de facto* without objective proof.

3. Through this methodological view, attention is concentrated wholly on the discourse process and on consensus, rather than at the method of adducing proof and at the empirical basis of the theses.

4. In actual reality, consensus is not always attainable, neither as a universal consensus nor as one of a strong majority. Does the question of rationality thereby become unsolvable or even meaningless?

5. In my opinion, two things are mixed up here: the problem field of rational motivation – which actually forms the justification of the acceptance of theses – and the democratic striving to arrive at a consensus and/or at compromises through discourses.

[16] I employ quotation marks here, as this term is not being used here in its customary sense.

3.6. Action and justification

It is a characteristic and essential feature of actions that justification is given for the type of behavior that makes up their content. "Justification" is not meant here in the sense of a conscious argumentation process, but rather as a reproduceable and endorsable – sometimes conscious or partially conscious – process of information-processing.

That actions, as a special type of behavior, are characterized by information-dependent determination and justification of behavior is something most action theoreticians have become aware of, even though they have, in their majority, rather strongly been influenced by a behavioristic approach.

As justification of actions, two elements occur: rules and ends.

If actions are conceived of as "behavior according to rules", then this may be understood differently, depending on how one conceives of the concept of the rule and of the manner of functioning of rules. If, as essence of a rule, particularly the similarity of the behavioral modes affected by it is emphasized, while the manner of functioning of the rule is viewed as an entrenched pattern set by habit, then the action is seen as something close to a result achieved through social drill. If the rule is understood as a behavioral norm, as an Ought addressing a volitional subject making decisions on what behavior to realize, then the rule is a determinant of the action within the context of the determination of action through information. To regard the action as a mere result of habit, socialization and drill is something I regard as incorrect, even though such moments de facto play an accompanying role in the process of action determination. The essence of the action is the process of the selection of behavior as justified by information-processing, not the mere habituation and drilling mechanism.

Action as satisfaction of normative rules is a special component of the justifying determination of the action in addition to the teleological determination of the decisions for the action. And since the normative rules are to be regarded as end-oriented themselves, the justification of actions by rules of Ought is to be regarded as a component of the teleological conception of action-determining decision.

The basic manner of justifying the action is provided by considerations of the end pursued. In the reflections preceding the action, actions are guided by the ends pursued by (and the preferences of) the agent; and from the perspective of the onlooker, actions are noted and explained through interpreting the intentions of the agent.

Action is said to be governed by end-oriented rationality. However, the talk of end-oriented rationality as a special manner of explanation is, in a way, deceptive. It creates the impression as if merely calling something (particularly an action) rational for the sake of some end already furnishes an explanation for the action.

However, calling attention to the determination of an action by an end will only then contribute to the determination or explanation of the action if the ends (the system of ends) of the agent are indicated. It must not be presupposed, as the general talk of end-oriented rationality implicitly does, that in a teleological consideration a system of immanent ends is finding application. Such an immanent realm or ends does not exist; rather it is a question here of a teleological analysis in which the ends set and preferences applied in the given case must be made explicit.

3.7. The characteristics of practical rationality

Here, now, I wish to briefly summarize my personal views in the matter or practical rationality.

I understand rationality in a structural and logical-operational sense. This applies in equal measure to the cognitive (purely descriptive) and to the practical field. This implies the separation of formal relationships – logical ties, so to speak – and premises of contents.

There is no material a priori, neither with respect to the observable world of facts, nor to the field of the practice. In practical philosophy the conception that immanent contents exist and are a priori binding is designated by the term "practical rationality". Just as there is no experience-independent knowledge of nature, there likewise is no practical rationality, no a priori valid reservoir of values and Ought principles of a contents nature.

Hence there is no practical knowledge as a cognitive path toward the grasping of objectively (and a priori) valid values and normative principles.

However, in the field of practical thinking, too, there exist structural ties and logically binding operations. The arguments of practical justifications and proofs are system-relative, attitudes which enter into the argumentation as stipulations by the subjects.

The recognition of practical rationality in the sense indicated here is not in conflict with the thesis of non-cognitivism. For the latter does not deny the logical ties existing in the practical field, but only the possibility of justifying practical sentences (norms, ends, values, preferences) without presupposed practical premises.

The structure of the action-related thinking operations is represented in systems of practical thinking: formal teleology, formal axiology, logics of preferences, logic of norms.[17] Between the practical disciplines mentioned there exist indissoluble relationships. Formal teleology shows e.g. that the selection of the optimal means from the set of possible ones is determined by preferential analyses. The teleological determination of action must take normative action determinants into account and explain their role within the framework of action determination on the basis of information. The logic of the practice comprises a complex of practical-logical disciplines among which a certain interaction takes place.

[17]Cf. O. Weinberger, *Rechtslogik* (The Logic of Law), 2nd ed., Duncker & Humblot, Berlin 1989, ch. 10, 11, 12.

Chapter 4

Design of an Alternative Action Theory

4.1. The ontological basis of the action theory

The concept 'action' is a generally familiar and on the whole understandable concept of everyday language. Highly controversial and not at all unproblematical, however, is the scientific explication of this concept, whose central position in many scientific disciplines and in the world-view of philosophy is something most modern thinkers are aware of. However, there is not a standard concept, no fundamental and undisputed definition of this concept, just as the picture presented by the "logic" and methodology of action theory is a far cry from a uniform one.

Von Wright distinguishes between two types of action theories, causalistic theories and intentionalist ones. "For reasons of expediency I shall call *causalists* those who deem it possible that intention is a Humean cause of behavior, and *intentionalists* those who regard the connection between intention and behavior as a connection of a conceptual or logical nature."[1]

[1] G. H. von Wright, Erklären und Verstehen (Explaining and Understanding), Fischer (Athaenäum), Frankfurt a.M. 1974, p.92.

Against the causalistic theories speaks the fact that intentions and motives are not causes in the sense of the usual explication of the causal law. The causalists are forced to expand the concept of cause to the point where it becomes mere figurative speech. They view a causal relationship not only as a regular and empirically necessary relation between observed (or at least in principle directly or indirectly observable) states of the system; rather, they regard elements of an informational nature likewise as causes. These elements, intentions, goals, preferences, are by their very nature no observable states – observable are only their effects, and this only under certain circumstances; they do not work materially, but as pieces of information.

The intentionalist, on the other hand, runs into the difficulty that he has to regard an action as a logical consequence and at the same time as a factual effect of a rational process. Action becomes a practical necessity. Intentions and goals are ideal entities. How can they give rise to real processes? How can a rational justification process bring about the occurrence of real – and, in the result, observable – events? Logical, – or, as some put it: quasi-logical – processes are hardly suited to explain physically discernible phenomena.

The alternative action theory which I will now briefly outline is in principle a finalist theory, hence a theory of the second type according to von Wright's classification; it avoids, however, the problematical conception that intentions and stipulations of ends can, in a quasi-logical way, bring about real processes.

Current action theories vacillate between (I) the view that action theory is an explication of a psychical phenomenon, namely of the behavior of acting individuals, and (II) the conception which looks at actions first and foremost from a sociological point of view. The sociologizing action theories regard actions as rule-controlled behavior. This rule-dependence can be understood in a two-fold way: (a) as a regularity of action established through habit, imitation and/or drill, or (b) as an institutionalized normative rule which addresses the individual as a free volitional subject. Conceptions (a) and (b) are not mutually exclusive. The normative rule can be regarded as having been institutionally established through a regularity conditioned by habit or drill.

The co-determining function of social moments is not disputable; a satisfactory action theory will have to take it into account. But the basic core of one's acting is formed by the act of choice whose direction is determined by ends and decisions of preference.

An important reason why I regard action as teleologically founded behavior – and not primarily as one that is determined by rules – is the fact that the rules themselves are justified, and sometimes criticized, by functional moments related to one's ends.

Relatively little attention is paid in the action theories to another social problem: that of social action, may it consist of actions by collectives, different institutions or by entire classes, social groups, or states. The fact that it makes sense to speak of such social action has not, of course, remained unnoticed, but the relationship between the acting individual and the social action – which justifies that one can speak in both cases of actions – has hardly been clarified. I believe that an adequate explanation can only be given by an information-theoretical structural theory of action. A so conceived action theory may be supplemented by an institution theory which understands institutions as frameworks for action.[2]

In modern psychology, and particularly in most action theories, the influence of the positivist-behavioristic conceptions is evident.

In the positivist view, on which behaviorism, too, is based, the acquisition of knowledge is nothing but the ascertainment of the behavior of things or systems of objects, or, as the case may be, the ascertainment of their behavior as it varies with time. In addition, knowledge may be acquired of certain ties between the states of the things or systems, or of certain regularities showing up in the time histories of the behavioral patterns studied. In principle, however, in

[2]Such a theory has been developed by *N. MacCormick* and myself. See chapter 9 of this book.

this world-view there is nothing but states of objects and systems, nor can there be anything else.

In the behavioristic view, the source of all knowledge is observation, which, according to the behavioristic conception, is interpersonally accessible and intersubjectively verifiable. Observation which is only subjectively accessible – the method of auto-observation (introspection), known above all from the field of psychology – is rejected as intersubjectively non-verifiable. What is only understood, but cannot be made accessible to observation, is not a field of scientific knowledge.

The behavioristic ontology and conception of knowledge as description by means of intersubjectively meaningful predicates produces a uniform image of reality which is closed in itself.

What does action mean in the world-view of behavioristic descriptivism, hence in a conception of reality in which only that exists which is the designatum of descriptions of behavior? In this world there is nothing but states of objects and systems as well as time histories of such states, which can be described by interpersonally controllable predicates. How can, in the framework of such a world-view, the concept of action be drawn up?

An action expresses itself in some behavior of a system, usually designated in action theory as the agent or subject of the action. Now in what does what is understood as action: a succession of states of a system, distinguish itself from all other states and trajectories of behavior in the world? Since the behavioristic world-view knows only behavioristically describable states and successions of such states, there is no characteristic here – nor can there be one – which would differentiate actions from other series of behavior. Ergo: The concept of action has no place in a positivistic-behavioristic ontology. The positivist-behavioristic world-view is a logically consistent conception which is closed in itself. This conception is not wrong, but inadequate if we want to introduce the concept of action. And I claim that for beings capable of action – which in my opinion is an anthropological basic quality of man – this world-view is not an adequate ontology.

To avoid misunderstandings I wish to state expressly that – if only observable behavior is taken into consideration – there is nothing in the world but observable states of systems, the time history of such states, and relations between them or between behavioral trajectories. And this view is closed in itself: nowhere does it present a "hole" where one would have to draw upon other elements for describing the events taking place in the world. The observable processes are linked together in the dimension of time and in those of space. If one considers only behavioristic determinants, then only they will be instruments for the explication of behavior. This does not mean that then everything will become clearly understandable and causally determinable within the framework of the behavioristc view. But there will be no point at which the overall view of the behavior of the systems of this behavioristic world would fall apart if non-behavioristic explanations would not come to stand in the breach. And yet it is an abstruse, one-dimensionally shortened world-view of the positivistic descriptions, which does not correspond to the *conditio humana* and does not permit us to understand ourselves as being capable of action. The behavioristic world-view does not supply us with an adequate basis for action-determining thinking.[3]

The action theoretician is struck first and foremost by two basic anthropological facts:

1. Man is a being capable of action. His behavior is determined in large measure by information and its processing.

[3]Ordinary language as a basis for behavioristic descriptions is deceptive insofar as various predicates are only seemingly descriptive and should actually be eliminated from among the descriptions presented as behavioristic. On the one hand,, value-predicates – such as "beautiful", "just", "good" (e.g. a "good knife") – occur as attributes as if they expressed observable behavior characteristics, while on the other hand many concepts are teleologically or normatively determined. A table is an object for which it is essential that it can serve as a basis, a support, a working surface and the like. The concept "table" is not purely descriptive; rather, it is defined also by a teleological characteristic. The property of "being married" can only then be meaningfully attributed to a person if the institution of marriage exists in society.

2. Man is a social being, and, having developed genetically from group animals, his basic attitude is socially oriented, and the development of the individual human being is physically and mentally community-bound.

The ontology is not a given fact of nature, but a construct which comes about, or is elaborated, in accordance with the given anthropological facts (if it is supported by philosophical reflection).

Man as an acting being is subject to the *epistemological primacy of the practice*[4], which can be characterized by the following points:

(a) Cognition serves action: We acquire knowledge in order to be able to act adequately. Primary purpose of the quest for knowledge is the making available of knowledge as a basis for action. Genetically, too, the role of knowledge becomes understandable from its relation to action and to behavior control. In the evolutionary process the cognition apparatus and an intensive striving for knowledge are developed so as to be able to display a behavior that will be advantageous in the struggle for life.

(b) The structure of the knowledge empirically gained is such that this knowledge can be used for action determination: it is directed at the investigation of causal relations. Causal knowledge can be used for discovering means to reach envisaged goals.

(c) Language systems are developed which enable us to carry out analyses that will help us determine our actions, to justify selective decisions and to explicate interpretatively the behavior of action systems. Language is not only an instrument for the representation and intersubjective communication about states of affairs, but also a means for action determination in decision processes and for interpersonal coordination of behavior.

(d) Cognition processes are, on the one hand, mental processes of hypothesizing construction and investigating analysis, while on the

[4]In *Kant's* philosophy this concept expresses the superordination of practical over theoretical reason. It means that the problem of correct action is superordinated to the problem of cognition. I do not interpret this principle entirely along Kantian lines.

other hand they are conscious activities of observation, experimentation and verification. Acquisition of knowledge is thus a function of end-oriented action.

(e) There is not only "knowledge for being able to act effectively", but it is also true that without activities no effective verification of opinions would be possible.

(f) Our practical action is tied up with a critical reflection: our presupposed conceptions are subjected to the critique furnished by our experiences with the results of our action, just as our value expectations are tested. It is tested whether the pre-set goals correspond in fact to the value expectation.

The action-determining process is based on cognitive information: knowledge about the situation in which an action is to be performed – knowledge of the situation of the agent and of the environment in which action is to take place – knowledge of functional interrelationships as a basis for the determination of means and for the drafting of action programs, furthermore information on intermediate results of the action if feedback programs are to be carried out.

Knowledge is – precisely because of the epistemological primacy of the practice – not a mere registration of facts,[5] but a systematic process of searching for information and adequately shaping it.

The ontological consequence: reality, the existing, is not only the totality of things and of the systems of things, hence what can be observed. And the existing is not only determined by purely descriptive predicates, but frequently in a far more complex way, as shown briefly in the following.

The empirical cognition of the material world surpasses the descriptions of behavior, for it aspires not only to ascertain regularities in the coexistence of characteristics and regularities of behavioral sequences, but is interested moreover in empirically recognized necessity, hence in the recognition of empirical laws. The difference between the

---

[5]Popper ironically calls such a conception of knowledge a "bucket theory of the mind". Karl R. Popper, *Objective Knowledge, An Evolutionary Approach*, Claredon Press Oxford 1972, p.111.

discovery of behavioral regularity and nomic relationships is striking. Nomic cognition postulates fact-transcendent validity, of which there is no question in the case of mere summarizing generalization of empirically given behavioral regularity. Only under the assumption that general propositions are valid as laws (i.e. of necessity) will there be a basis for prognoses and retrodiction.

Only then will it be permissible and meaningful to speak of the possible and impossible, or to justify disposition assertions and contrafactual theses.[6]

If, of a system, I know all the states it passes through from the moment it came into being until its collapse I do not know everything that can be known about that system. The system might under certain circumstances, which, however, have not or will not come about, assume other states than those actually realized. I know far more about the system if I know also the possibilities as to what states it might assume, namely under circumstances which might – or might have – come about, even if *de facto* they will not or have not come about. The positivist image is not all one can know about real systems.

Such reflections are not philosophical trifling, but essential reminders of the fact that an ontology (and epistemological conception) of acting human beings must not be conceived of positivistically, merely as a description of behavior. This applies also to factual knowledge (not only the knowledge about institutions and practical theses). Every analysis for decision-taking purposes is based on a transcendence of the knowledge of the merely factual; it is based on well-founded theses (conceptions) about possible continuations of the trajectories of behavior. Only if on the basis of nomological knowledge several possibilities are available to select from will planning, choosing, deciding and the designing of programs be meaningful.

[6]Cf. N. Rescher, Lawfulness as Mind-dependent, in *id.* (ed.), *Essays in Honor of Carl G. Hempel*, D. Reidel, Dordrecht 1969, p.178–197; furthermore O. Weinberger, Der nomische Allsatz (The Nomic Universal Proposition) in: *Grazer Philosophische Studien* (Graz Philosophical Studies) 4, 1977, p.31–42.

Knowledge of the necessary and possible is one of the prerequisites of action-determining thinking, and the development of a theory of the modalities: "necessary", "possible", ..., is a postulate of the epistemology based on the primacy of the practice, for practical thinking moves necessarily within fields of possibilities.

In the social world in which we, as acting persons, live, objects are not always characterized merely descriptively, but often rather by characteristics that correspond to the institutional function of the given objects.

The human agents who find themselves within the radius of action of institutions must take cognizance of institutional objects (e.g. banknotes or chessmen) not only as objects of observational descriptions, but must also know and understand them as institutional objects whose institutional properties they must understand in taking characteristics of the objects into account that cannot be reduced to positivist descriptions of behavior. This is, of course, not a matter of a "duplication" of the object – the colorfully printed piece of paper and the banknote as an object in an institutional function are one and the same thing –, but what I know about this object is more than might be represented by a factual description, no matter how subtle.

The universe of the objects in the ontology of human agents comprises not only material objects. It also comprises ideal entities which cannot be observed by the senses and which are grasped not by observation, but by understanding. Ideal entities occur as contents of mental processes, but frequently they have, in addition, real existence. Reality – the existence of entities – is therefore not always based on observability through direct or mediated observation by the senses as is the case with material objects, but it is always connected with the fact that the entity existing in reality can be attributed temporality (time coordinates of existence or presence). The existence of ideal entities does not always consist in that they are contents of mental experiences of persons. The reality of life comprises, besides material things, also ideal matters as components of the really existing: e.g.

the knowledge of society, values, norms and the like, which form part of social reality.

For important reasons the thinking of people must also take into account ideal entities in their spiritual being, regardless of the real being of these mental contents (of these ideal entities).

A mental complex (e.g. a theory, a poem or a mathematical proof) is an entity which is understood without determinations of time and whose validity is independent of mental acts with the corresponding content. It is important to view this sphere as ontic being independent of any mental happenings, for the corresponding meanings are to be conceived independently of communication processes and mental acts. And only in this conception will logical relations and logical operations be valid. That (or to what extent) mental acts of persons who experience these thoughts and carry out these operations will take place in logically correct fashion is not always and not necessarily the case.

This so-called spiritual existence need not be understood as an immanent entity in the platonic sense. These mental matters (and the logical relations) need not be regarded as immutable structures of the nature of the mind (of the sphere of ideas); they may rather be understood as constructs whose structure is fixed and which, usually tied to language, lead their own ideal lives and, precisely because of this ideal fixation and conceptual detachment from mental acts, follow their own structural and logical nature.

This objectified conception of ideal contents under abstraction from the mental acts is also a precondition for the possibility of intersubjectivity, for functioning intersubjectively is something within the exclusive capability, not of act contents as such, but only of structures that have been made independent of mental acts and have a linguistic-semantic determination. Whether among the language-users concerned the understanding of a sentence or of any utterance is perfect, i.e. whether the participants in a communication process attach one and the same meaning to a sentence or any utterance, is not yet assured by the fact that the communicatum must be conceived of as an ideal object rather than as the mere content of psychic acts.

The pragmatic question of the verification of the interpersonal identity of the meanings which two language users ascribe to an utterance or a sequence of characters is a difficult problem which will not be examined here in detail.

In the field of practical philosophy it is indispensable that ideal entities of a position-taking character should be included into the universe of the existing. Existence is to be ascribed to values, preferences, ends and norms, namely real existence of a different type than that which the ideal entities of cognitive nature possess. The ontology of practical philosophy will comprise, besides the cognitive sphere, ideal entities whith a practical (action-related) meaning. Norms, values, ends, preferences, relations can be understood, interpersonally communicated, and analyzed semantically as well as logically. To practical contents can (but need not) be ascribed real existence, too. To a norm, e.g., can be ascribed social existence, it can exist (be effective, have been accepted) as an ideal component of an institution. Really existing practical contents are always really existent relatively to a system (e.g. an institution) to which they belong.

4.2. The information-theoretical approach to action theory

I believe that there is only one meaningful way to arrive at a useful action concept: to regard actions not only as transformations of states – these can in principle be represented behavioristically – but as results of an information process, without it being presupposed, in this information-theoretical approach to the action, that this information process is always linked with consciousness, nor that the behavior of the agent is materially brought about by these information processes as a mental operation.[7]

[7]Cf. in this connection the considerations in Chapter 5, p.96 et seq.

Through this information-theoretical approach the action becomes definable as an information-determined behavior of a specific structure characterized by this information process. This information process is of a teleological nature.

From the information-theoretical perspective in the sense as just described, the following further basic features of the action theory as I see it result:

1. The action is always attributed to a subject (agent).
2. To this agent, a system of ends and preferences is assigned.
3. The subject is capable of realizing (himself or indirectly) information processes.
4. If the information process is to be action-determining, then the agent must have a scope for action: he must have some alternatives as to his future behavior at his disposal between which he can decide. Thus there exists a forking of the future behavioral trajectory, and the subject performs a selection from the field of possible alternatives on the basis of the information processes.
5. The action-determining information process must incorporate – in addition to descriptive information – also position-taking (practical) information expressing criteria (reasons) for selection processes.
6. Precisely the point just mentioned is the reason why action theory – and in fact all practical philosophy – must be erected on a dichotomous semantics that distinguishes between cognitive (descriptive) and practical sentences.

4.3. The semantic basis of action theory

An analytic theory of choice and decision works necessarily with position-taking information that makes it possible to conceive of volitional processes, not as mere unfounded acts of decision, but rather as justification processes determined by practical information contents. Only under this analytical precondition can a genuine, information-theoretically founded action theory be built up.

If the volitional decision is interpreted as pure arbitrariness, then there remains only the fact of the choice between possibilities, without taking into account the fact that selections must be first justified, namely by optimization analyses. Optimization always is a process governed by criteria expressed as practical information: goals, values, preferences, norms.

A genuine analytical action theory is necessarily based on a duality of types of information: cognitive and practical information. And therefore the language of action theory and of all practical philosophy must be built up on a dichotomous semantics which categorially distinguishes descriptive (cognitive) sentences from practical ones.

Practical sentences – unlike cognitive ones – are subject-related: they characterize the attitudes of the subject (of a system) to which the practical sentence is assigned. They have no descriptive meaning, i.e. they do not state what is the case; their pragmatic function is of another kind: they constitute selection functions, or attitudes of the system which serve for the determination and justification of decisions (selective acts). The categorial semantic difference between cognitive (descriptive) sentences and practical ones rules it out that identity of meaning could exist between them, or, in other words: A practical sentence can never be expressed by a descriptive one, nor conversely, a descriptive sentence by a practical one (mutual non-translatability of descriptive and practical sentences).

4.4. Action theory as a structure theory

The information-theoretical approach alone suggests that it may be promising to conceive of action theory as a theory of the structure of action-determination. In addition there are two further reasons for such a conception: 1. The factually realized processes of action-determining decision are not identical with the operations of end-oriented rationality, for as a rule they are pragmatic simplifications. This implies that from the behavior of people and the thinking operations accompanying it, one cannot directly read the relevant structures, but will rather have to work, in action theory, with the concept of rational decision as an "idealization" of the processes actually realized. 2. In many cases of importance for the practice, actions by non-psychophysical persons will be encountered, as well as interpersonal social relationships of such a nature as makes them difficult to grasp if action is tied to acting human individuals: deputyship, guardianship and the like.

Thus, in my opinion this theory is not a "descriptive natural history" of the human volitional and decision processes, but rather a theory of the rational structure of such processes and of the manners of argumentation valid in them.

It is not the task of this theory to ascertain the factual selection procedures of individuals, collectives and institutions, but rather to characterize the structure of the arguments resorted to in decision-making.

Human attitudes, preferences and activities are, as experience teaches us, to a high extent variable. That which remains is the structure of these processes, which can be carried out with various contents. On the basis of a formal action theory, changes of contents – e.g. changes of the objectives set or the value standards employed – can be understood and treated without changing the formal theory.

This formal approach makes it possible to relate the decision and action structures not only to the actions of the human individual; rather, it is valid also for other systems if they can realize, by means of their organs, the corresponding operations. The formal action theory is, therefore, not merely an analytical instrument of individual action, but at the same time an adequate basis for the analysis of collective action and of the theory of institutions.

This formal theory does not permit one to regard certain ends, value concepts or norms as immanently valid simply on the grounds that they are held to be anthropological data and/or mental ones valid a priori. A separation of form and content comes about. The formally conceived theory is, as a matter of principle, open for wholly different settings of ends or preferences. The accepted (presupposed) ends and value standards are – varying with one's perspective – things ascertained or stipulated, but no yardsticks required a priori.

This formal action theory makes it possible to apply one and the same formalism in methodologically and epistemologically highly different fashions varying with the problem situation, as I will show in the next chapter. And this methodologically differentiated application of the schemes of action determination through information overcomes basic difficulties of the traditional action theories.

4.5. *Action deliberation and motive interpretation*

Actions and the associated processes of information processing are dealt with in two – wholly different – situations:

1. Either one is confronted with the task of determining what one should do and how it could best be done (*action deliberation*),

2. or one observes the behavior of a subject and tries to grasp and to understand it as an action (*motive interpretation*).[8]

To this basic methodological alternative of the action analyses, secondary considerations, particularly evaluations and/or justifying argumentations, may come in addition.

Action deliberation is a process of searching for action possibilities conforming to the teleological system of the agent, and of selecting optimal means or programs for the satisfaction of ends envisaged. The essence of deliberation is optimization from teleological and

[8] *H. Lenk* evidently focuses only – or primarily – on the observing and interpreting point of view when he defines action as an interpretation construct. Cf. H. Lenk, Handlung als Interpretationskonstrukt (Action as an Interpretation Construct), in: *id.* (ed.) *Handlungstheorien interdisciplinär* (Interdisciplinary View of Action Theories), vol.2, 1st half-volume, Wilhelm Fink Verlag, Munich 1978, p.279–350.

preferential points of view and, in some cases, with action-determining norms being resorted to.

When we observe agents (acting subjects) we are faced with a wholly different problem situation. We must realize (and possibly justify) why we regard the behavior of the agent as action; furthermore we must try, through interpretation, to answer the question how and to what ends the agent acted. The mere understanding of the specific type of the action is based already on interpretation. The understanding of the type of action and of the motives for the action interprets the observed behavior as the result of an action-determining information process and tries to interpretatively reconstruct the teleological reflection which led to the action.

4.6. Summary of the basic features of the alternative formal-finalistic action theory

Summarizingly I can now explain why in the title of this book and of this chapter I am speaking of an "alternative action theory". This term is not primarily meant as a contrasting position to von Wright's doctrine, with which I share a number of elements (although I am looking in a different way for an access to the logic of norms and to action theory), but rather as a position which would confront the ruling trends in action theory with a markedly different alternative. Its main features are:

1. *An information-theoretical approach.* Action must be considered from an information-theoretical perspective, for it constitutes not only factual and observable hehavior, but a behavior which comes about as the result of an intentional information process.

2. *A constructivist view.* Action theory is not a descriptive theory along natural-historical lines, but rather a construction resting above all on the interrelation between causality and teleology. Causal cognition is so structured that it can serve for the determination

of means and thus for the selective decision-making, and teleology exploits this relation for justifying the teleological relationships.

3. *Action theory is a structure theory.* From the information-theoretical approach it follows that action theory is formally conceived of, i.e. that it clearly distinguishes between forms of thinking and contents (ends, preferences) to be inserted. The formal theories of action-related thinking: teleology, axiology, logic of preferences and logic of norms, form the logical basis of this theory.

4. *Norms as determinants of action.* Within the framework of the teleological basic structure it is explained how autonomous and heronomous norms work in action-determining fashion.

5. *The problem-dependent conception of the application of the action-determining formalisms.* Considerations determining selective decision-making (action deliberation) are contrasted to the processes of understanding and interpreting actions (motive interpretation). These methods are differentiated according to the problem situation, but both are founded on the same formalism, namely the one on which the action is based.

Chapter 5

Fundamental Concepts and Theses of the Formal-Finalistic Action Theory

5.1. Introduction

Like any other explicative theory, the formal-finalistic action theory, as I call my theory, is based on previous experiences and analyses of the field considered and is therefore some sort of rational reconstruction of the pre-scientific experience field. In my conception of action theory it is decisive for the character of the theory that I am not limiting my studies to actions by individuals, but am rather considering the overall field of action, so that, already in its fundamental structure, the theory is designed to serve also as a basis for the explication of collective action, social action, and actions by institutional bodies.

At this point I will present, in a brief survey, the most important concepts and theses of the formal-finalistic action theory. To obtain an overall overview I fear I cannot avoid repeating certain things that were already referred to before.

5.2. The definition of the concept of action

Action is information-determined behavior, and it is by indicating the structure of this information-processing that the action concept is explicated.

The structure of the action-determining information process is a rational explication model, and not, by any chance, a presentation of the results of consciousness analyses of those processes which may go hand in hand with certain actions, namely with conscious action by individual human agents. The elements of the structure model need not, by any means, always be experienced contents of consciousness. They may, even when actions by individual persons are considered, be non-conscious moments or not fully conscious ones. And in the case of actions by other agents – e.g. in that of social action –, no such carrier of a consciousness is present here to whom such states of consciousness might be attributed.

5.3. Two kinds of information as a basis for action

Essential for the model, envisioned by me, of action-determining information processes, is a splitting-up of the information into two categories, different as to their function and their semantic characteristics: cognitive and practical information.

Action is necessarily based on factual information, which of course can be available in a great variety of ways. It need not be present as consciously experienced contents of the mind. It may be in the nature of situational knowledge about the field upon which the action is going to impinge, or of causal knowledge permitting one (a) to perceive alternatives to the future states of the object (or system) upon which the action might impinge, and (b) to find means for attaining envisaged goals.

Knowledge of the reality is nevertheless an indispensable prerequisite for the possibility to determine actions and perhaps to realize them. Within the framework of action-determining thinking it is also necessary – if rarely talked about – to introduce the notion of logical modalities. *It is only if the concepts of the necessary and the possible are introduced that one deal with scopes for action.* The idea of a scope for action means that the object or system impinged upon by the agent can, in the future, assume different states, depending on how it is impinged upon. The scope for action deals with the possibilities of the development of the object (or system) within the framework of given necessities.

Action determination means: to decide between alternative possibilities and to select the means or acting programs to be realized for the attainment of envisioned ends.

Action theory must not confine itself to noting that such selection processes for determining the manner of action to be taken do take place (as e.g. Luhmann notes in his system-theoretical approach); on the contrary, in action theory it is precisely a matter of analyzing how the selection made is determined by given pieces of practical information (goals, preferences, norms) and/or by decisional acts. *The action-theoretical analyses center around the justification of the selection.*

From factual information alone, the determination of a selection will never result. (This proposition can be regarded as an alternative formulation of the principle of non-cognitivism.) If selection needs to be justified, pieces of practical information must be drawn upon as determinants.

When an agent chooses between objects O_1, O_2,[1] this can be realized by a global act or on the basis of a justifying analysis. The global act is, as a rule, not analyzed in detail. It can, however, if it is to be understood more deeply (psychologically or sociologically), be presented in an interpreting analysis as a motivated action through a

[1] "Object" is to be understood here quite generally as a certain something (a state of affairs, a thing, or something else).

modeling reflection. (Such an interpretation of course always remains hypothetical.)

From an observed selective act in which an agent A selects O_1 from the set of possibilities $\{O_1, O_2\}$ it can be inferred that the agent A does not prefer O_2 to the object O_1. It cannot be inferred, however, that the agent prefers O_1 to O_2, for it may well happen that O_1 and O_2 are rated equal, in which case the selection between O_1 and O_2 will be made arbitrarily (by pure chance).

If the selection is based on reasons (rather than only the result of the act being noted), then practical information (as to ends, preferences, norms) must be available by which the option (selection from the set of possibilities) is justified.

Hence the action-determining information process is necessarily always based on practical information as well.

If the results of the selective acts are observed "from the outside", i.e. by an observer differing from the agent, then the practical information leading to the selective acts is not explicitly articulated and hence not expressly indicated as justification in any given case, but if one wishes to understand the selection – or explain it by interpretation –, then one must – hypothetically, through understanding interpretation – try to find out what practical information may have been "behind" the selective act.

We can therefore formulate the thesis: *Action-determining operations are always based both on cognitive information about facts and on practical information.*

5.4. Scope for action

It will only then be meaningful to speak of an action if there exists a certain scope for action, i.e. if the agent perceives alternatives for his future behavior and takes a decision as to the action alternative to be realized. The making of a selection on the basis of a real or only imagined field of possibilities is an essential characteristic of action.

5.5. *Optimization analysis as basis for action decisions*

Where alternatives for possible behavior exist, a mechanism must come into play which determines from among these alternatives the one that will be realized. This selective process is, in action theory, not only noted as a fact, but also conceived of as a justifying process of information-processing. It is a matter here of choosing on the basis of an optimization analysis. The reasons for the selection are pieces of position-taking (practical) information: ends, preferences, norms.

The justification of the selection depends (besides on cognitive data (knowledge)) always on practical information. When several alternatives do in fact exist, the selection is always based on an *optimization analysis*. The sometimes quite complicated optimization reflection can schematically be reduced to a simple relationship. In one way or another, criteria (e.g. the stipulation of a definite end) must be available according to which the alternatives are lined up in order of preference. The criterion of preference employed may be a global one (i.e. not analyzed in greater detail) or an analytical-rationally determined one. Since the lining-up in order of preference constitutes a semi-order, exactly two cases can occur:

1. There is exactly one optimum alternative, i.e. *one* alternative which is preferred (in the strong sense) to all others.

2. There are two or more alternatives which according to the relevant criterion are both, and equally, rated optimal.

In case 1 the alternative preferred to all others is regarded as selected. In case 2 the determination through a preference consideration according to the given criterion is only a partial one. One of the alternatives rated as – equally – optimum ones (i.e. as deserving equal preference) will be selected. The selection from among this set will be made arbitrarily (through some process of chance).

A plurality of equally optimum alternatives will not lead to a "standstill", to a balanced position of rest, but to an arbitrary (random) selection.

Some thinkers have been of the opinion that reasons (motives) for action are action-determining *forces*. These forces can work in the same direction, thus mutually strengthening one another, or in opposite directions, thus producing a motivation in the direction of the stronger motives, which then, however, will work only with the differential intensity. In the case of opposite forces of equal strength, the result will, in this view, be a motivational equilibrium and thus a standstill.[2] This image, in which the determination of action is comparable to forces at work, is not adequate. My action theory stands in clear contrast to this mechanistic explication of action.

If one and the same object (or state of affairs) will be of exactly as much use as a possible action alternative as it will do harm, then a zero evaluation can come about. It will then be completely up to the agent's discretion whether the alternative to realize the given manner of behavior will be selected, or rather the alternative not to realize it.

Optimization considerations belong to the very essence of action. Of course there will be wide variation in the degree to which they are carried out consciously, often even systematically and with methodological care. For us this question is not of prime interest here, for we are concerned only with the structure of such considerations and with the argumentations employed in them.

In the practice of value considerations there are transitions between global position-taking and evaluations on the basis of criteria that are analytically made explicit. Even in cases where an analytical rationalization of the criteria has been realized, a rest of a global evaluation will often remain behind. When speaking e.g. of the quality of life in a narrower sense one will usually mean a characteristic of the social life situation which, although important, is not, in detail, clearly determined and measurable, but which should nevertheless, although not clearly defined and broken down into single features, command attention as a relevant moment of the evaluation. Like any

---

[2]Cf. the famous case of "Buridan's donkey", which is based on the force model of motives. The donkey standing between two equal and equally far removed hay bushels starves to death because the motivating forces cancel out.

other global consideration, the quality of life, too, can under certain conditions be analyzed and more closely determined.

The rankings according to preference on the basis of single criteria can usually be clearly determined by a rational process, and frequently they are also measurable. The optimization analyses, however, must as a rule be carried out within a system of several ends and value criteria. While an overall optimization from the point of view of a complex system which takes into account several points of view at the same time is evidently dependent on the partial evaluations according to the various criteria, it is, logically, not yet determined by the evaluations according to the partial criteria. The partial evaluations enter with different weightings into the global preference determination; and the relative weighting need not be constant throughout the field under consideration.

The selection processes take place in a field of alternatives that have been recognized as possible. The determination of the possibilities is a purely cognitive process. The recognition of these possibilities need not, in fact, be complete, and is not always free of errors (possibilities may be assumed that do not in fact exist, and possibilities that do de facto exist may not be recognized).

A rational optimization analysis is dependent on the criteria taken into consideration and on their relative weighting. If recourse is had to additional criteria and/or the weighting of the criteria, is changed, then a wholly different ranking of the possible action according to preference will frequently come about.

A further moment which may greatly change the result of the optimization analysis is a limitation or expansion of the considered field of the consequences to be expected of the various possibilities of action.

Examples: If, in a political analysis, only the Gross Domestic Product is taken into consideration one will obtain a different result than when other points of view – e.g. social distribution criteria, consequences for the employment market, etc. – are considered as well. – When we evaluate a top sport training program as an element of a life plan we may arrive at a positive evaluation, which, however, in certain cases can turn out quite negative when taking a long-term view.

5.6. The admissibility of means (of modes of action)

In the practice of deciding and choosing, the selection is not always made from among the entire set of given possibilities, but often rather from the subset of the *admissible possibilities*. Every personal system and every social system knows "taboos", a limitation of the possible means for attaining one's ends to those means which are deemed morally admissible. Such moral restrictions lead to the set of the permissible means or action alternatives, from among which the selection is then made.

I think it is quite important to realize that this restriction is interpolated *prior to* the actual selection of the means (or of the mode of action).[3] Wherever morality comes into play, a limitation of the possible to the permissible comes about. Moreover, I also wish to claim that a certain type of moral restrictions exists (or is recognized) in all personal and all social systems.

Remark

There is, however, the problem whether these moral limitations are always imposed with absolute validity, or whether they can rather be softened when they must compete with certain ultra-urgent goals that have been set.

[3] This view has nothing to do with the natural law or with an objectivistic theory of morality, for we do not lay down in any way according to what standards the limitation to the permissible is to be carried out.

5.7. The agent (Subject of the action)

Actions are always understood as the behavior or activity of an agent (subject of the action). As one might also put it: the action is attributed to an agent. Some think that man, as an individual, is the natural subject of any action and that any talk of other subjects as agents can be understood only figuratively, since only the individual human being has the ability to act. Here the formal-finalistic theory takes a different view. For it regards as a possible agent any subject which (directly or indirectly) can realize the appropriate functions. Now what properties must an agent have, and what functions must he be able to satisfy?

If something (an entity) is to act as subject of an action, he, she or it must have the following properties:

(I) This entity must possess (or be assigned) a certain practical orientation. Depending on the circumstances, the associated practical system may be more or less explicitly present, or its existence is assumed, and then it is determined by the observer in a process of understanding interpretation.

(II) The agent must have a certain measure of cognitive capacity at his disposal which permits him to secure information about the given situation, about the action possibilities available and about existing causal relationships.

(III) The agent must be able to realize in one way or another selective acts, doing so on the basis of cognitive and practical information, both of which – as I outlined before – are required for action determination. These elective acts are either global position-takings or analytically characterized decisions of preference. Generally it may be said that the determination of the action is realized by acts which move between these two poles.

Practical life experience proves the existence of various types of subjects of actions, for which capacity not only individual persons can qualify, but also collectives and various institutional bodies.

Subjects may also act on behalf of other subjects or of institutions. Someone acting as a deputy, a guardian or an organ of an institution is expected, not to realize his own goals, but to conduct the action-determining preference analysis, and the optimization of the process of selecting the action possibility to be realized, in accordance with the orientations and needs of the subject on whose behalf he is acting.

The social fact that action on behalf of someone else is institutionalized proves that the rational-analytical representation of the action-determining information processes as required by my action theory is not only a demand of the theoretical construction, but is also in agreement with the processes existing in reality. If action were only a result of reactions by the agent to the circumstances of his life, and if the position-takings were recognizable only as selective acts, but not in their justification structure, then there could be no action on behalf of another subject.

Likewise, the customary social processes of consultation with someone else about the question how I should act are only possible because the process determining the action decision can to a high degree be expressed rationally-analytically. The objectives set and preferences entertained by the agent must be made accessible to his consultant; only then will it be possible, on the one hand to critically appraise, in the consultation, the practical orientations themselves, while on the other hand, particularly owing to the consultant's knowledge, ways and means can be shown as to how the optimization of the selection of means (in accordance with the agent's goals) can be achieved.

5.8. Action and program

Action usually is not just one single act posited by one single, punctual – as it were – impulse; action usually means the realization of a series of successive individual acts which can to a greater or lesser extent form a unity. Hence the content of the action decision frequently is not just one single act, but an action program comprising a sequence of acts. The structure of such a program may vary. Interesting and important are such programs as will make the determination of subsequent acts dependent on the result (effect) of preceding ones. In such cases a number of cognitive ascertainments must be made as to what situations were realized by the preceding activity, whereupon the next act is determined on the basis of these results (feedback program, a program which is dependent on the result of the previous acts). Here, therefore, a further, secondary form of information processing comes into play which is not concerned with the basic decision to act, but with realization decisions concerning the implementation of the action program.

5.9. Action deliberation and motive interpretation

Depending on the problem situation, the formalism of the action theory is applied in two different ways:

First there is the problem situation of the agent, who carries out the relevant information process for arriving at the action decision. This perspective is characterized by its orientation to the recognition of the possible action alternatives and to the determination of the choice on the basis of a relevant preference and optimization analysis. This analysis of the action, hence the carrying-out of the action-determining reflection, is termed by me *action deliberation.* Meant by this is of course the structure of the problem situation and of the operations, regardless of who carries out this analysis, the agent, his organ, or someone else. This follows naturally from the non-psychologistic approach for which we have opted.

Different is the outlook of the observer who tries to recognize, understand and interpret the actions as such. All he can directly observe is a certain behavior of a subject, or impingements of this subject upon the object of the action. Everything else is interpretation by the observer. There must be reasons present which make this behavior of the subject appear as action, i.e. as a behavior that can be understood as the result of an intentional action-determining information process. The recognition that the observed behavior is an action is no recognition yet of the action observed, but actually only the ascertainment of the existing problem situation consisting in that one is confronted with the task of understanding a behavior as action. For the action to be recognized, the ascertainment of the behavioral sequence must be joined by an interpretative reconstruction of the considerations leading to the action. What needs to be understood (interpretatively reconstructed) are the ends (purposes, intentions) of the action. Since the ends as determined by interpretation may be called motives, this perspective from which the action is observed may be called *motive analysis*.

Evidently this approach to actions is quite complex, a matter of interpretative construction, and thus by its very nature always hypothetical. For interpretation is never objectively verifiable in its entirety.

Motive interpretation is a process quite familiar to us from everyday life. We try to understand actions, which is only then possible if we grasp the reason for the action, the agent's motive. One can even say that a person's behavior will only then be regarded as action if we regard this behavior as the result of an intention, i.e. as motivated. To understand actions always means: to ask a 'Why?' question that will be answered by recognition of the motive. It is also plausible that this recognition is based on interpretation, i.e. that it constitutes an explanatory construct.

Motive analysis as understood by the formal-finalistic action theory is essentially different, however, from the customary conception. Usually the 'Why?' question is answered by the indication of *one single* motive. Although simple and plausible, this is hardly adequate to the subject. From the formal-finalistic theory it is evident that the action is not always the result of one single end, but must rather be understood as the resultant of a teleological assessment not dominated, as a rule, by one single goal. The motivation of the action will have to be understood as a decision of preference on the basis of various and differently weighted ends. Though far more complicated, this interpretation presents a much more adequate picture of the real justification of the action. In my opinion an action by an agent also means an insight into his complex system of ends and an understanding of the complex justification of his behavior.

Motive analysis is rendered even more complicated by the fact that the role of internalized norms should be taken into consideration. Depending on the ethical attitude of the agent the class of permissible means will be different, and in his selective decisions the agent's behavior will be determined, besides by teleological moments and preference assessments, also by fixed normative attitudes.

When we observe e.g. that otherwise quite normal people, citizens like you and me, will in certain situations commit terrible atrocities which may even be of no direct use to the agent himself, an explication will hardly be possible without having recourse to internalized ideological factors (e.g. nationalist postulates). A great many positive ethical patterns of conduct, e.g. care for others, will hardly be explainable without taking normative moments into account in the determination of the action.

5.10. The justification of actions

In addition, a third approach to actions often will be important, even though it evidently does not occur independently of the action deliberation and/or the motive interpretation: namely the confrontation with the problem of justifying actions, i.e. of appraising them. Here a host of new problems presents itself which result on the one hand from the selection of the evaluating point of departure (for an ethical, legal or other appraisal), while on the other hand having to take into account in any event the dual aspect of the action: consideration of the result of the action, and evaluation of the intention underlying it. In justification analyses, both aspects must be considered; the evaluation may turn out wholly different depending on whether the action is evaluated on the basis of its result or of its intention.

In practice there will be no great problems here; usually one will have no doubt as to whether the processes observed are actions. However, the theoretical treatment of this question is particularly difficult. It cannot be directly seen from a process whether it is intentionally founded, hence whether it is an action by a subject.[4] What permits us to interpret certain processes as actions by an agent are analogy considerations with respect to our own experienced actions. From the observation itself this does not strictly follow. Decisive for our pertinent considerations seems to me to be the fact that we are agents ourselves and, from this perspective, also know the "backside" of the action. The information-theoretical approach permits us to find, at least partially, empirical reasons for the volitional nature of observed processes. The influence of information indicates that the assumption that it is a case of actions here can be made empirically plausible.

5.11. The institutionalist aspect of actions

In the field of actions, the relationships between agent and community are of essential relevance. The practical attitudes of the subject of the action are determining factors for his action. Yet these attitudes themselves are not "prime causes" of human volition, action and abstention from acting, but rather to a high extent functionally dependent on institutions and social influences on the individual or collective agent. And while the institutions are relatively fixed

[4]This question plays a part in the philosophy of religion, too. Since all processes – including those conceived of as realizations of a (divine) project – take place as being governed by natural law, it cannot be seen from the observed data whether they are only real causal processes, or at the same time effects of a divine world plan, too.
Intentionally produced processes are based on causality, as is evident from the structure of the teleological relationship and its dependence on causality.

social realities with which the agents are confronted, they are on the other hand also changeable by the actions of people and through the development of the institutional realities. The institutionalist theories of society and of human action are very well aware of this interaction. An adequate action theory is therefore necessarily closely related to institution-theoretical considerations, as the institutions are by their very nature frameworks of social action.

Within the framework of the finalistic action theory normative action determinants can be explained in plausible fashion. And they also form the basis for explaining the relations between agents and social institutions. The formal-finalistic action theory, in combination with normativistic institutionalism (or neo-institutionalism), also appears to furnish, in my opinion, a solid basis for a theory of law and of society.[5]

5.12. The theories of practical thinking

The information processing lying at the basis of action has given rise to a class of "logics of the practice". While being interrelated to a certain extent, they are relatively independent disciplines. *Formal teleology* is the one which, as basic structural theory of action-related information processing, corresponds to the finalistic character – the intentionality – of the action; it comprises the following topics: ends, means and their relationships, the structure of the system of ends, the determination of possible means and programs, and the justification of the decisions consisting of the selection of means (or programs) according to the criteria of the system of ends and of the preferences. The elements of the teleological relationships – ends, means – are value-determined. The *theory of values* (axiology), or more precisely: its formal characterization, constitutes therefore a field of the theory of practical thinking, just as the *logic of preferences*, which constitutes the rational core of the justification of decisions and of the selection

[5]Regarding the institutionalist theory of society and of law, see ch. 8.

of means. For various reasons, norms appear on the scene as action-determinants. This explains why the *logic of norms* likewise belongs to the group of the disciplines of action-related thinking. The chief functions of the norms as determinants of action lie (a) in the fixation and regulated shaping of action, (b) in the influencing of behavior by social moments and considerations, and – last but not least – (c) in the limitation of possible means to (morally or socially) permissible ones.

On the logic of norms (or deontic logics), which has developed into an established and much discussed logical discipline, I will come to speak separately in chapter 7. Here I will now make a few remarks on the basic thoughts of the other practical logics.

5.13. The practical system

The formal-finalistic action theory does not occupy itself with the agents themselves and does not investigate their psychic or sociological constitution; rather, the agent is assigned a practical system which in practical argumentation represents the subject of the action. Varying with the type of consideration as resulting from the problem situation the practical system comprises ends, value standards, preferences and norms.' As fundamental for the action analyses I regard the system of ends which – in order to be able to arrive at decisions – is coupled with a preference system. (If the order of preferences is not given explicitly – or not perfectly so given – the application of the teleology requires the intervention of decision acts by which the selections are made and the decisions taken.)

What is essential is that the practical system should be based on a dichotomous semantics, namely one differentiating categorially between descriptive and practical sentences.[6]

[6]See p.88 et seq.

5.14. Non-derivability postulates

Connected with this dichotomous structure of the semantics of practical philosophy are two requirements:

(I) The methodological requirement always to make clear at what points of the argumentations decisions will occur, or where perhaps practical premises (possibly in addition to cognitive-descriptive ones) will come into play.

(II) The metapostulate for the construction of practical-logical systems, stipulating that from a class of purely descriptive premises (i.e. without practical premises) no practical conclusions shall be drawn, and that from a class of practical premises no descriptive conclusion shall be derivable.

These metapostulates for the construction of logics of practical thinking mean an essential barrier to systems that are to appear in this role. For practical-logical systems the non-derivability principle forbidding (a) the derivation of practical conclusions from purely descriptive premises, and conversely, (b) the deduction of purely descriptive sentences from purely practical ones, will always be valid. Non-derivability postulates are necessary if the categorial separation of descriptive and practical sentences is to be ensured.

5.15. On formal teleology

Action is conceived of as end-determined behavior. Therefore it suggests itself naturally to concentrate first and foremost on a category of sentences which can express teleological determinants. The end/means relationship (teleological relation) exists between willed states of affairs. If certain ends are presupposed (assumed) as willed, then the teleological relation indicates that certain means for attaining or promoting this end are derivable as willed. The concept 'end' must be viewed in the context of the action. Ends are not entities existing by and for themselves, but conceptual elements of informational action-determination. Ends are ideal entities of a practical nature which play an essential part in the decision process of the action. In the process of the determination of means and action programs, as well as in the selection between possible means they function as elements of the justification of the decision.

By indicating the end (or ends), the attitude of the subject, the direction of his will, is expressed.

Telos, goal and similar terms that are identical with or at least related to the concept of end (which of the two is the case depends on linguistic conventions) seem to indicate that the stipulation of a goal or an end specifies a situation to be achieved, a "finis" or "final state of affairs". This, however, is not an essential characteristic of an end at all. The end postulate may have reference to a characteristic of a process, or constitute a target value for a behavior or an action in the course of time, and does not always express a final point of the action.

Formal teleology is the theory of the teleological relationships and the intellectual operations of the end/means analysis, the selection and the action-determining operations. In this theory the structure of possible systems of ends is investigated and a typology of the ends according to their formal properties is discussed. Not investigated or discussed, however, are the ends actually accepted by individual human beings or groups, nor is it attempted to propagate an ideal realm of ends.

Formal teleology (just as the finalistically-founded formal action theory) speaks of a bearer of the teleological system (an agent or subject of the action), but meant by this is not the psychophysical subject as a biological (or, in the case of collective actions, social) entity, but only a point to which the teleological system and the operations according to the formal theory of teleological thinking are attributed.

To subjects as empirical realities – e.g. acting persons – can, in the application of formal teleology, be assigned certain systems of ends in such a way that the subjects are conceived of as actual bearers of the systems of ends and of the teleological thought-operations.

In the formal analyses of the teleological operations there occur cognitive elements – situational recognitions, causal knowledge –, for these are indispensible elements of the action-determining operations. Teleological thinking, particularly the finding of suitable means to given ends – or, from a more complex viewpoint, the elaboration of action programs – presupposes modal thinking, i.e. the development of the concepts "possible", "necessary" and "contingent". This also means (I) that fact-transcendent knowledge must be formed (namely nomological insights), and (II) that constructions of modes of behavior (of programs) in possibility fields are developed. Teleology – just as action theory in general – presupposes a scope for possible action, not only as an anthropological fact of human existence, but also, and particularly, as a rational-constructive framework of deliberation as governed by given ends.

Teleology is oriented to justifying action decisions (selective acts). This is done on the basis of optimization analyses. Teleological thinking is therefore also dependent on evaluations and preferences. A behavioral possibility occurring in the decision process (or as selection alternative) is not visualized here by the agent (the subject of the teleological system) as a mere factuality, or an envisaged one, but is rather viewed in an evaluating perspective. It is evaluated under the aspect of the end or ends of the teleological system. To arrive at a justification of selection decisions one needs a relative evaluation (ascertainment of preferences or a possible value-equivalence) of the alternatives A and non-A between which we are to choose.

In teleological analyses one always proceeds from a system of ends that can be assigned to the subject of the action as a volitional characteristic. Between the ends of a system of ends there exist various relationships: ends can be abstract or concrete to different extents, can be vaguely or clearly determined in different measure, and an end can be a means to another end (e.g. the end "to bake bread" to the end "to appease hunger").

5.16. *The weighting of the ends*

The various ends of the system are each attributed a relative weight: in a given system an end may have greater weight than in another one. Of importance is the following thesis which emphasizes the significance of the assignment of relative weights to different ends: Two systems of ends which comprise the same ends will nevertheless be different if the ends are attributed different weights. For they may lead to different decisions.

Furthermore I am of the opinion that the various ends will not always be assigned weights that are constant throughout the field of their relevance. It may e.g. happen that a certain system of ends rates freedom of opinion higher than economic utility, but only up to a certain point, namely to the point where economic shortages (e.g. acute hunger) occur, from which point on the relative weighting of the ends "freedom of opinion" and "economic utility" will change so that "economic utility" will now have priority above "freedom of opinion".

A special case of the relative weighting of ends is the ranking of ends. This occurs when one end is given priority, as a matter of principle, above all other ones. Then everything which serves the end ranked first will have priority, and the ends so outranked will only acquire their secondary relevance if this does not – or at least not essentially – interfere with the primary end.

An example of this ranking of ends is *J. Rawls's* stipulation that his principle of maximum possible freedom will under certain conditions lexically outrank the principle of the permissibility of social and economic inequalities – namely if these inequalitites are to everybody's advantage and if there is a fair equality of opportunity.

In the case of lexical (hence, as it were, absolute) ranking, lower-ranked end principles can only then come into play if the higher-ranked principle has already been satisfied, hence if it is only a question of taking secondary differences into consideration which do not upset the preference of the higher-ranked end.

It seems to me that this ranking of ends and guiding ideas is as a rule not applied in this ultrastrict sense – nor, probably, should it be so employed. If a certain end is singled out as guiding idea, one believes that the most important goal is the orientation of the action towards this end. Everything else then appears less important. But this manner of according preference to a main end does not rule out that in certain borderline situations simultaneous consideration of both the main end and other goals will after all be possible. In fact, one may even find oneself involved in a consideration where a certain competitive relationship will come about between the main end and other objectives: in consideration of a major advantage for a secondary end a certain curtailment of the satisfaction of the main end may, in such borderline situations, be found acceptable.

5.17. System of ends and logical consistency

In most cases where one speaks of systems this concept is so understood that a system is a non-contradictory (logically consistent) complex of sentences or thoughts. Nothing analogous applies to the system of ends. (Perhaps I should therefore preferably have chosen another term, but I prefer to stick to the usual terminology.) One and the same system of ends can contain incompatible ends. In such a system, e.g. the postulated ends "Now to go for a walk" and "Now to stay at home" can co-exist (i.e. in essence: be desired at one and the same time). Teleological assessment has precisely the task of deciding between divergent (and incompatible) ends, or between possible action alternatives that serve different – including mutually incompatible – ends.

The system of ends cannot be criticized according to the criterion of logical consistency; it does not aspire to be a system of logically consistent theses at all, for its function is wholly different from the role of an objective image of a reality (which image would of course have to be consistent).

In teleological reflection, ends indicate as a rule only the "direction" of the action: that which is striven for. Its realization usually does not consist in a direct attainment of the contents of the end, but in the ends being realized in an indirect way, namely through the use of means which will accomplish what is striven for. Frequently, and mainly in view of the complexity of the task posited as an end, the means are expanded into action programs opted for from the point of view of the ends.

The determination of (possible) suitable means depends on causal relationships. A means M_1 can bring about that which is striven for as an end. The causal relationship indicates a possible way for realizing the end. [Some have therefore regarded teleology as a mere reversal of causality. This, for all the evident essential relationship between causality and teleology, is not the case, however. The terms of the teleological (i.e. end/means) relationship are postulates, something that is willed and is to be realized directly or indirectly, whereas the terms of causal relationships have no volitional meaning. Causal relationships are valid (or are considered to be valid) regardless of whether the causal consequence is willed or not willed by some subject.]

Since a given end may usually be attained in different ways, there often are different means to the envisioned end. This situation calls for a further step in teleological thinking: the selection of the optimum means (according to the criteria of the system of ends) from among the set of the possible means. This implicitly means also that the possible means are evaluated relatively and that a decision will be taken according to this preference. The criteria determining the preference vary and comprise particularly the extent of satisfaction of the goal, the certainty of satisfaction of the goal (with the means of course also being determined on the basis of stochastic causality), the attainability of the means (the volume of expenditures required), etc. Equivalence of possible means is solved by arbitrary (random) selection between the alternatives that are equivalent in value.

5.18. Possible and permissible means

The class of possible means is – particularly where moral or ethical-political points of view are involved – limited by moral postulates. One may e.g. reject drug traffic as a means for procuring income, with the effect that this way of maximizing one's income – although possible and effective – is excluded from the class of possible means, thus arriving at a class of possible and at the same time morally permissible means.

Remark

The limitation of the possible means to the (morally) permissible ones has major consequences for the success of the agent. One who in comparison with other people (in particular business competitors) has limited possibilities of action will probably be less successful than his competitor. One who has moral scruples would on that account most probably be greatly handicapped in his chances of success. And in many cases – as we know from experience – this is indeed the case. Drug dealers and traders in arms get rich, intrigants often win the game. Nevertheless, this pessimistic view of things is not correct. While calling attention to a very important social fact, it overlooks the social mechanisms that work in the opposite direction. Everyone is in search of, and is greatly interested in finding, dependable partners (including business rivals) and in this endeavor one must – as many do – favor the partners and fellow-citizen of high moral standards. This attitude of people in society compensates to a high degree the negative effects of the limitation of one's actions to the morally permissible.

In the usual presentations of teleology the relationship between the determination of action through the finding of suitable means and the selection of the optimum means is, as a rule, presented in somewhat simplified fashion. In reality it often is a matter here of invention and construction, of the working-out of programs, of course not only through the application of known causalities, but through the invention of structured sequences of actions which introduce an interaction of elements permitting programs to be brought into existence that will accomplish the end pursued.

Problem solutions do not merely depend on a multitude of known causal relationships; what is decisive, rather, is a purpose-oriented organization of elements which needs to be invented so that an approach can be realized by which the end will be satisfied.

In the case of actions according to programs the decision reached does not exhaust itself in selecting the program. Also, in the course of the acts, further, successive action impulses will be provided. In some programs, namely those with a feedback, intermediate results are ascertained on whose basis decisions will be taken as to how to continue the procedure.

5.19. Remarks on formal axiology

Evaluating sentences are in the main determined by two moments: 1. By the points of view or criteria of the evaluation, and 2. by the scale of values that is decisive (or is stipulated to be so) for the evaluation. By the points of view the type of preference is defined. Hence, categories of values (evaluations) can be distinguished that vary with what criteria were resorted to. One may distinguish e.g. moral, economic, esthetic, and other values. Just what criteria happen to be relevant for value considerations is a question of the material value theory; formal axiology is satisfied with noting that value categories can be distinguished that vary with the points of view. A direct comparison of evaluation attributed always refers to *one* category only. It is only through the constitution of complex criteria that a comparative value consideration of categorially different evaluations can likewise be carried out.

An evaluation according to a stipulated point of view is measured against an associated rating scale. It is possible to associate to one and the same evaluation viewpoint various rating scales. An evaluation system will be defined only by a criterion together with the stipulation of a rating scale.

Let us assume that we are dealing with a subject field whose elements can meaningfully be attributed values according to the given criterion. This field we can call *evaluation field*.

The rating scales can vary widely. They may consist of punctual individual values or present a graduated, possibly even continuously variable value characteristic. I believe that only the following minimum requirements need to be fulfilled:

(a) A zero point must have been determined for the evaluation, i.e. the case must have been defined in which objects of the field are assigned the zero value (meaning that it is granted that such an object can be meaningfully evaluated according to the criterion under consideration, but with the result that it is attributed the zero value, hence neither a positive, nor a negative value of this category).

(b) The direction of the rating scale is stipulated, i.e. it is laid down which value shall be regarded as positive (or as negative) or which axis of the scale shall be characterized as positive (or as negative).

A few examples may serve as illustrations of possible forms of the scale.

One can stipulate a rating scale of moral values comprising only the values "good", "evil" and "(ethically) zero-valued", with "good" being regarded as the positive value.

One may also, however, assume a different scale of morality, namely a valuation from "extremely evil" to "(ethically) zero-valued" to "ethically extremely good". The extreme values may be conceived of as points or as open-ended half lines. Instead of a continuous scale, scattered points may be fixed on the half-lines of the positive and negative values.

Economic values may be mapped on a half line from zero to positive values. Such a continuous scale is possible e.g. for the rating of usefulness (or of monetary value). It is also possible, however, to introduce a double half-line as scale in case we introduce "negative utility" (damage) as an evaluation possibility.

The stipulation of the scale does not, as a rule, come about arbitrarily, but rather as the result of a theoretical conception of the given field, and the scale will then also have effects on the consequences derived from the evaluation system.

A well-known example from philosophy: *Schopenhauer* proceeds from the theoretical conception that motivation for action (for activities) always comes forth from a desire to satisfy needs (or overcome shortcomings). Thus there are only different degrees, different intensities of the needs, hence of what motivates us to eliminate these shortcomings: hence only negatively-valued motivators with the zero point ("freedom from want", absence of needs) as limiting value. It is from this construction of the motivation for action that the pessimism of Schopenhauer's philosophy of life and his supreme goal directly result: minimization of the motivation for action, hence of the needs motivating to activity, the conception of absolute absence of needs in a purely contemplative Nirwana.

These examples are only cited to show two things: the essential influence of the stipulation of the rating scale for the evaluation system, and the effects of the theoretical constructions of the methodological consequences of the evaluation system on the practical-philosophical doctrines advocated.

By introducing the concept of different value categories we have opted for a rational-analytical approach to axiology. It would, however, be a distortion of the axiological reality and its problems if we were to come to a full stop upon arriving at this view. Two considerations are necessary to place this view, correct though I deem it to be in principle, in the proper light.

(I) There is not only rational-analytical evaluation as made evident by the criteria and rating scales. There is also such a thing as *global evaluation*, which in many cases is even the primary thing which will only be "cultivated" by rational analyses and specified by criteria into value categories. Such global, not systematically reflected evaluation also has its applications and will often be transformed into a clear structure only by analysis. Global evaluation decides between the taking of a positive or a negative stand; cases of global zero-valuedness rarely evoke evaluating comments, and from a global perspective the difference between zero-valuedness and indifference (non-ratability) hardly comes to mind.

(II) Under certain circumstances a summarizing evaluation on the basis of a complex criterion composed of two or more criteria will be meaningful and perhaps even necessary. It may e.g. become necessary to evaluate things simultaneously from both moral and esthetic points of view [cf. the idea of the kalokagathos (the beautiful and good) in Greek philosophy]. Here a methodological remark is essential: From the partial evaluations according to the individual criteria the overall evaluation will not yet logically result; this resultant will be co-determined by the relative weighting of the components.

5.20. On logic of preferences

Logic of preferences works either with (a) two relators of two places each, or (b) with one relator of two places: "p is (strongly) preferred to q" and "p is rated equal to q" in case (a), and "p is weakly preferred to q" in case (b). The weak preference is defined as disjunction "p is preferred or rated equal to q". These two conceptual stipulations can be transformed into one another. Since the selection is determined by strong preference it is simpler, for action-theoretical considerations, to start out from terminology (a).

Analogously to what can be done in the case of one-place evaluating sentences, various categories of relative evaluating sentences may be distinguished, and here, too, these categories are characterized by the evaluation criteria. The various criteria according to which preferences are stipulated can have different relationships to one another: they may be comparable or, rather, non-comparable. They will be comparable when they differ from one another only with respect to the degree of abstractness (e.g. well-being vs. satisfaction of the need for food). Where they are non-comparable (e.g. moral vs. esthetical value), the value criteria create categories of relative evaluation or of preference relationships.

Through such relative evaluation a ranking of the evaluated object according to the criterion used is generated. Since as a result of the relative evaluation, in addition to preference determinations, the ascertainment of equivalence may likewise come to pass, there comes about, through such relative evaluation, a semi-ranking in the evaluation field, i.e. relations of preference are introduced, with the particularity, however, that among some elements of this classification there may be equivalence.

Preferring some element to another may be justified on various grounds: more extensive or more intensive satisfaction of the criterion; since frequently not only strictly deterministic processes, but also stochastic relationships are resorted to to attain the ends, the higher or lower probability of the ends being satisfied by the means may justify the preference given. Since, with the alternatives considered, negative consequences are possible as well, the risk – the probability and the weight of a possible damage – also plays a part in the preference determination. The probabilities and the magnitude of undesirable results of alternatives are, in principle, cognitively ascertainable, but the evaluating reaction to risk is a matter of position-taking and, in the final instance, not rationally justifiable.

The preferential relationship, i.e. the stipulation that the state of affairs p is preferable to the state of affairs q, says nothing about the "distance" between the relatively evaluated objects or states of affairs. When one says "p is better than q", nothing is said as to by how much p is better than q. From determinations of preference, quantitative value-relationships between the terms so related cannot be derived. What, in relative evaluation, was found to be true of one-place evaluation will apply analogously to global evaluation and complex evaluations. But it is particularly from considerations on preferential evaluations that it is possible to justify why complex preferences, too, must be determined from incompatible criteria.

If a well-founded choice between alternatives is to come about, then the preferential rankings according to different, mutually incomparable criteria alone are not sufficient for this purpose. Rather, notwithstanding the non-comparability, a ranking according to preference should be realized, this according to a complex criterion comprising different factors, including non-comparable ones. [If, for example, I have to take a purchasing decision between objects G_1 and G_2, with, say, G_1 being more beautiful than G_2, but G_2 of better quality than G_1, then a summarizing evaluation according to the double criterion "beauty/quality" must be made. Now this complex relative evaluation, while having to be carried out with the "partial evaluations" being taken into account, is logically not yet determined by the partial preference; rather, it requires an additional decision.]

5.21. Ordinal and cardinal preference

Preference can be ordinally and cardinally determined. The relative evaluation that determines the selection between possible alternatives through preference determination (as limited in the case of value equivalence) is to be understood ordinally. Which means: the terms of the preference relationship are not assigned numerical values (or: no such values need be assigned), and the stipulation of the preference takes place without determination of the distance between these terms. If, on the contrary, the terms of the preference consideration do have numerical values, then the preference claim can be derived from the quantitative relationship of the evaluations. Conversely, from the preference "A is preferred to B" no quantitative determination of the evaluation of A and of that of B is derivable. All that can be said is that – provided that such a quantitative evaluation is meaningful and that an appropriate value rating scale has been introduced – A is rated higher than B.

For many problem-solving methods and calculations, quantitative value determinations are useful, but is does not form part of the nature of teleology and of purpose-oriented thinking that the evaluations must be cardinally determined. This is important for at least two reasons: (a) the numerically determined evaluation need not always be meaningful, and (b) decisive for the determination of the choice is the (strong) preference, regardless of the numerical (quantitative) distance between the alternatives to choose from.

Chapter 6

On the Idea of Practical Inference

Simultaneously a study on the relationship between mental operations and actions

6.1. The concept of practical inference[1]

Practical inference (PI) is the term used, following reflections by and examples from *Aristotle*, for a figure of thought of the following structure:

---

[1]I have dealt with this problem field in an earlier study: Handeln und Schliessen. Überlegungen zum Begriff der praktischen Inferenz (Action and Inference. Reflections on the Concept of Practical Inference), in F. Van Dun (ed.), The Law Between Morality and Politics, *Philosophica* 25, 1979, p.5–36. Reprinted in : O. Weinberger, Moral und Vernunft (Morality and Reason), op.cit. p.380–411. In the following I will quote a few paragraphs from this study (partly in modified form).

Premises:	Comprise the ascertainment of the existence of an intention of an agent, and the claim that a certain action (or: only this action) will lead to the fulfillment of this intention;
Operation result:	The performance of the action (or the thesis that it is necessary to perform this action).

This definition characterizes the problem field, but it is not as clear and unequivocal as one expects a logical theory to be.

The problem of PI is only a partial question from that general sphere of fundamental questions of practical philosophy which is essentially linked up with the conception of the relationships between cognition (knowledge), volition (action) and reflection, and which comprises also norm-logical, preferential-logical, action-logical, decision-logical and similar investigations. While the following investigations will be limited to those moments which are directly connected with the PI concept, the results will also cast some light on the general problem field of the fundamentals involved.

Is PI a logical conclusion, or in what is it similar to logical conclusions? The importance of this question is not to be found in only one direction: it is not merely a matter here of explaining whether and in how far PI is identical with or similar to logical conclusions, but also of characterizing more precisely the nature of deduction itself, either by integrating thinking operations of the practical field into the field of logical-deductive operation, or by delimiting logical deduction from action-related operations.

The central question of the investigations following below is, on the one hand, the comparison of PI with deductive operations, and, on the other hand, the question whether the action itself can assume the part of a conclusion in logical deductions, or whether one should perhaps rather regard PI's as a kind of deductions where the result of the operation is constituted by an action.

One of the examples of *Aristotle* may serve as illustration of the PI:

	Dry food is suitable for every human being.
	I am a human being.
	This is dry food.
Hence:	this food is suitable for me.

6.2. Comparison of practical inference with conclusions in descriptive language

a) There are striking parallels between conclusions in the usual sense and PI's. Both are linguistically representable. Even if it is said of PI that its result is an action, this action occurs in PI theory in a linguistic cloak, i.e. the result is a linguistically characterized action.

b) PI can be schematized analogously to conclusions.

Just as we have inference schemes, logically valid inference schemes – and correspondingly: inference rules –, valid PI schemes and PI rules can be drawn up. Hence PI is a formal relationship, and PI theory can be regarded as a kind of logic.

c) Analogously as in the case of conclusions, the result of a PI comes about in compelling fashion. This moment of inevitability, i.e. the inevitability with which the result is obtained from premises, can be regarded as the decisive characteristic of logical operations. It is valid not only for the realm of descriptive language as necessary heredity of truth, but is also e.g. the moment which leads to the recognition of logical relationships and deductive operations in the field of the norm-sentences or in the complex field of descriptive and norm-sentences.

d) In a PI, the causal premise can be understood either as objectively valid truth or as subjective opinion of the agent. Does this have an influence on the logical character of the PI? Is a PI a logically valid scheme, despite these two different possibilities?

e) In logical inferences in the customary sense (i.e. in descriptive language) the validity of the inference scheme is, as a matter of principle, independent of facts, in particular independent of the factual truth of the premises and conclusions. It is only through the relative dependency of the truth of the conclusion on the truth of the premises (if the premises are true or are assumed to be) that the truth of the conclusion is asserted by the deductive relationship. Most formulations of the PI as given in the pertinent literature comprise factual elements (e.g. the fact that there exists a subject who has a certain intention). If the PI is to have validity as a logical scheme or a logical rule, its formulation must be made free of such references to facts.

f) Unlike the usual logical deduction operations, which are defined in fields of objects to which both the premises and the conclusions belong, the action as resulting from the PI is an object totally differing in nature from the premises.

g) The semantical status of the elements of the PI can be regarded as problematical. On the one hand the concept 'intention' is not a purely descriptive concept, for practical terms must be resorted to in order to define it. Nor, on the other hand, can the result of the PI be represented purely descriptively, for the action concept is not definable as a pure description of an event or process without using typically practical concepts as e.g. intentions, ends, and the like.

6.3. G. H. von Wright's contribution to the theory of Practical Inference

G. H. von Wright has devoted two writings to the PI's.[2] In them, the author presents a variety of practical inferences. By means of a few fundamental distinctions, the realm of practical deduction is split up into logically different fields.

A distinction is made between primary PI's and secondary ones, with the latter – unlike the former – containing already among the

[2]G. H. von Wright, Practical Inference, *The Philosophical Review* 72 (1963), p. 159–179; German translation "Praktisches Schließen", in *id.*, *Handlung, Norm*

premises a practical necessity (or as I would say: an Ought or Must).[3] With primary – but not with secondary – PI's the problem exists whether the PI's are compatible with the principle of the non-derivability of Ought from Is.

For the field of the primary PI's, which interest us here first and foremost, the author indicated a non-personally formulated basic scheme from which he derives two logically wholly different conclusion forms: the scheme of the PI in the first person and that in the third person.

The basic scheme is illustrated by the following example:

(1) One wishes to make the cabin habitable.
Only if the cabin is heated will it become habitable.
Hence the cabin must be heated.

Schematically:

(1') One wishes to attain x.
Only if y is done will x be attained.
Hence y must be done.

The corresponding PI in the first person reads:

(2) I wish to make the cabin habitable.
Only if I heat the cabin will it become habitable.
Hence I must heat the cabin.

The PI in the third person speaks of the Will and the (practical) Must of a person A:

und Intention, Untersuchungen zur deontischen Logik (Action, Norm and Intention, Studies on Deontic Logic), de Gruyter, Berlin/New York 1977, p.41–60; On So-called Practical Inference, *Acta Sociologica* 15 (1972), p.39–53; German translation "Über sogenanntes praktisches Schließen", in: id., *Handlung, Norm und Intention, Untersuchungen zur deontischen Logik* (Action, Norm, and Intention, Studies on Deontic Logic), op. cit., p.61–81.
In this chapter I only treat von Wright's theory of the PI's. The paper cited in Footnote 1 contains also analyses of the contributions by *Jarvis, Kenny, Kim, Rescher* and *Wallace*, which I prefer not to repeat here.

[3]Cf. von Wright, *Praktisches Schließen* (Practical Inference), op.cit., p.56.

(3) *A* wishes to make the cabin habitable.
Only if *A* heats the cabin will it become habitable.
Hence *A* must heat the cabin.

The relationship between (1) on the one hand and (2) and (3) on the other hand is probably understood by *von Wright* in such a way that (1) is replaced by the explications (2) or (3) as differentiated according to the possible problem situations.

PI's of the type (2) are regarded by *von Wright* as the true practical inferences: The first premise is an articulation of one's own intention, the second one a causal assertion subjectively regarded as true; the conclusion follows with subjective practical necessity – subjective, i.e. valid-for-me, because the causal premise may be objectively wrong. The conclusion is not a sentence (not a proposition), but actually the corresponding action.[4]

The inference in the third person consists of propositions. The second premise is understood objectively, so that the conclusion is reached with objective practical necessity. This objective practical necessity actually finds expression in a theoretical conclusion:[5] "Practical necessity is that necessity to do something definite to which an agent is subject when striving to attain one of his objectives", with a special case being given when the goal can only be reached by learning (mastering) the activity.

In his 1972 essay *von Wright* distinguishes between the retrospective and the prospective use of PI, without, however, abandoning the distinction between PI's in the first and in the third person.[6]

---

[4] "If the second premise is wrong, it is still prossible that I (erroneously) *believe* it to be true. And then I will believe the conclusion to be true", ... "If, therefore, I base my reflections on the two premises, then the conclusion will be *valid for me*, even if the second premise, and hence also the conclusion, is wrong. This is a peculiarity of practical inferences in the first person." (G. H. von Wright, *Über sogenanntes praktisches Schließen* (On So-Called Practical Inference), op.cit., p.69.)

[5] Cf. G. H. von Wright, op.cit. p.67.

[6] Cf. G. H. von Wright, op.cit. p.76 et seq.

If the inference is used retrospectively, then we start out with the conclusion and reconstruct a class of premises, as it were, from which the conclusion follows.

An agent did *A*. Why did he do it? We explain his action in considering it from a "teleological perspective" by noting that he strove for a specific goal and had a specific cognitive orientation with respect to the requirements of the situation, i.e. that he regarded the action concerned as a practical necessity for the attainment of this goal. This is a model case for what is generally called 'teleological explanation of the action'.

I did *A*. Now someone impels me to reflect why I did it. I can justify my behavior by telling that this or that was my goal and that I believed it was a practical necessity for me to do *A*.

Used prospectively, the PI ends in the first person with the announcement of my intention to do something specific, and in the third person with the prediction of an action.

Von Wright's merit in having, through subtle analyses, called attention to the fact that it is from the field of the practice – both there where action is taken and there where action needs to be understood – that logical analysis has to start out is indisputable. Nevertheless I doubt the correctness or adequacy of some of his theses and conceptions. My comments will move in two directions: (I) I will analyze von Wright's distinctions in the field of the PI and criticize his deduction scheme of the PI, and (II) I will plead for another approach in the analysis.

Ad (I):

Distinguishing between PI's in the first and in the third person does not, in my opinion, hit the core of the differences in nature of PI's. The linguistic distinction between sentences in the first and those in the third person cannot, of and for itself, constitute the decisive moment for an essential difference between the schemes, for one can interpret the I-sentence as a sentence on the person of the speaker (a sentence in which his name would take the place of 'I').

The essential difference lies in the problem situation: on the one hand it is a matter of the situation of an agent (subject of the action) who guides his behavior through a reflection, and on the other hand of the situation of an observer who wishes to understand an agent and who interprets his behavior as action. It strikes me as adequate to consider a non-personally formulated scheme of the practical-logical relationships which will be applied in methodologically different ways, depending on the problem situation.

Von Wright cites *Kant's* dictum: "He who wishes the end, will also (provided rationality decisively influences his actions) wish the means lying within his power that is absolutely required to this end",[7] which expresses the principle of the "transfer of intentions from ends to means".

The property of the means to be striven for (desired) stems from the end-oriented intention and is mediated by the causal relationship saying that the means will lead to a situation intended as end. It strikes me as only natural to regard this relationship, occurring as it does in all PI's, as the common core of the practical structures investigated and to ascribe the epistemological and methodological differences to the various application conditions, as determined by the problem situation, of this basic structure. The thing of importance here is to crystallize out those relationships which have analytical validity. And this, it seems to me, is possible only in the general scheme – the neutral scheme with respect to persons, as it were. The variety occurring in the analysis, e.g. the objective or subjective positing of the causal premises, can be understood as different ways of applying one and the same analytically valid arsenal of instruments.

To my view one might object that purely linguistically alone PI's in the first and in the third person are fundamentally different: 'I have the intention A' and the ascertainment 'The person P has the intention

[7]I. Kant, *Grundlegung zur Metaphysik der Sitten* (Foundations of the Metaphysics of Morality), 1st ed. 1785, I. Kant, *Werke* (works), ed. W. Weischedel, Suhrkamp, Wiesbaden 1956, Vol.VII, p.46.

A' are categorially different.[8] In the former case we are dealing with a declaration of intent, and in the latter one with the recognition of a fact. This recognition, however, is not a pure description insofar as what is asserted contains – in indirect speech, as it were – a determination of intent. It seems to me that, for this reason, one cannot purely and simply regard the practical inference in the third person as a pure descriptive-inference form. For: the linking-up of the premises with the conclusion sentence is given precisely by the teleological-causal connection, hence by a relationship between the elements contained in the indirect speech.

The second premise is, with *von Wright*, always a sentence of the 'if and only if' type. The existence of one single means for satisfying the end is, however, merely a special case, to which practical thinking most certainly will not limit itself. In *von Wright's* conception, the practical necessity comes about precisely by this circumstance, the existence of one single means.

A sentence stipulating B to be a necessary means for attaining A (the end A) is all by itself (without further premises) certainly not a sufficient reason for doing B (or: for wishing to do B, or for wishing B).

In *von Wright's* example it follows by no means from the premises "If the cabin is to be made habitable" and "Only if the cabin is heated can it be made habitable" that the cabin is to be heated. Let us assume the cabin has a leaky roof. Then heating may be a necessary, but will not be a sufficient measure for making the cabin habitable. Who would think the cabin should be heated in any event if one does not or cannot carry out the second measure, the roof repair necessary for making the cabin habitable?

The intention transfer is based on causal relationships to which sufficient conditions correspond. The necessary condition alone is no guaranty for the validity of the intention transfer in the PI.

Von Wright's conception of the practical necessity springs precisely from the uniqueness of the means. "The conclusion (of inference (1) –

[8] A. J. Kenny, Practical Inference, *Analysis* 26 (1965/66), p.65–75.

note added by me, O. W.) I would like to term a *practical necessity*, namely the practical necessity to apply the means mentioned in the second premise in order to reach the goal mentioned in the first premise."[9] If one changes the inference scheme by deleting in the second premise the word "only", the moment of necessity will be eliminated. Where several means are available to realize an end, there is no necessity to apply precisely the one means mentioned in the second premise.

For the following reason the PI schemes are not conclusive, i.e. they do not precisely hit the core of the logically (analytically) valid relationship. It may be that one acts because the action itself is willed. But in all actions taken into consideration in PI's it is a matter of action with the aid of means: If A is intended (willed as goal), then A is assigned a certain positive value, a usefulness, or whatever one wants to call this characteristic of being willed, which is of the half-order type. One may assume that the means will not always be value-indifferent. If at all, they will be value-indifferent only by way of exception. If, e.g., heating is a means for making the cabin habitable, then this heating will involve effort and some expense.[10]

If B is the sole and also sufficient means for attaining the goal A, then evidently B should be done if and only if the value (usefulness) of A and B combined is positive, i.e. if the end situation striven

[9] A more adequate translation would read: "namely to apply the means mentioned in the second premise". G. H. von Wright, *Handlung, Norm und Institution* (Action, Norm, and Institution), op.cit., p.43. A passage from "Erklären und Verstehen" (Explaining and Understanding) shows even more clearly that, with *von Wright*, practical necessity is precisely viewed as a consequence of the uniqueness of the means. "If A believes that the performance of a is the sole thing sufficing for reaching his goal, then the case is unproblematical. For then the performance of a is, in his opinion, also necessary." (p.95).

[10] It may of course happen that someone takes joy in this effort, hence does not attach to it the negative value usually associated with the expenditure of means. For our considerations it is not decisive whether the means is evaluated positively, negatively or at zero usefulness. In any event it does not fall outside of the evaluation. And this suffices for our argumentation.

for and the expenditures for attaining it are, together, still evaluated positively.

Von Wright perceived this problem partially himself,[11] but he fails to see that as a result the practical necessity inherent, in his construction, in the unique means is called into question in any event, i.e. is not a necessity. Since the PI has, as its object, always an action with the aid of means, the validity of the conclusion as to the action is always dependent on the evaluation of the end and means together. Now since this evaluation may also turn out to be negative, namely when the negative value (the expense) of the means outweighs the positive value of the end striven for, the consequence has no general validity, hence is not a necessity.

Of the complexity of the ends system the author speaks only relatively little. He remarks that several ends may be pursued at the same time, and that ends (or wishes) may be mutually incompatible. Conflicts between ends pursued must – so the author thinks – be excluded by stipulation a limine.[12] In my opinion this is not a propitious path. Ends that logically contradict one another should, to be sure, be excluded. But the co-existence side by side of ends whose simulataneous pursuit is inherently contradictory should not be excluded. For example, one may simultaneously cherish the ends of dining exquisitely and saving money. If a more expensive meal is believed to be a better one, then the pursuit of the one end provokes a limitation of the other one. The problem should not be solved through limitation of the ends in the system, but though decision from the complex point of view of both ends.

---

[11] "If he (the agent, O. W.) recognizes what he necessarily should do and feels a strong aversion to it, he may change his intention and cease to strive for the original good." G. H. von Wright, *Über sogenanntes praktisches Schließen* (On So-called Practical Inference), op.cit., p.70.

[12] G. H. von Wright, *Handlung, Norm und Institution* (Action, Norm and Institution), op.cit., p.64.

Ad (II):

If I understand *von Wright* and his intentions in the analysis of PI's correctly, the famous author's concern is the proper description of the phenomenon of acting persons and the determination of the action by rational operations. In this endeavor he tries to schematically pin down the differentiatedness of the linguistic representation of those situation in which PI's occur, with the guiding star of his analytical efforts being those elements which can in this process be obtained through in-depth analysis of the corresponding linguistic game. My approach is different. I am concerned with formally characterizing the role and structure of the action-determining thinking. These schemes – here the schemes of the PI – are to be examined for structural validity. They are not generalized images of the factual, action-related thinking. They are "rational reconstructions" of the action-determining information processing,[13] not generalized descriptions of acting persons.

6.4. Practical inference and formal teleology

Practical inference as represented in the PI schemes is connected with formal teleology, as the logical theory of end/means relationships might be called. But the nature of teleology is disputed. Should one view it as a theory of specific practial forms of thinking, or does it merely give a description of actual relationships as read from experience?

In my opinion, teleology must be presented as a system of schemes of thought to which formal generality may be attributed. It is not as a generalization from observations about the behavior of people that teleology is won; rather, it is built up as a system of analytically valid forms and operations. These schemes are to be regarded as compellingly valid. The teleological schematism can be used both for

[13] Cf. Chapter 4 of this book.

the representation of the structure of the reflection guiding the action and as an interpretation scheme for the explanation of actions.

If one proceeds from the teleology so conceived as basis of the PI's one can gain a few insights about the PI's. Their first premise articulates the stipulation of an end, an intention. For the validity of the rational operations it is not relevant whether this stipulation of an end appears as the intention of the speaker, of his interlocutor or of any other subject. If the scheme and the operations are to be regarded as rationally valid operations, then the end must be linguistically formulated and intersubjectively understandable. The end as stipulated is expressed by a description of a certain state of affairs which indicates the content of the will. Thus a state of affairs determined as desirable is posited as premise. The second premise of the PI must not be understood as an arbitrary 'if/then' sentence, nor as an arbitrary general conditional sentence; rather, it must be a sentence which expresses a causal relationship, for it is only through such relationships that means to given ends will be determinable.[14]

There are actions (acts) which are performed for their own sake. This can be presupposed, although in the analyses the quality of being willed for its own sake often recedes into the background, making the action to appear instead as justifiable for the sake of something else. Besides, there are also willed ends that are realized indirectly, namely through the use of means that bring about the willed result. Actually it is precisely such indirect action which constitutes the field of teleological analysis. Since there are effects of causes to be found in the world, the possibility of indirect action exists, i.e. the possibility of realizing ends through the employment of means.

[14]Acquaintance with the concepts 'causal relationship' and 'causal law' is assumed here. From a philosophical point of view a mutual interdependence of causality and teleology can be perceived, for the causality concept is so structured that the recognition of causality can be used for the determination of means. See "Excursion on the recognition of causality and causal explanation" in Chapter 8 of this book.

The subjective prerequisite for indirect action is the knowledge of causal relationships, or, perhaps, the belief that the subject possesses such knowledge.

In the teleological schemes the end (a willed state of affairs, an intention determined as to its contents), is presupposed as premise. It need not be asked – but, in some cases, may be asked in a different consideration – whether this presupposed end is willed primarily (for its own sake) or can itself be justified by other ends.

Willing in the sense of formal teleology is an evaluating position-taking. The end stipulated is assumed to have a positive value. The evaluation of the willing need not be quantitatively (numerically) given, but the following theses will be valid in any event:

(1) If something – a state of affairs S – is stipulated as an end, the state of affairs S is assigned a positive value.

(2) While the evaluation need not take place in the form of assignment of a numerical measure, it can be performed in relation to other evaluations (relative valuation). A state of affairs S_1 may be preferred to a state of affairs S_2, or vice versa, or, finally, S_1 and S_2 may be rated equal.

(3) The evaluation and relative evaluation may be in the nature of a global-decisionist position-taking or be based on cognitive determining rules. The acceptance of such rules always contains an element of decision, however.[15]

How does one explain, from the point opf view of formal teleology, the transfer of the intention from the end (stipulated as a premise) to the means, and the selection between possible means for reaching a given end? Here a two-step process is realized:

1. the determination of the means,
2. the choice between possible means.

[15] It is in this that non-cognitivism expresses itself in teleology and axiology.

Ad 1:

Whatever can causally bring about the end E is a (possible) means to the end E. Varying with the problem situation, certain limiting conserations may be added here:

(a) Sometimes only such measures will be taken into consideration as means as lie actually within the power of the acting subject.

(b) In the reflections of a subject determining his action only those causal relationships will come into play which the subject knows, including, however, causal relationships that are actually invalid, yet are believed by the subject to be true (cognitive subjectivization of the teleological reflection).

(c) Not only deterministic causal relationships will find application, but also stochastic causal relationships. In the case of such stochastic causality the evaluations and selection processes are far more complicated. The following investigations proceed, for simplification purposes, from the assumption of a deterministic causality wherever a probability relationship is not expressly taken into consideration.

Every possible means is attributed *prima-facie* willedness – precisely because of the teleological scheme of indirect action. According to this scheme, indirect action makes use of a causal relationship.

The *prima-facie* willedness is, as it were, a determining element in the deliberation process, not a willing in the definite sense, not a quantity directly guiding the action.

Ad 2:

The decision of the will comes about only through the second step. From the class of the possible means the optimum one (or one of the optimum ones, in case several ones are equally optimal) is selected. A precondition for this is that the means can be evaluated and that their relative valuation can be carried out. This relative valuation is to be understood as greater or lesser suitability of (or greater or lesser probability of the goal being realized) the means for the goal to be attained. For example: the means M_1 will lead with greater (lesser, equal) probability to the end than (as) the means M_2.

No means at all, exactly one means, or several ones may be available in any given case. If a plurality of means is available, the choice will be made on the basis of a relative weighing of the means. If the negative value of a means outweighs the positive value of the end, so that, in other words, the complex 'End plus Means' is valued negatively, then the application of this means is out of the question, as it has been found unpracticable because of its uselessness. If the resultant value of 'End plus Means' is zero (neutrality of the means), then acting by applying this means is just as good as not acting at all: no rationally justified decision will come about, and the decision will be purely arbitrary.

The selection will always be made from among the means vallued as practicable, and the action alternative selected will be the one in which the complex 'End plus Means' is given an optimal rating. Since two or more alternatives 'End plus Means M_i' may be rated equal, this analysis does not always lead to a clear decision.

Summing up, it can be said:

1. If the class of the means valued as practicable is empty (i.e. if the resultant value 'End plus Means M_i' is negative for every M_i), then there is no realizable action alternative for attaining the goal.[16]

2. If there are only means which are valued neutral (no resultant value 'End plus Means M_i' is positive, at least one is neutral), then it is left to the agent's discretion whether one (and which one) of the neutral alternatives is realized.

3. If the class of the positive resultant values 'End plus Means M_i' contains exactly one element, then this means should be employed.

4. If the class of the positive resultant values 'End plus Means M_i' contains two or more elements, then the one of highest value should be realized, or, in case this optimal value is shared by several elements, any of the means with this optimum resultant value can be selected.

The system of ends assigned to an acting subject is usually complex. In the schemes of the PI and in formal teleology, usually only

[16] There is, of course, also the case where no means at all exists or is known that will lead to the realization of a meaningful goal.

elementary relationships are represented which proceed from one single end. Now while such technical analyses are undoubtedly important, they are, when viewed against the practical situations existing in reality, only to be understood as partial analyses.

6.5. The system of ends and logical consistency

A rationally constructed system of ends contains no logical contradictions, i.e. it contains no logically false states of affairs as ends, nor at one and the same time ends that are contradictorily opposed, such as 'p is intended' and '$\neg p$ is intended'. In the field of teleology there do exist, however, so-called conflicts of ends: the system of ends may comprise ends whose simultaneous satisfaction is logically or factually (practically) impossible. (E.g. I would like to go for a walk now and also finish my work.) It is precisely by this that occasions for selective acts are constituted whose rational analysis is the object of formal teleology. If – as proposed e.g. by *von Wright* – one would view the system of ends as not only as free of logical contradictions, but also as free of conflicts, i.e. regard only such ends as elements of the system of ends as can be realized all together, then the rational schematism of the choice would be removed from the realm of formal teleology and transferred into the structure of the system of ends. The reflections about the construction of a conflict-free system of ends would then have to work with *prima-facie* ends to obtain the system of ends as a result of conflict elimination. This approach strikes me as unsuitable.

6.6. Some conclusions on practical inferences and on the relationship between mental operations and actions

Do practical inferences exist? They do in the sense that thinking schemes with practical sentences as terms are formally of general validity and that on these schemes compelling (logical) rules can be based.

All this, however, only if all ends, practical attitudes, preferences, etc. are expressed explicitly. Otherwise one might possibly speak of inference-like operations, meaning such rational chains of thought in which at certain points decisions not determined by the premises are necessary.

Is the action to be regarded as a result of the practical inference? I do not think it adequate to regard the action itself as a result of the practical inference. True, it would be possible to view the action as an expression of the conclusion (to regard the action as an assertion), but in my opinion it is better to represent the rational operations entirely in the framework of a language in the usual sense, with the action then joining them as realization. The linguistically formulated thinking scheme can then not only be used for action determination, but also for motive interpretation.

The realization process will then not appear as a (quasi) logical operation with realistic effect.

The intentions (ends) are expressions of the active orientation, given by nature, of the agent, as rationalized expression, as it were, of this primary orientation. The information process, represented in the form of the PI – or more precisely: as teleological analysis and preference-determined decision (choice between alternative means or alternative action possibilities) –, is interposed here to give the active behavior the end-oriented direction under optimization points of view. The action as resulting behavior does not spring from the mental operations, but from the immanent activity of the agent. (Thus the puzzle of intentionalism resolves itself.)

To what extent is the practical inference (or the thinking determining the action) objective deduction and to what extent is it subjective decision? PI and teleological reflection are inference, not, admittedly, in the sense of truth-conserving deduction, but in the sense of formal conclusiveness. In the case of perfectly explicit representation of the system of ends, of the analysis of means and of the choice-determining preferences, everything will be rationally conclusive; in the problem situations as practically given it will usually be a matter of an interaction between rational frames and decisions at specific stages in the reflections.

Is there a practical necessity? There will be practical necessity if and only if we are dealing with operations in which all determining elements are represented explicitly. This practical necessity is rationally conclusive relative to the premises. Most problem situations in practical thinking do not permit a totally logicized manner of presentation, however.

What status do the elements of the teleological relationship have? The elements of the teleological relationship – the determinations of ends and means – are to be regarded as practical sentences, regardless of whether the scheme is formulated in the first, second or third person.

Are conflicts of ends to be regarded as logical (in certain cases: practical-logical) contradictions? No. The system of ends is, on the contrary, to be regarded as a class of determinations of intentions which as a rule cannot all be satisfied at the same time and in the same measure. It is precisely the task of teleological analysis to solve these conflicts of ends through rational selection (or rational decisions).

Can teleological schematism be regarded as a formal theory? I believe it even must be so regarded, for only then can it be used as an instrument of action guidance and motive explication, in making use of premises having a specific content (stipulations of ends, causal relationships, preferences).

Are von Wright's practical-inference schemes valid rules of practical analysis? I do not regard *von Wright*'s schemes as valid in this form, but *von Wright* has the wholly special merit of having clearly formulated the problems and having recognized the fundamental importance of teleological analyses. The problems of the action-determining thinking operations require a detailed formal theory of teleology, including a logic of preferences. Since the decision and action processes are not limited to the putting-up of individual acts, but comprise complex action as well, the development of action programs (as complex means, as it were) must be included in the calculations. The operations that become necessary for the realization of programs, particularly feedback decisions, form a supplementary field of action-determining thought operations, which depend of course on further additional empirical information.

The PI schemes and formal teleology show on the one hand an essential relationship between cognition and the determination of actions (since causal relations appear everywhere in the schemes), while on the other hand it becomes evident that thinking (conclusive rational operations) is by no means only at home in the realm of cognition, but equally in that of action. It is manifest, however, that the schemes usually presented as PI are far removed from exhausting the field of action-determining thinking (of information-processing).

Chapter 7

From Deontic Logic to the Genuine Logic of Norms

Undoubtedly it was the intention of the creators of deontic logic to produce a theory of sentence structures and of logical operations which was to be applied as an instrument for the regulation of thinking and rational argumentation in the normative disciplines (ethics, jurisprudence, etc.). That this was the task envisioned is clear and undisputed; whether and to what extent this task was accomplished will have to be examined. This critical examination of deontic logic will have to be carried out on two levels: on the level of the philosophical preconditions, and on the level of the applicability of deontic logic as logic of the normative fields.

7.1. The concept 'Deontic Logic'

The following features are characteristic of the systems of deontic logic:

1. The deontic logics are conceived of as theories of the normative terms (prescription, prohibition, permission, etc.) and of the sentence structures of Ought and May, and are built up in a loose analogy to the alethic modalities: they are regarded, as it were, as offsprings of modal logic. Linguistic analysis is in the center of attention.

2. The deontic logics comprise deontic sentences and (ordinary) descriptive sentences.

3. The elementary deontic sentences consist of a deontic operator with an argument expressing the description of a state of affairs.

Expressions occurring as deontic operators are: 'It is prescribed …', 'It is forbidden …', 'It is permitted …', and 'It is indifferent …'. The arguments (contents) of deontic sentences may be action variables or arbitrary state-of-affairs variables.[1]

In deontic sentences, negations can occur at two places: (a) before the deontic operator[2], (b) before the description of the state of affairs. Varying with this placement of the negations, there thus arise four types of elementary sentences ('O_d' designates a deontic operator; 'p' a description of a state of affairs):

$O_d p$

$O_d \neg p$

$\neg O_d p$

$\neg O_d \neg p$

4. Mutual definability of the deontic operators 'prescribed', 'prohibited', 'permitted' is assumed, so that any one of them may be assumed as fundamental (and the other ones as defined).

5. The deontic sentences are treated as descriptive sentences capable of being either true or false. They occur as arguments of truth functors: they are negated in the same way as other descriptive sen-

[1]The two types of forms of deontic logic, namely those forms working, as contents of deontic sentences, with (a) a designation of the action, or (b) descriptions of states of affairs, have both been paid attention to and contrasted with one another. 'Action' has, in this process, mainly been regarded as a transformation of a state of affairs, rather than in the sense of a behavior determined by intention and information-processing – as would conform to the formal-finalistic action theory. The early works on deontic logic are based primarily on conception (a), the later ones on conception (b). The difference between both construction procedures is not important for my critical observations.

[2]The negation of the deontic operator is rated equal to the negation of the sentence formed by it. $[(\neg O_d)p = df(O_d p)]$. Here, too, the deontic sentence is treated as a descriptive sentence that can be subjected to the truth-functional negation.

tences; double negation will cancel out, and by means of truth functors complex sentences are formed. The transformations and deductions are carried out according to the rules of two-valued propositional logic.[3]

6. The contents of elementary deontic sentences may likewise be of molecular nature. Such composition will be truth-functionally determined, so that truth-functional transformations within the contents are permissible, whether occurring through equivalent transformations [e.g. '$O_d(p \wedge q)$' – '$O_d(q \wedge p)$'] or through weakening deductions [e.g. '$O(p)$' – '$O(p \vee q)$'].

What was it that led to deontic logic being viewed as a system analogous to the alethic modal logic of the necessary, possible and contingent? Mainly, I believe, two moments: (I) The linguistic pictures of the deontic and alethic modal sentences are wholly analogous; Operator – state-of-affairs argument, together with the possibility to negate either of these elements. (II) the mutal definability, assumed in both cases, of the operators.

The necessary is put in analogy to the prescribed, the possible to the permitted, as well as the definitions:

$$Mp = df \neg N \neg p \qquad\qquad Pp = df \neg O \neg p$$

It was immediately recognized, however, that the deduction rules of modal logic cannot be simply adopted by deontic logic too:[4]

The following differences in the deduction rules were recognized immediately:

In alethic modal logic the following is valid:

(1) From 'p is necessary' there follows 'p'

(2) From 'p' there follows 'p is possible'.

In deontic logic however, the analogous deductions are not valid:

---

[3]The creators of deontic logic do not meritorily discuss Jörgensen's dilemma, nor the caesura between descriptive and practical sentences or the philosophical and methodological problems connected with dichotomous semantics.

[4]De facto, however, certain analogies to alethic modal logic have influenced the building-up of deontic logic. Cf. in this connection von Wright's remark in the discussion of '$Ep \leftrightarrow \sim O \sim p$' in his book "*Normen, Werte und Handlungen*" (Norms, Values and Actions), Suhrkamp, Frankfurt a.M. 1994, p.75.

(1') From 'p is prescribed', 'p' *does not follow.*

(2') From 'p', 'p is permitted' *does not follow.*

Disputed, on the other hand, are above all the following deduction rules, recognized by the adherents of deontic logic, but not accepted by its critics:

(3) From '$O(p)$' there follows '$O(p \vee q)$' (called *Ross's paradox*).

(4) From '$O(p \wedge q)$' there follows '$O(p)$' and '$O(q)$' (*the splitting-up of the conjunction in the Ought content*).

Remark 1

The difficulties – insurmountable for classical deontic logic – involved in the representation of conditional norm-sentences led to the development of dyadic deontic systems. In them, the conditional norm-sentence is taken as a primitive concept, and the categorical (not conditional) norm-sentence is defined as a conditional norm-sentence with a tautological condition. For details on this problem, see below in the section on the conditional norm-sentence.

Although Jörgensen's dilemma was generally known, the semantic character of the deontic sentences was hardly felt to be a problem and was not discussed in detail; rather, one simply assumed that deontic logic represented the structure of and the logical operations within the normative systems. Deontic sentences were regarded as values of propositional variables and therefore unconcernedly introduced into the fomulae of propositional logic. Only secondarily, upon reflecting that norm-sentences cannot claim any truth values, was it realized that deontic sentences (being descriptive sentences capable of being either true or false) cannot be identified with norm-sentences. Hence one began to interpret them differently, namely as descriptive sentences about norms or about a normative system under consideration. Now one also had to face the question of what relations exist between the rational relationships within the normative system and the relationships, as represented by deontic logic, between sentences about norms. Does deontic logic adequately represent the logical relationships within the normative system?

The justification of the logical relations in deontic logic rests on the logical relationships within the normative system, and they will be justified if, and only if they correctly portray the relationships and operations within the normative system. This approach re-orients the logician's view from the deontic systems to the genuine logic of norms which is the standard for judging the adequacy of the deontic logics.

Remark 2

Some skeptics with regard to the logic of norms deny the existence of logical deduction within the normative system and contend that deductions exist only within the realm of the sentences about norms (or about the normative system under consideration). This point of view is inconsistent. Let us assume that within the realm of the sentences about a normative system Sn the inference is valid "From 'In S_n N_1 holds' there follows 'In S_n N_2 holds'". Now let in S_n the norm N_1, but not the norm N_2, have been stipulated. Then the following descriptive sentences about S_n are true in case, in accordance with the premise, no normative inferences exist within S_n: 'In S_n, N_1 holds' and 'In S_n N_2 does not hold.' Thus the inference within the realm of the descriptive sentences about S_n leads from a true premise (that N_1 is valid in S_n) to a false conclusion (since, according to the premise, N_2 is not valid in S_n). Hence it is not possible to recognize consequences within the realm of the sentences about norms while, in contrast, denying them within the realm of the norms themselves (cf. p.19).

7.2. *A valuation of the importance of deontic logic*

I have always been skeptical about deontic logic, and by now doubts have begun to occur even among the advocates of this approach to the problems of a logic of norms.[5]

[5] O. Weinberger, *Die Sollsatzproblematik in der modernen Logik* (The Problems of 'Ought' Sentences in Modern Logic), Rozpravy ČSAV, vol.68, no.9, Prague 1958

Despite my doubts, which I will explain and justify in greater detail below, I wish to underline the positive sides of occupying oneself with deontic logic. The positive moments lie in two directions:

1. The conviction has been strengthened that a logical theory of thinking in the field of norms is possible and necessary. This was achieved, not by profound philosophical and methodological reflections – these have, rather, been lacking –, but purely by the existence of the comprehensive body of literature on the subject. The question of deontic logic (and thus, indirectly, also that of the logic of norms) has been made a problem of current research. Although resting on a problematical philosophical basis, deontic logics have strengthened the awareness that formal deduction with normative sentences is possible, so that therefore the task exists of creating a corresponding theory. The semantic peculiarity of normative sentences (as a semantic category contrasted to descriptive sentences) was not clarified, but it became clear (a) that a purely formal manner of representation of the normative sentence structures and of the rules about how to deal with them (equivalent transformation, derivation of consequences) is possible and forms part of the scientific working program, and (b) that the derivation of consequences is analogous in nature to deduction in the field of the logic of descriptive language: The deduction of consequences is determinable by formal rules; the derivation of consequences is, as a matter of principle, non-creative in the sense that they cannot contain anything new over and beyond the content of the premises.[6]

(reprinted with an epilogue in: Studien zur Normenlogik und Rechtsinformatik (Studies on the Logic of Norms and on Legal Informatics), Berlin 1974, p.59–186); *id.*, The Concept of Non-Satisfaction and Deontic Logic), in: *Ratio* 14/1972, p.16–35.

[6]To avoid misunderstandings, be it noted here that this "Not-being-permitted-to-contain-anything-new" is to be understood as exclusion of a More or New in information; but it is not excluded that the conclusion may contain terms (namely in a weakening function) that are not contained in the premises. This is the case e.g. with the conclusion "from p there follows '$p \vee q$'".

2. Through the presentation of problematical steps it may also have extremely sensitized the critical-analytical attention of the researchers interested in the logic of norms, so that what prima facie had appeared plausible now also came to be carefully analyzed (e.g. the interdefinability of the operators of prescription, prohibition and permission).

7.3. The generalization of the deduction concept

As I already explained in the first chapter under the heading "Take Jörgen Jörgensen seriously!", it is necessary to pay attention to the semantic and logical independence of the norm-sentences as distinct from the category of descriptive sentences, and hence also, if one wants to arrive at a norm-logical deduction theory, to generalize the deduction concept in such a way that deductions with normative sentences (premises, conclusions) will likewise become possible. This can be done in two ways:

(i) By proceeding from the consideration that deduction consists in formally operating with assumed premises according to such rules as will lead to conclusions that possess a certain hereditary property of the premises. In the case of deduction in the descriptive language this hereditary property is the quality of being true, so that it is ensured by the deductive relationship that the conclusions will be true if all premises are true (determination of the relative truth of the conclusions through the premises). The generalization of the deduction concept so as to make it applicable to descriptive and norm-sentences consists in introducing a hereditary property which is a split concept: when attributed to descriptive sentences it means their being true, but when attributed to norm-sentences: their being valid.[7] If we introduce "positing" as superordinate concept of 'being true' (of

[7] Criteria of normative validity need not be discussed here, no more than criteria of being-true need to be discussed in the logic of descriptive language. Both concepts play the part of markings for the positing as a premise, respectively for the derived, logically obtained, deduced positing of the conclusions.

descriptive sentences) and 'being valid' (of norm-sentences), then the generalized deduction process is the passing-on, according to formal deduction rules, of the "positing" from the premises to the conclusions.

Deduction in the descriptive languages is then a special case of the generalized deduction concept.

(One may, of course, perform the same generalization also without introducing the positing concept. A descriptive conclusion is true if obtained according to the deduction rules from true descriptive premises and valid norm-premises; a norm conclusion is valid if obtained according to the deduction rules from true descriptive premises and valid norm premises.)

(ii) By introducing the consequence concept through rules that are valid for classes of consequences and abstractly (without using the concept of truth) [Let '$Cn(A)$' designate the set of consequences of A]:

1. $A \subset Cn(A)$
2. $Cn(A) = Cn(Cn(A))$
3. If $A \subset B$, then $Cn(A) \subset Cn(B)$[8]

With similar effect, I have characterized the relation of inference – likewise without recourse to truth relationships, hence applicable also to norms – by the following properties (with 'A', 'B', 'C' and 'D' being arbitrary sequences of sentences):

1. Every sentence contained in the class of the premises is itself a consequence of these premises. From $A(A = \{x_1, x_2, \ldots x_n\})$ there follows x_i for every i (i = 1, 2, ..., n).

2. If the relation of inference 'From A follows B' is valid, then 'From A, C follows B' will likewise be valid; in other words: Addition of arbitrary premises to a valid relation of inference will again yield a valid relation of inference.

3. If the relation of inference 'From A, B, C, D follows E' is valid, then 'From A, C, B, D follows E' will also be valid, in other words:

---

[8] C. E. Alchourrón, A. A. Martino, Logic Without Truth, in: *Ratio Juris*, vol. 3/1990, p.46–67.

Changing the sequence of the premises will leave the validity of the relation of inference intact.

4. If the two relations of inference 'From A follows B' and 'From A, B follows C' are valid, then the relation of inference 'From A follows C' will also be valid: in other words: premises which follow from other stipulated ones can be left out without the relation of inference thereby becoming invalid.

5. If 'From A follows B' and 'From B, C follows D' are valid, then 'From A, C follows D' will also be valid.[9]

There is – as one sees – no conceptual difficulty involved in working in logic with a generalized concept of inference which can also be applied to those elements of the relation of inference which are not capable of being either true or false.

The important thing, in my opinion, is to base all reflections about the construction of a logic of norms on the semantic caesura between descriptive and practical sentences, i.e. on a dichotomous semantics, rather than insisting on a definition of inference that depends on the notion of truth. In his essay "Gibt es eine Logik der Normen?" (Is there a Logic of Norms?, 1993), von Wright writes: "Refusing to agree that from a command there follows logically a corresponding permission is simply blockheadedness." Equally blockheaded, in my opinion, would it be not to recognize as a logical inference the individualization from a general norm or the detachment of the satisfied condition of a hypothetical norm-sentence.

In contrast to deontic logic, however, norm-logical deduction – although it fulfills the general principles of relations of inference – must be regarded as a special kind of deduction, since it comprises two semantic categories of sentences rather than only descriptive sentences.

[9]Cf. St. C. Kleene, Introduction to Metamathematics, Wolters-Noordhoff, Amsterdam 1952, p.88 et seq; O. Weinberger, Teorie důsledkových vztahů a hypothetická normativní věta (Theory of the relations of entailment and the hypothetical norm-sentence), in: id., Studie k logice normativních vět (Studies on the Logic of the Norm-Sentences), Rozpravy ČSAV, Prague 1960.

7.4. The extensionality of the norm content

In the case of Ought sentences (commands or prohibitions) it is essential that they can be satisfied as well as violated. An Ought sentence will be satisfied if and only if that which it commands (its content) is a fact; it will be violated if this is not the case. It appears only natural that one should permit truth-functionally composed contents of Ought and May sentences. However, this involves a few problems, too.

What sense does it make to make tautologies or contradictions the content of norm-sentences? To command (or permit) something tautological (or logically necessary) is futile: such a command (is it a command at all?) cannot be violated, nor can it play any regulative part whatsoever. Permitting the logically necessary can neither limit a true Ought, nor does is ensure a scope of action.

If the logically impossible is made the content of an Ought (or of a permission), then one stipulates something non-satisfiable, or, better formulated, something which cannot meaningfully be regarded as action (or behavior). To permit the logically impossible is certainly superfluous, and it is problematical whether one should regard this as a permission at all.

But how about the admissibility of truth-functional transformations of Ought contents? If the content is a logically equivalent transformation, then nothing will be changed in the content of the norm-sentence. If 'I_1' is logically equivalent with 'I_2' then '$O(I_1)$' means the same as '$O(I_2)$', for these two Ought sentences are identical as regards their satisfactional functionality.

It is problematical, however, whether from an Ought sentence '$O(p)$', '$O(q)$' will also follow if q is a logical consequence of p. For example, does '$O(p \vee q)$' follows '$O(p)$'? This inference scheme accepted as valid by deontic logic has been made out as absurd by Ross through the following example: If "You shall send off this letter" is valid, there should follow from this that "You shall send off this letter or burn it".

It has been tried in a variety of ways to justify Ross's paradox, i.e. to show it to be non-paradoxical. In my opinion this problem is situated on a wholly different level. For the following reason this deduction procedure is paradoxical:

If a command "You shall p" is valid (or has been stipulated as an Ought in a normative system), and if according to the rules of deontic logic "You shall $(p \vee q)$" is valid as a derived norm, then the paradox arises from the circumstance that by the premise "You shall p" it has by no means been ensured that p (or that the norm "You shall p") will be satisfied; and if p is not satisfied, a norm will have been derived which can be satisfied only through realization of q.

The difference in comparison with the deduction according to descriptive logic is clear. In the latter, the premise will be true (satisfied) if and only if p is a fact; the premise '$O(p)$' of the normative conclusion can be valid, however, even if p is not a fact. The normative conclusion '$O(p \vee q)$' will then only be satisfiable through realization of q. Hence the paradoxical lies in the fact that through factual circumstances (not excluded by the premise) an Ought can come into existence that is not justified by the established norm.

Alf Ross's amusing example merely obscures the actual reason why this deductive procedure is inadmissible. It is invalid for the simple reason that here, in contrast to the conclusion according to descriptive logic, the stipulation of the premise 'Op' does not ensure the satisfaction of $(p \vee q)$. If one then regards '$O(p \vee q)$' as a norm of the system, with p not being in fact the case, then one can fulfill one's duty only by doing something not prescribed at all by the norm-giver.

The objections to the other controversial deductive procedure of deontic logic (a procedure not illustrated by similarly impressive examples as Ross's paradox) likewise result from the possibility that the Ought will not be satisfied. "From '$O(p \wedge q)$' there follows according to the rules of deontic logic 'Op' and 'Oq'." Is the possibility of splitting up the Ought content a valid rule? A conjunctive Ought content does not justify the Ought attributed to a part of the conjunction. Undoubtedly every deontically perfect world will contain, under the condition that '$O(p \wedge q)$' is valid, both p and q. Hence if 'Op' or 'Oq' is not satisfied, the premise will not have been satisfied. This, however, does not suffice for justifying the disputed conclusion. The stipulation of the premise '$O(p \wedge q)$' does not ensure the satisfaction of the parts of the Ought content. If, however, e.g. p is not satisfied, then there is no reason for regarding the satisfaction of 'Oq' as a duty. Under this condition it may even be forbidden to realize q. [E.g. "You shall fill the steam-boiler with water (p) and heat the boiler from below (q)"; to deduce therefrom "You shall heat under the boiler (regardless of whether or not it has been filled with water)" is obviously wrong, for in this case q is even forbidden.]

In the case of Ought premises the possibility of non-satisfaction must always be taken into account. Inferences of the type as cited are therefore invalid. Not everything which is a necessary condition for the satisfaction of the norm will be a normative consequence of the Ought premise.[10]

7.5. The deontic operators and the problem of their mutual definability

The deontic logics have been erected on the principle that the elementary deontic sentences consist of a one-place operator and a description of a state of affairs. This appears generally acceptable inasmuch as the character of the sentence is represented through the deontic operator, while the content of the Ought or May finds expression through the description of the state of affairs. The formulation of the contents of the deontic sentence (or of the norm-sentence) may be differently structured, but just what is prescribed or permitted must always be indicated. As mentioned already before, the only problem here is whether in the case of complex contents tautological or contradictory contents should also be permitted. (In my opinion this problem is

[10] O. Weinberger, The Concept of Non-Satisfaction and the Logic of Norms, in: *Ratio* 14/1972, p.16–35.

more of a philosophical one.) The stipulations that refer to the deontic operators are disputed, however, and these doubts are of essential importance for the assessment of deontic logic.

What we are concerned with here are the Ought, Forbidding and Permitting operators (O, F and P). In addition there is an Indifference operator, defined as conjunction of Pp and $P\neg p$. For the time being it can be left out of consideration.

The deontic operators are regarded as mutually definable, which appears prima-facie (judging merely by linguistic feeling) as plausible. The interdefinability of the three operators 'O','F' and 'P' implies that one may at one's discretion regard one of them as primitive term and the other ones as derived ones.

The mutual definability of command and prohibition presupposes the possibility of the negation of the content, while the interdefinition of command (or prohibition) and permission also presupposes the negation of the deontic operator. Since the negation of the operator is defined by the truth-functional negation of the deontic sentence, deontic sentences are assumed here to be a kind of descriptive sentences. In his essay "Gibt es eine Logik der Normen?" (Is There a Logic of Norms?) von Wright too called the equivalence '$Pp \equiv \neg O \neg p$' into question. "The relationship between permission and absence of a prohibition is not a *conceptual* relationship but a *normative* one. Now there may be good reasons for making a normative codex (a normative order) a closed one by stipulating that anything not forbidden by the norms of the codex will *ipso facto* be permitted. But to declare permitted what is not forbidden is a normative act."[11] This equivalence is, in any event, valid only in a closed normative system.

If one proceeds from an action- and institution-theoretical conception, a normative system will appear as a behavior-regulating system, as a system of thought destined to regulate the behavior and action of people. Only Ought sentences, i.e. sentences expressing commands or prohibitions, can achieve this.

[11] G. H. von Wright, *Normen, Werte und Handlungen* (Norms, Values and Acts), Suhrkamp, Frankfurt a.M. 1994, p.75.

Since permissions cannot be violated, a permission does not exclude any manner of behavior. And since regulation always means the exclusion of possible behavior, a purely permissive system would not be a normative system in the role of a regulative instrument. Taking permission as a primitive concept of the normative field is therefore problematical.

Deontic sentences as descriptive sentences do not themselves determine actions, they do not (at least not directly) offer selection criteria for action.[12] Coordination of the contents of descriptive sentences and deontic sentences (or of norm-sentences) is important, because it forms the basis of the determination of what is to be done or not to be done, as well as of the determination of permitted behavior. The coordination of Ought contents and descriptive contents is realized by satisfaction functions: 'Op' is satisfied if and only if p is a fact. The contents of permissions cannot be realized by an analogous stipulation for 'Pp'.

Furthermore there are many reasons which will be discussed in the next section, why the concept of permission is not unambiguous, which disqualifies it as a primitive concept of the logic of norms.

The mutual definability runs into difficulties if a normative system is inconsistent or open.

If in the system both the command p and the command $\neg p$ are valid, then the permission of p cannot be defined as $\neg O \neg p$, since in the system $O \neg P$ is valid, whereas the condition of Pp is $\neg O \neg p$.

If the system is inconsistent, because it contains both Op and $P \neg p$, then the permission of p cannot be defined by $\neg Op$, since the system contains Op.

If the system is open, i.e. if it is not decided in it whether a certain state of affairs p is obligatory, prohibited or permitted, then one cannot infer from the not-being of p that $\neg p$ is permitted. If the system is closed (i.e. if the normative status of every state of affairs p

[12]This would require a transformation into a prescription, which might read approximately: "If a deontic sentence stipulates that p shall be, then p shall be."

is determined), then, conversely, one can also infer from the fact that p is obligatory that $\neg p$ is not permitted.[13]

Deontic logic thus presupposes that normative systems are consistent and closed. This is an important limitation, for most normative systems are open. And it is also desirable that the concepts 'command', 'prohibition', and 'permission' should be so defined that they can also be applied in open or inconsistent systems.

7.6. Note on the iteration of deontic operators

It is only in passing that one sometimes speaks of the possibility of iteration of deontic operators (which would give rise to sentences of the form 'OOp', 'POp', etc.). For one thing, interesting interpretations of these sentence forms hardly suggest themselves (despite earlier assumptions to the contrary, they have been found unsuitable for the representation of empowering norms), and, for another thing, this iteration is conceptually a problematical matter. The formation of the deontic sentences would have had to be defined as an operation with descriptive sentences (inclusing deontic ones) if an iteration were to be meaningful. However, it will be preferable to regard the structure of the deontic sentence as a determination of contents by a state of affairs, in which connection 'Op', 'Pp', ... are not to be regarded as instances of such states of affairs.

In deontic logic, therefore, the iteration of deontic operators can be excluded.[14]

[13] O. Weinberger, *Rechtslogik* (Logic of Law), 2nd ed., Duncker & Humblot, Berlin 1989, p.233.

[14] It is even more evident that in a genuine logic of norms the iteration of normative operators is out of the question, since in that case "p ought to be (may be)" belongs to another semantic category than p.

7.7. The problem of permission. Nature and function of permissive norms

Apart from the fundamental objection that the deontic logics, although aspiring to represent a logic of the normative field, treat deontic sentences as descriptive ones, there are in particular two problem fields, discussed within the framework of these logics, which have caused grave doubts as to the adequacy of these systems: (I) the permission problem, and (II) the representation of the conditional norm-sentences. The former problem I will characterize in the present section, while the hypothetical norms will be discussed in the next one.

I cannot help feeling that with respect to the concept of permission our logical intuition is far less clear than in the analysis of Ought, possibly also for the reason that in the whole context of action the function of May is not as readily understandable as the role of Ought, which evidently is entitled to a regulating function (and secondarily to the role of a yardstick for valuation).

Is permission only a consequence of the non-existence of a prohibition, or is there also such a thing as permission as content of norm-setting acts? And if one answers this latter question with Yes, one will then face the question of what function such acts have. And if one doubts the definition '$Pp = df \neg O \neg p$' (or '$Pp = \neg Fp$'), the definition of the contents of the permission will likewise be rendered problematical, since a direct recourse to satisfaction functions is not possible here. Because of various circumstances one is faced with the problem of whether there exists a uniform permission concept, or whether differentiations appear to be justified.

A few things appear to be intuitively clear:

1. From the command p it follows that p is also permitted. (From the prohibition p it follows that $\neg p$ is permitted.)

2. If a normative system were to contain the command p and simultaneously would permit non-p it would be inconsistent, and correspondingly the prohibition of p excludes the permission of p

(prohibition of p and permission of p means an inconsistency of the normative system).

3. The permission p is compatible with the permission $\neg p$. There are no logical contradictions between permissive sentences.

A permission p is not always justified by the non-existence of the prohibition p. It is inadequate to conceive of a permission only as a consequence of the non-existence of a corrresponding prohibition. There is also such a thing as permission on the basis of volitional acts: either because an express permission was given, or because from a command there follows the corresponding permission.

Sometimes one speaks of bilateral permission, namely when both p and $\neg p$ are permitted.[15] Bilateral permission means the same thing as indifference ('I') in deontic logic. It is inexpedient to work with the bilateral permission concept instead of with the normal (unilateral) one as fundamental permission concept, for through 'P' it is possible to define'I', but not the other way around.

Von Wright differentiates between strong and weak permission:[16] p is permitted in the weak sense if it is not forbidden, p is permitted in the strong sense if p is not forbidden,[17] but nevertheless is normatively determined, i.e. the norm-giver has decided on the normative status of p by permitting it. This can evidently occur in a twofold way: by a permissive norm p or by a command p (from which the permission of p follows logically).

In his book "*An Essay in Deontic Logic and the General Theory of Action*" (Acta Philosophica Fennica XXI, Amsterdam 1968) the same author speaks in a wholly different sense of weak and strong permission. For the weak permission '$P(p \vee q) \equiv (Pp \vee Pq)$' is valid, while for the strong (or free-choice) permission '$P(p \vee q) \equiv (Pp \wedge Pq)$'

[15]Kelsen e.g. in his later period views negative permission as bilateral permission.

[16]G. H. von Wright, *Norm and Action*, Routedge & Kegan Paul, London 1963, p.85 et seq.

[17]This condition appears superfluous: it merely excludes – unnecessarily so here – that the normative system will become inconsistent through the stipulation of the permissive norm.

is valid. Here the indecisiveness of logical intuition with respect to the permission concept becomes evident.

The sentence "What is not forbidden is permitted" must be judged differently, depending on whether it refers to an open or a closed normative system. The system is closed if with respect to every state of affairs of the volitional field of the normative system there is a decision as whether it is forbidden or permitted. Otherwise the system is open (which is the normal case). In a closed system one can infer from the not-being-forbidden of p that p is permitted. [Then it will conversely also be valid that we can infer from the permission of p the non-existence of a corresponding prohibition.] If, however, one speaks of permission in the open system on the grounds that in the system there exists no prohibition p, then this is a wholly different permission, one that for the time being can only be assumed, since because of the openness of the system it has not been decided whether p is not forbidden after all.

Proceeding from the contrasting of "norms" and "norm-propositions" (conforming in my terminology to "norm-sentence" and "descriptive sentence about the norm" respectively), Alchourrón and Bulygin have distinguished between prescriptive and descriptive deontic operators.[18]

In the field of the prescriptive concepts they abide by the interdefinability of the deontic operators, whereas for the descriptive permission they introduce two different concepts: strong permission of p [$\mathbf{P}s\alpha p$], which exists if it follows from the normative system that p is permitted, and weak permission [$\mathbf{P}w\alpha p$] if no prohibition of p is valid in the normative system.[19]

It is correct to represent the norm-sentence and the descriptive sentence about norms through different linguistic means and not to

---

[18]C. Alchourrón, E. Bulygin, Permission and Permissive Norms, in: W. Krawietz et al. (eds.), *Theorie der Normen* (Theory of Norms), op.cit., p.349–371.

[19]The definitions read ('α' designates the normative system):

$\mathbf{P}s\alpha p = df\,\text{“}Pp\text{”} \in Cn(\alpha)$

$\mathbf{P}w\alpha p = df\,\text{“}Fp\text{”} \notin Cn(\alpha)$

present them merely as different interpretations of one and the same sentence. Nevertheless, the problems of the logic of norm-sentences are not yet solved here. Here the authors remain at the interdefinability of the deontic operators, although in the open or inconsistent system the interdefinition cannot be carried out ('$\neg O \neg p$' is e.g. not equivalent with 'Pp'). From a genuine logic of norms such a system also differs in that the negation of the operator is defined as a negation of propositional logic, so that the sentences can be understood as deontic ones rather than as genuine norm-sentences.

Since the strong and the weak permission are consequence-logically defined and the normative system is only globally designated with 'α', this distinction of two types of permission-denoting sentences about a normative system would even then remain valid if the normative system were to consist of norm-sentences.

However, there is the following problem: The descriptively interpreted deontic sentences will be true if and only if the prescriptive system contains the norm which the descriptive sentence quotes. Hence if the two descriptive permission sentences are introduced there must exist, in the prescriptive system, a normative situation which conforms also to the weak permission. While the weak permission as a consequence of the not-being-forbidden is not justified by norm stipulation, it constitutes nevertheless a normative situation of the normative system concerned. Hence one can also speak of weak permission of p in the normative system itself, a permission in the open normative system, a "permission until further notice", as it were, which will be revoked when a prohibition p, not stipulated so far, joins the system.

True, the authors endeavor to create two systems, a genuine logic of norms and a logic of statements about norms, but they cannot succeed in this, since they have failed to recognize that the principles of deontic logic are unsuited for a logic of norm-sentences. In particular the treatment of deontic sentences as descriptive ones and the assumption of the mutual definability of the operators render this impossible.

Once having noted that permissive sentences have no regulative function we will then be confronted with the question what part they play instead. Through permissive sentences an Ought can be limited or cancelled. E.g. "Abortion is forbidden, but in the first three months of pregnancy it is permitted" limits the prohibition. In a dynamic perspective, what was so far forbidden may in future be permitted.

It makes sense to stipulate the permission of p, even if this does not regulate the behavior of the duty-bound subjects. The duty-bound subject enquires after the May so as to obtain a framework for his decision of how to act. In open systems the May is not unambiguously determined, since something not explicitly forbidden need not, for that reason, necessarily be permitted. Explicit permission is therefore meaningful. In hierarchical norms systems, permissive sentences may serve for the establishment of freedom rights.

While permissive sentences, as genuine norm-sentences, have the functions mentioned, this is not true of the deontic sentences of the form 'Pp', which must be interpreted as descriptive sentences about norms. The function of the permissive norm-sentences constitutes the justification for the fact that permissive operators, in addition to Ought operators of the commanding or prohibitive type, also have their place in the logic of norms.

7.8. The conditional norm-sentence in deontic logic

In classical deontic logic, two forms have been proposed as expressions of the conditional norm-sentence:

'$O(p \rightarrow q)$' and '$p \rightarrow Oq$'

Both forms are unsuitable.

'$O(p \rightarrow q)$' does not permit a rule according to which the satisfied condition might be detached and the unconditional Ought sentence be won. Equivalent transformations of the content show the sentence to be only seemingly a conditional one. Who would understand '$O(\neg p \vee q)$' as a conditional sentence? If '$O(p \rightarrow q)$' were to represent the hypothetical norm-sentence "If p, then q ought to be", then

'$O(\neg q \rightarrow \neg p)$' "If $\neg q$, then $\neg p$ ought to be" should mean the same thing as the original hypothetical norm-sentence. But this evidently is not the case.

From the formula '$p \rightarrow Oq$' it cannot be seen that the sentence as a whole is a norm-sentence. It is likewise questionable whether the transposition of the sentence, namely '$\neg Oq \rightarrow \neg p$', can be regarded as a hypothetical norm-sentence. The *modus-tollens* inference

$$\begin{array}{l} p \rightarrow Oq \\ \underline{\neg Oq} \\ \neg p \end{array}$$

is suspect if the first premise were really understood as a norm-sentence (which, however, is at variance with the structure of the sentence), for in that case a descriptive sentence would be derived from two normative premises, which would contradict the underivability principle.

For solving the problem of the conditional sentence in the framework of deontic logic, the dyadic systems have been proposed. Fundamental here is a two-places deontic functor, with one argument having reference to the prescribed (or permitted) content, while the other one expresses the condition. To the unconditional deontic sentence, the deontic sentence of the system is assigned whose condition is tautological. Thus to every categorical deontic sentence an infinite class of sentences is assigned, all of which stipulate the same contents as prescribed (or permitted) and impose a condition that is tautological. Logically equivalent to such a sentence is also every sentence with this same consequence and an analytically or factually true condition. The proof of the validity of the unconditional Ought (or May) is different, however, depending on how the true condition is expressed. Thus it may consist in proof that the condition is a logical law, in proof of the condition by drawing upon definitions, or in proof on the basis of facts.

In principle a rule functionally analogous to the detachment rule can be formulated: The proof of the truth of the condition can serve as proof of the unconditional validity of the matter conditioned.

The sentences of the dyadic deontic logic are likewise statements about norms, for they are used as arguments of extensional functors.

The solution of the problem of the conditional deontic sentences is purchased in the dyadic system at the price of a complicated representation of the categorical sentences; otherwise the problems of the deontic logics will remain the same as in the monadic systems.

A certain lack of "elegance" of the dyadic systems entails the fact that an internally complex basic concept is used which should be analyzed itself, and the otherwise simple categorical sentence becomes complicated: it is recognized as such through examination of the tautological structure of the antecedent.

7.9. The interpretation of the deontic logics and the possibilities of their application in the normative disciplines

The fact that the deontic sentences occur as arguments of truth-functional functors forces us to regard them, not as norm-sentences, but as propositions about norms. Deontic logic thus is not a genuine logic of norms.

The stipulation of the mutual definability of the deontic operators entails a limitation of the interpretation (and applicability) of these systems: deontic logic pertains only to consistent and closed normative systems. And finally it is assumed that what is prescribed will be satisfied, since otherwise the conclusions "From 'Op' there follows '$O(p \vee q)$'" and "From '$O(p \wedge q)$' there follows 'Op' and 'Oq'" valid in the system cannot be accepted.

Thus there results a highly limited field of application of these systems in the normative disciplines.

The normative systems are as a rule open systems, only a few are closed by normative stipulation, such as e.g. material penal law.

The classical deontic logic has no adequate form for the representation of conditional norm-sentences. True, the dyadic deontic logic solves these problems in a certain way by introducing a conditional norm-sentence as a primitive term. An ingenious trick, which, however, hardly throws light on the nature of the conditional norm sentence, while the categorical norm-sentence becomes complicated.[20]

If deontic logic is to be interpreted as theory of the sentences about norms, then it appears only natural to first of all ask the question what a genuine logic of norms looks like. The structure of the logic of norms would then be the justification of the relationships in deontic logic as the logic of the descriptive sentences about norms. Would such a theory then still be necessary or useful in any way?

7.10. The path toward a genuine logic of norms

The development of the logic of norms was dominated by two trends: On the one hand there was the trend to emphasize the semantic peculiarity of the Ought sentences as contrasted to descriptive sentences, while on the other hand there was an interest in analyzing the logical relationships between certain linguistic operators of the normative field.

The trend aiming at a study of Ought revealed the necessity to develop a logic of Ought (or of the imperative[21]) which was to do justice to the semantic peculiarity of Ought.

[20]The interpretation of the categorical norm-sentence as a conditional norm-sentence with tautological condition is probably motivated by the idea that such a condition could be detached as being always true, i.e. that according to a *modus-ponens* rule a categorical norm-sentence could be obtained. Such a rule is not a component of the dyadic system, however.

[21]In these reflections the concept of the imperative is not understood as a relation between those commanding and those subjected to commands, but first and foremost as expression of an Ought. When Kant speaks of the categorical imperative he is not concerned with the relationship between one commanding and one obeying, but with the category of Ought.

Hume points out, in a much-cited passage, that in argumentations designed to justify morality there is an erroneous transition from facts of Is to conclusions of Ought. Here a different way of justifying an Ought is demanded, namely in argumentations which lawyers would call justifications *de lege ferenda*.[22]

Kant and the philosophy taking its cue from him have made us fully aware of the semantic-logical peculiarity of the Ought sentences. The contrasting of Is and Ought became the point of departure for the normativistic philosophy of law and analytical ethics. Ought-sentences (or norm-sentences) became a semantic category; Ought-sentences (or imperatives) cannot meaningfully be characterized as true or false, no more than prime numbers could meaningfully be characterized healthy or sick (*W. Dubislav*).

The mainstream of logical research was interested in the logical relations between the relevant sentence-forming operators of the normative sphere which express command, prohibition or permission. The elementary sentences of this type consist of a deontic operator and a state-of-affairs argument. They permit of two types of negations: an operator negation and a state-of-affairs negation, and these negations

[22]The passage reads: "I cannot forbear adding to these reasonings an observation, which may, perhaps, be found of some importance. In every system of morality, which I have hitherto met with, I have always remark'd, that the author proceeds for some time in the ordinary way of reasoning and establishes the being of a God, or makes observations concerning human affairs; when of a sudden I am surpriz'd to find, that instead of the usual copulations of propositions '*is*' or '*is not*', I meet with no proposition that is not connected with an '*ought*' or an '*ought not*'. This change is perceptible; but is, however, of the last consequence. For as this *ought*, or *ought not* expresses some new relation or affirmation, 'tis necessary that is shou'd be observ'd and explain'd; and at the same time that a reason should be given, for what seems altogether inconceivable, how this new relation can be a deduction from others, which are entirely different from it. But as authors do not commonly use this precaution, I shall presume to recommend it to the readers; and I am persuaded that this small attention wou'd subvert all the vulgar systems of morality, and let us see, that the distinction of vice and virtue is not founded merely on the relations of objects, nor is perceived by reason." (D. Hume, *A Treatise of Human Conduct*, Harmondsworth, Middlesex, England: Penguin Books Ltd. 1985, p.52)

are understood truth-functionally. It was in this way that the branch of norm-logical research came into being that is usually designated as deontic logics and that regards the deontic sentences as being capable of being either true or false, i.e. as a kind of descriptive sentences. This outlook leads to the modal-logical approach to the problems of the logic of norms. The modal-logical view was emphasized by the express contrasting of various modal-logical systems to one another (*Höfler*, *von Wright*, *Gardies*[23]).

A genuine logic of norms must take its cue from the tradition of the demand for a logic of Ought-sentences which regards norm-sentences as a semantic category categorially different from descriptive sentences.

This means three things:

1. In conformity with von Wright I reject the view that there can be no logic of norms because the traditional concepts of consistency, contradiction and inference are believed to be inapplicable to norms.

2. With von Wright I reject the introduction of sentences expressing norms as arguments of truth-functional functors.[24]

3. I regard the Ought-sentence as a fundamental concept of the (genuine) logic of norms, and I introduce permissive norms only secondarily.

In the following sections I will discuss a few principles for the construction of a genuine logic of norms and call attention to a few peculiarities of this logic in comparison with logic systems of the

[23] A. Höfler, Abhängigkeitsbeziehungen zwischen Abhängigkeitsbeziehungen (Dependency Relations Between Dependency Relations) *Sitzungsberichte der kaiserlichen Akademie der Wissenschaften in Wien* (Proceedings of the Imperial Academy of Sciences in Vienna), Vienna 1917, vol.181, no.4, p.41; G. H. von Wright, *An Essay in Modal Logic*, North-Holland Publishing Co., Amsterdam 1951; J. L. Gardies, *Essai sur la logique des modalités* (Essay on the logic of the modalities), Presses Universitaires de France, Paris 1979.

[24] G. H. von Wright, Gibt es eine Logik der Normen? (Is there a logic of norms?) (1993), in: *id., Normen, Werte und Handlungen* (Norms, Values and Actions), Suhrkamp, Frankfurt a.M. 1994, p.65.

descriptive language, but I shall not try to present a technically fully worked-out system of the logic of norms.

7.11. Ought and May. Negation in the genuine logic of norms

The genuine logic of norms proceeds from the conviction that the regulation of behavior is the basic function of norms and normative systems. Ought-sentences expressing commands or prohibitions are therefore regarded as the fundamental type of norm-sentences. Only Ought-sentences – but not permissive sentences – can be satisfied or violated.

One can work with one single Ought operator (e.g. in the form of an exclamation mark '!') or with two Ought operators, namely the command and the prohibition operator. Between these two operators the following definitory relation obtains:

$$Op = df F\neg p, \text{ or } Fp = df O\neg p$$

The content (the argument of the Ought operator) is a state of affairs. The content indicates what ought to be or not to be (is commanded or forbidden).

There must be a coordination of contents between Ought sentences and descriptive ones. The Ought sentence 'Op' will be satisfied if and only if p is a fact, i.e. if the descriptive sentence 'p' is true.

The content of the Ought sentence can be defined as a satisfaction function correponding to the content of descriptive sentences. But not every content of descriptive sentences need be admitted as Ought sentence content.

The relation between descriptive sentence and norm-sentences can also be described by proceeding from a neutral state-of-affairs description (with *Hare*: "phrastic") which can be made the content of a descriptive or norm-sentence through a corresponding operator (with *Hare*: "neustic").

Using the negation of the norm-sentence content is unproblematical, as is the use of the truth-functional connectors in the content of norm-sentences.

A certain problem is formed by the tautologies and contradictions as Ought contents. A tautological command, e.g. '$O(p \vee \neg p)$', has no regulating function, since it does not exclude any state of affairs. Such a command is pointless, but does not do any harm either. A contradiction, i.e. the prescription of something logically impossible, obviously makes no sense, for such a norm cannot be satisfied.

Since the content of Ought sentences is defined as a satisfaction function, logically equivalent transformations in the contents are permissible, for they do not change the satisfaction conditions.[25]

'Op' and '$O\neg p$' are termed *complementary Ought sentences (commands).* In contrast to the two-valued propositional logic, where always one of the two propositions 'p' and '$\neg p$' is true, one of two complementary Ought sentences will not always be valid. If in a given normative system both are valid, the system is inconsistent.

It is worth noting that complementary permissive sentences 'Pp' and '$P\neg p$' are compatible. Hence the logical incompatibility of complementary norm-sentences depends on the operator and not only on the relations between the contents of the norm-sentences.

Although it is evident that permissive sentences have no directly regulating functions, it is not only a fact that permissive sentences are created by normative acts, they also have important functions.

Permission is the negation of Ought. When a permission p is given it is excluded that non-p is commanded (or – which means the same thing – that p is forbidden).

The relation between 'Pp' and '$O\neg p$' ('Fp') is that of a negation norm. If a normative system contains at the same time 'Op' ('$F\neg P$') and '$P\neg p$', it is inconsistent.

---

[25]It is not a valid inference, however, that if 'q' follows from 'p', then 'Oq' will follow from 'Op'.

Permissive sentences are norm-sentences that (just as Ought-sentences) are stipulated by norm-generating acts,[26] although they have no direct guiding function. The normative stipulation of 'Pp' can also occur through stipulation of the Ought norm 'Op', since 'Pp' is valid as a logical consequence of 'Op'.

The content of the permissive norm is defined by stipulating 'Pp' as the negation norm of 'Fp' ('$O\neg p$'). ['Pp' may also be said to be the permissive sentence that can cancel '$O\neg p$' ('Fp') according to the *lex posterior* principle.]

The stipulation of permissive norms means a limitation of the Ought. If this limitation is stipulated simultaneously with the stipulation of the Ought to be limited, then an exception from or limitation of an Ought rule can be decreed by permitting part of the cases which otherwise would fall under the general rule. If the permission that limits the Ought is not decreed retroactively, but simultaneously with the stipulation of the Ought itself, then it will always be possible to re-formulate the Ought sentence in such a way that the exception is taken into account through suitable subsumption conditions, without the permission concept being resorted to. E.g. "Abortion is forbidden" and "Abortion within the first three months of pregnancy is permitted" produce the Ought sentence "Abortion after the first three months of pregnancy is forbidden".

Normative systems are as a rule open systems. It is not excluded that there also exists a not expressly stipulated Ought. In that case it may, also from a static point of view, be important to declare expressly just what is permitted. By the permission, a prohibition of the matter permitted is excluded (otherwise there would exist a contradiction within the normative system).

It is only natural for a duty-bound subject to ask, when faced with a normative system, what it can do or not do without violating the normative system. If the normative system is a closed one, the answer is: that and only that which is permitted in the system. But if the

[26]This does not apply to the so-called weak permission of p, which is inferred from the absence of an (explicit) prohibition p in the (open) norms system.

system is an open one, the answer will be more complicated: that which can be proven to be permitted in the system (i.e. that which is commanded or expressly permitted) and perhaps also everything which is not (expressly) forbidden. This component of the May will remain uncertain, however: it is not based on a normative decision of the system, but on the will of the duty-bound subject to stake out its scope of action (its May) as broad as possible, hence to regard as permitted (in the weak sense) everything not declared by the system to be forbidden.

Whether a weak permission concept should be introduced into the logic of norms I prefer to leave open.[27] A weak permission cannot be the content of a norm-generating act.

If the function of the permissive sentences (or the relation between Ought and May) is looked at in the course of time, one will be led to a discussion of the derogation problem.

The dynamic view is meaningful for every norms system, not only for the legal system, for which this view is particularly important, however, since the legal system establishes the norms for the origination of new norms and the changing of Ought with time.

Derogation can mean: (a) Cancellation of a norm (deletion of the corresponding norm-sentence), or (b) Cancellation of the norm through the stipulation of another regulation which is in conflict with the existing norm.[28]

The cancellation of a norm through an act of deletion [in the broad sense of the term; as such an act (*contrarius actus*) one may also consider a social process with cancelling effect, not only an explicit act by a volitional subject, cf. the concept of becoming obsolete] has the effect that then the state of affairs concerned will not be governed

[27]Permission in the weak sense – as being "permitted, since not expressly forbidden", – can also be conceived of as a proposition about the normative system examined.

[28]These two cases correspond by and large to the juridical distinction between formal and material derogation.

by any normative regulation; it will neither be commanded, nor be forbidden or permitted.[29]

Derogation through the stipulation of new norms with different contents depends of two questions: (I) of the determination of the norm-logical conflict, for this derogation will occur if and only if – and to the extent that – the new norm is logically incompatible with the norms that existed so far, and (II) of the normative stipulation of a rule of norm dynamics.

The ascertainment of norm-logical incompatibility is based on the contradiction between a prohibition and a permission of the same content (or, in appropriate cases, on norms with logically incompatible contents being prescribed at the same time). The solution of this conflict from the point of view of norm dynamics is not a logical question, but a pragmatic one that is decided normatively. For practical reasons one will as a rule decide in favor of the *lex posterior* principle.

One may also, however, decide on the contrary in favor of the conservative solution: new norms will only then acquire validity if they are compatible with the norms already existing.

In this way one might stipulate inalienable basic rights. In practice a change by dynamic processes is not absolutely excluded. A preference for the existing norms (human rights) is achieved by making the conditions for the changing of constitutional norms more difficult.

In linguistic practice and in deontic logic, negations of the normative (deontic) operators are used. In deontic logic this negation is defined by the negation in the sense of propositional logic. Since in the genuine logic of norms the norm-sentences are not regarded as capable of being either true or false, it needs to be examined just what the negation of the operator – or of the norm-sentence formed with it – means. The matter at issue here cannot be the assertion that the norm-sentence is not a component of the norms system under consid-

[29]The deletion, too, is dependent on a *lex posterior* principle, which permits the changeability of the system by later norm-giving.

eration (this is expressed by the corresponding deontic sentence, which can therefore be negated in the sense of propositional logic), but rather the derogation (deletion) of the norm-sentence. The derogation consists in the cancellation of a norm-sentence through a cancelling act of norm-giving (*contrarius actus*). The result of this kind of derogation is that in the normative system under consideration there will be no norm of this content. Usually, however, the derogation is not carried out as a pure cancellation, but as stipulation of the negation norm: That which was forbidden is now permitted, or that which was permitted is now forbidden.

7.12. The norm-logical consistency postulate

Norm-logical incompatibility (inconsistency, the norm-logical contradiction) must not be interpreted in the sense of propositional logic. One cannot define it as non-satisfiability of the conjunction '$N_1 \wedge N_2$', for this conjunction is not meaningful inasmuch as the norm-sentences N_1, N_2 are not capable of being either true or false.

Norm-logical inconsistency must be defined by a specific definition. Let 'α' and 'β' be contents of Ought-sentences. '$O\alpha$' and '$O\beta$' are incompatible if the conjunction of the Ought contents '$\alpha \wedge \beta$' is non-satisfiable in the sense of propositional logic.

If one takes into account both the Ought operator and the permissive operator, then the norm-logical inconsistency is defined as the co-existence of '$O\alpha$' and '$P\neg\alpha$' (or of '$F\alpha$' and '$P\alpha$'). A normative system is inconsistent if it prohibits and permits the same thing (prescribes something and permits the opposite).

[Since from the command 'Op' there follows 'Pp', it will be sufficient to stipulate a command plus the permission of its opposite as the definition of norm-logical incompatibility. Since it is conceivable that one will take only Ought-sentences into consideration, one should make both stipulations for the concept of norm-logical incompatibility: both the principle that one and the same thing cannot be simultaneously commanded and prohibited, and the principle that one and the same thing cannot be simultaneously prohibited and permitted.]

It is a logical requirement that normative systems should be consistent. However, this norm-logical consistency postulate is not of the same nature as the prohibition of inconsistency in descriptive language. An inconsistent descriptive system has no model; there can be no reality which it describes. But normative systems containing inconsistent norms may very well exist. Norm-logical inconsistency does not exclude the existence of such systems. Inconsistent normative systems are logically deficient, however.

Remark

In the legal order the following problem exists: Decisions may be taken – be it erroneously or for other reasons – which do not conform to the general norm which should find application in them. This has the result that the normative system becomes inconsistent, for that which is valid for the given case by virtue of the decision contradicts that which follows with the conclusion for this case from the general norm. It is therefore expedient to distinguish between the consistency of the rules of law and the consistency of the entire legal order. For this inconsistency produced by decisions at variance with the law, Merkl's "error calculus" seeks to find a practical solution.

7.13. Norm-giving and deduction

Varying with the type of the normative system, the stipulation of the norm will be different. No matter whether the norm is a result of law-generating acts or of certain social processes (as in the case of rules of customary law), or rather of normative stipulations by the autonomous moral subject, the point at issue is always that norms have been laid down as the basis for norm-logical deduction. The variety of origins of norms is not relevant for the logic of norms. Essential, however, are the following two moments: 1. the system-relativity of the norm-logical consideration, and 2. the principle that the stipulation of a norm also gives validity to its norm-logical consequences.

The system-relativity expresses itself above all in the fact that the consistency postulate is valid with respect to *one* single normative system, while different systems may contain mutually incompatible norms.

Norms can also be said to be stipulated by norm-generating acts if the concept of these acts is so broadly conceived of that collective volitional acts and other social processes (e.g. in the origination of customary law or in the genesis of social ethics) likewise qualify as norm-generating acts. It is misplaced, however, to define the norm as the meaning of generating acts and to assume that a norm will only then exist if there is a generating act to this effect – as *Kelsen* does in his later period.[30] For, on the contrary, validity must be ascribed also to the norm-logical consequences of stipulated norms, e.g. to the individual norm as a consequence of a general one.

Ought-sentences that have a contingent content can be satisfied or not satisfied (violated). Their validity is independent of their satisfaction. For the validity of a permission it is irrelevant whether use is made of it.

Through norm-logical inference under the assumption of stipulated norms, logically derived norms are determined. Premises of the norm-logical inference relations are on the one hand norm-sentences, on the other hand descriptive sentences.

For norm-logical inference, the following principles are valid:

1. A normative consequence can only be won from a set of premises which contains at least one norm-sentence.

---

[30]Cf. H. Kelsen, *Allgemeine Theorie der Normen* (A General Theory of Norms), posthumously edited by K. Ringhofer and R. Walter, Manz, Vienna 1979, and O. Weinberger, *Normentheorie als Grundlage der Jurisprudenz und Ethik*. Eine Auseinandersetzung mit Hans Kelsens Theorie der Normen (A Theory of Norms as Foundation of Jurisprudence and Ethics. An analysis of Hans Kelsen's theory of norms), Duncker & Humblot, Berlin 1981.

2. Norm-logical inference is non-creative: no Ought (no duty) can be logically derived which was not at least implicitly contained in the premises.

3. If the set of premises is consistent, then so are the conclusions.

The stipulation of an Ought premise does not guarantee that the prescribed content is a fact. [This in contrast to the inference in propositional logic, where the premise is an argument in proof of something if and only if its content is a fact.] The Ought conclusion will be valid only if the derived Ought is valid also in the case of non-satisfaction of the content of the premise or of a part of this content. Therefore, from 'Op' there will not follow '$O(p \vee q)$', since the conclusion would only be satisfiable through realization of q if the premise 'Op' is not satisfied. '$O(p \wedge q)$' does not justify the conclusion 'Op', since 'q' need not be realized and the partial duty p does not exist if the second part q is not realized.

7.14. The conditional norm-sentence

Anyone familiar with the thinking and argumentation practice in the normative disciplines will agree with von Wright that an adequate theory of the conditional norm can be regarded as a touch stone of a norm-logical system, for a conditional Ought and the operating with conditional norms – to think only of the subsumption conclusion – form the core of juridical thinking.

When does one speak of a conditional sentence? The characteristic nature of such sentences should not be tied to the occurrence of certain connectors such as 'If ..., then ...', but rather define them through those inferences which can be carried out with conditional sentences. Stipulating something as conditional (asserting, prescribing, permitting it, etc.) is to be understood as a stipulation which justifies an unconditional conclusion if the condition is satisfied. It is on these basic thoughts that the definition of the conditional norm-sentence rests. In addition there is the semantic precondition that the logic of norms distinguishes two sentence categories, descriptive sentences and norm-sentences.

The functor of the conditional norm-sentence is defined by the following stipulations:[31]

1. It is a functor for the formation of norm-sentences. The conditional norm-sentence is a norm-sentence which hence has system-relative validity, is generated as a norm-sentence and is not capable of being either true or false.

2. It has two sentence arguments, with one of them expressing the condition and the other one the conditioned. The conditioned has normative meaning. The conditioning sentence part can have descriptive or normative meaning. Usually the conditioning argument is of descriptive nature. (Here we will consider only this case.)

The functor of the conditional norm-sentence I write as '¿'. '$p > Oq$' can be read: 'If p, then q ought to be'. Hypothetical permissive sentences can be formed in analogous fashion.

3. For the (descriptively conditioned) conditional sentence the following two deduction rules are valid:

(1) $p > Oq,\ p \succ Oq$

["From 'If p, then q ought to be' and 'p', there follows 'Oq'"]

(2) $Oq, p \succ p > Oq$

["From 'q ought to be' and 'p', there follows: 'If p, then q ought to be'"]

(1) we can call a norm-logical detachment rule, (2) the conditioning rule.

This manner of introducing the conditional norm sentence is independent of truth functions.

The detachment rule is valid ex definitione. Something analogous to the transposition of the implication '$(p \rightarrow q) \equiv (\neg q \rightarrow \neg p)$' does not exist here.

[31] Cf. O. Weinberger, Teorie důsledkových vztahů a hypotetická normativní věta (A Theory of Deductive Relationships and the Hypothetical Norm-Sentence), in: *Studie k logice normativních vět* (Studies on the Logic of Norm-Sentences), Prague 1960 (in Czech, with a summary in German).

When is there logical inconsistency between hypothetical Ought sentences? The answer: when under identical or equivalent conditions one and the same thing is both commanded and forbidden (or when incompatible states of affairs are prescribed): $p > Oq$ and $p > Or$, with '$q \wedge r$' being logically non-satisfiable; or: $p_1 > Oq$ and $p_2 > Or$, with '$p_1 \equiv p_2$' being valid and simultaneously '$q \wedge r$' being logically non-satisfiable.

Between conditional permission sentences there is no logical contradiction. When a conditional Ought-sentence and a conditional permission sentence coincide, a logical contradiction will arise if under the same conditions a state of affairs is commanded and its negation simultaneously permitted. E.g.: '$p > Oq$' and '$p > P\neg q$' are inconsistent.

In the case of conditional norm-sentences it is necessary to distinguish between potential inconsistency (as long as the condition is not satisfied) and actual inconsistency (after satisfaction of the condition). Logical inconsistency is to be avoided in any event, but potential inconsistency will have no effects in practice. Logical inconsistency may (potentially or actually) exist also between elementary norm-sentences and conditional norm-sentences, e.g.: 'Op' and '$r > O\neg p$'. If 'r' is satsfied there is an actual inconsistency, otherwise a potential one.

The *normative rule* is a generally addressed conditional norm-sentence. It may symbolically be written as '$\bigwedge x(Fx > OGx)$'. The normative rule permits the subsumption inference that comes about through individualization and application of the norm-logical detachment rule. The second premise expresses the ascertainment of a subsumable state of affairs.

The *rule for norm generation* is a hypothetical norm-sentence of a special kind. The antecedent contains, as subsumption condition, a special state of affairs: as condition, a volitional act of a subject authorized to generate norms is stipulated. If we designate as '$A(Op)$' the state of affairs that a volitional act has as its content the norm 'Op', then the rule for norm generation may symbolically be presented as follows:

$\bigwedge A \bigwedge p[A(Op) > Op]$,
or in words: For every act A and every state of affairs p the following holds: If the act A, prescribing that p ought to be, is given, then p ought to be (namely as derived norm of the authorizing normative system).

The special feature of this conditional sentence is the tie between the content of the act in the antecedent and the content of the consequent; this tie does not exist in the normal conditional norm-sentence. Hence the rule of norm-generation does not simply come about through substitution into the formula of the normative rule, but is represented only through the additional tie between the content of the act and the content of the consequence.

7.15. Quantifiers in norm-sentences

In the quantification of norm-sentences, a distinction must be made between internal and external quantification.

If the content of a norm-sentence is quantified, then we are dealing with an internally complex norm-sentence: the internal universal Ought-sentence can be written as '$O \bigwedge x(Fx)$', which (for a finite universe of quantification) means: '$O(Fx_1 \wedge Fx_2 \wedge ... \wedge Fx_n)$', i.e. the state of affairs consisting of '$Fx_1 \wedge Fx_2 \wedge ... \wedge Fx_n$' ought to be.

And analogously for the existential quantifier: '$O \bigvee x(Fx)$' means '$O(Fx_1 \vee Fx_2 \vee ... \vee Fx_n)$', i.e. the state of affairs '$Fx_1 \vee Fx_2 \vee ... \vee Fx_n$' ought to be.

The external universal quantifier corresponds to the juxtaposition of norm-sentences: '$\bigwedge xOFx$' means '$OFx_1, OFx_2, ..., OFx_n$'.

The external universal quantifier justifies the individualization conclusion, but the internal universal quantifier does not. Normative rules are universalized by means of external universal quantifiers.

The external existential quantifier '$\bigvee xOFx$' means that at least one of the norm-sentences 'OFx_1','OFx_2', ... 'OFx_n' is valid.

7.16. Norm-logical inference

After having, in his 1993 essay “Gibt es eine Logik der Normen?” (Is there a Logic of Norms?), taken up the program of creating a genuine logic of norms, von Wright formulated the following rule for proving a norm-logical consequence from a non-contradictory system of norm-sentences:

(i) The concept of the negation norm: The negation norm of a command is the permission with the opposite content, and the negation norm of a permission is the command with the opposite content. Symbolically: ‘$P\neg p$’ is the negation norm of ‘Op’, and ‘$O\neg p$’ is the negation norm of ‘Pp’.

(ii) An O- or P-norm is a logical consequence of a consistent set of norms if the addition of this O-norm (or of this P-norm) renders the originally consistent set inconsistent.[32]

Now we have to examine whether this rule as to how the validity of norm-logical inferences can be proven is adequate.

Von Wright invokes this rule for proving that ‘Op’ follows from ‘$O(p \wedge q)$’, since ‘$P\neg p$’ and ‘$O(p \wedge q)$’ are inconsistent. It is indeed inconsistent to prescribe a conjunction as content, while simultaneously permitting the non-satisfaction of a part of the conjunction. I believe, rather, that it speaks against the proposed rule for justifying inferences that it justifies this deduction. If q is de facto not satisfied – which is possible and is not excluded by the premise ‘$O(p \wedge q)$’ – then the duty p does not exist. In fact, p may, in case q is not satisfied, even be forbidden. ‘$O(p \wedge q)$’ and ‘$\neg q > O\neg p$’ are compatible norm-sentences.[33] Von Wright's rule for justifying a norm-logical inference is, in my opinion, problematical because of the fact that it leaves the possibility of the non-satisfaction of duties out of consideration. And

[32] G. H. von Wright, Gibt es eine Logik der Normen? (Is there a Logic of Norms?), in: id., *Normen, Werte und Handlungen* (Norms, Values and Actions), Suhrkamp, Frankfurt a.M. 1994, p.67 and 70.

[33] I have given the following example of the logically non-conflicting co-existence of such sentences: “Leave the window closed and play the piano”, “If the window is not closed, you may not play the piano.”

in case this occurs, duties are derived which otherwise would not exist. Thus the principle is violated that inference is non-creative. If the lawgiver wishes to stipulate the duty p and the duty q, independently in each case of the satisfaction of the other one, then he must stipulate 'Op' and 'Oq' instead of '$O(p \wedge q)$'.

It disconcerts von Wright that substitution of '$\neg p$' for 'q' renders the deduction of 'Op' from '$O(p \wedge q)$' problematical. This I do not regard as serious from the point of view of his theory, since the definition of the inference was related only to consistent normative systems, whereas the author regards '$O(p \wedge \neg p)$' as an inconsistent norm.

Now on Ross's paradox von Wright says the following: "The sole way in which the addressee can *jointly* satisfy the two commandments 'Send off the letter!' and 'Send off the letter or burn it!' hence consists in sending off the letter and *not* burning it." This is indisputable, but the problem does not consist in how the premise and the conclusion can be jointly satisfied, but in what happens to the conclusion if the premise is not satisfied, i.e. if p is not realized; in that case the conclusion can only be satisfied through realization of q. And that would be a new duty (and one with arbitrary content).

As highly problematical I regard what von Wright terms a "misunderstanding of the inference relation": "That from a norm another one follows means *neither* that if the former is true, then the latter will likewise be true, *nor* that if the former was stipulated (exists, stands), then the latter would likewise – at least implicitly – have been stipulated. That from a command to send off a letter there follows a command to either send it off or burn it means 'only' that the first command is (or would be) incompatible with a permission to leave the letter unsent and do something else". (p.82)

The methodological meaning of inference always consists – both in the cognitive and in the normative field – in uncovering what is stated implicitly in the premises. The point of von Wright's rule, too, is the justification of the conclusion; forming the negation norm and noting that it would render the formerly consistent normative system inconsistent is a method of proving the validity of the conclusion relative to the normative system from which the conclusion follows. The recognition that the negation of the consequence is incompatible with the normative system shows that the consequence is at least implicitly contained in the normative system. Although the normative consequence of stipulated norms may not have been expressly stipulated, it does exist as a logically deduced component of the normative system. A (genuine) logic of norms will be meaningful if and only if one assumes that together with the expressly stipulated norms their logical consequences will be valid as well.

Jean-Louis Gardies believes to have overcome the peculiarity of the norms and of norm-logical inference through a transition from the syntactic point of view to a semantic analysis.

Proceeding from the idea of possible worlds, with Saul Kripke, he introduces the concept of permissible worlds as a normatively determined subset of the possible worlds.

The norm "*p ought to be*" will be defined as true in the actual world if and only if *p* is true in all those worlds from the set of all possible worlds which are declared permissible. (Hence the set of the permissible worlds is an explication of the Ought content.) The Ought-sentence defined in this way is a practical sentence (as I understand this term), for it expresses a selection, or demands it by dividing the possible worlds into permissible and impermissible ones.[34]

Not plausible at all, however, is the explication of the permissive sentence: "It is permitted that *q*" will be true in the actual world if and only if *q* is true in at least one permissible world. If we take only this one permission into consideration, then the set of the permissible worlds will not have been lifted out of the set of all possible worlds, i.e. all possible worlds will be permitted. Also, one wholly fails to see why the permitted should have to be true in at least one permissible world. *q* may be permissible even if it is not realized in any world. To define the meaning of the permission through the truth in a permissible world

[34]Cf. J.-L. Gardies, *L'erreur de Hume* (Hume's Error), Presses Universitaires de France, Paris 1987, p.27 et seq.

presupposes that the permission is made use of at least once. That does not make for a plausible explication of the concept of permission.

The inference theory proceeding from this semantic analysis of the Ought-sentence recognizes as valid all infernces from the content of the Ought-sentence, hence both 'Op' $\succ$ '$O(p \vee q)$' and '$O(p \wedge q)$' $\succ$ 'Op', 'Oq'. Of course, my objections raised in the investigation of deontic logic apply here, too.

The conditional norm-sentence is treated in this semantics as an extensional conditional sentence: permissible are all those worlds which contain $\neg p$, as well as those p-worlds which are also q-worlds. Does this adequately represent the conditional Ought of q? The sentence is satisfiable not only by bringing about q in an actual p-world, but also by preventing p (bringing about non-p). The conditional norm-sentence explicated as a material implication does not satisfy the pragmatic function one expects of the conditional Ought.

Gardies's proposal does not, in my opinion, lead to a logic of the normative field by extensional means.

Normative systems contain, besides categorical norm-sentences, also conditional norm-sentences, in particular normative rules and – where it is a matter of dynamic norms classifications of the legal-system type – rules for norm generation. Therefore, also those conclusions must be taken into consideration whose premises comprise, besides norm-sentences, also ascertainments of facts (hence descriptive sentences). It would be elegant, of course, to formulate a uniform rule that would determine all norm-logical inferences, but the insight we have gained so far is restricted to the indication of a few valid inference rules.

I believe that one can cast light on the problems of norm-logical inference by considerring first the inferences from Ought premises and then those from permissive ones; next, consideration must be given to Ought and permissive premises simultaneously, and finally to inferences in which, besides norm-sentences, fact-ascertaining descriptive premises also occur.

Inferences from Ought-sentences. An Ought-sentence gives expression to the fact that a certain state of affairs or set of states of affairs ought to be. From the Ought-sentences stipulated as premises, those and only those Ought-sentences can be derived as consequences which express a genuine or not genuine subset of the states of affairs stipulated by the premises. Instead of prescribed states of affairs (i.e. falling under the Ought) one might speak of duties and sets of duties. The set of duties occurring in the conclusion must be a subset of the one stipulated in the premises.

The Ought-sentences 'Op_1' and 'Op_2' are normatively equivalent if they stipulate the same set of states of affairs as prescribed (i.e. falling under the Ought). Then 'Op_2' will also be a consequence of 'Op_1', and vice versa.

Inferences from permissive sentences. If 'Pp' is stipulated as a sentence of a normative system, then a set of states of affairs, namely all those states of affairs which correspond to the set of the consequences of '$\neg p$', will be excluded as Ought contents. By the stipulation of 'Pp', all Ought sentences whose contents are in conflict with p are cancelled, or a logical contradiction will arise in the system (if the permissive sentences are valid simultaneously with the Ought sentences).

What permissive sentences can be derived from the premise 'Pp'? Those and only those permissive sentences which exclude a genuine or not genuine subset of the set of the Ought contents excluded by the permissive premise.

If '$C(p)$' is the set of the consequences of 'p', then the permissive sentence 'Pp' excludes the prohibition of any element of $C(p)$. From the permissive sentence 'Pp', any permissive sentence 'Pp_i' in which p_i is an element of $C(p)$ can therefore be derived.

Permissive sentences with logically equivalent contents are semantically equivalent, and therefore mutually derivable.

Inferences from Ought-sentences and permissive sentences. If Ought and permissive sentences are considered simultaneously it is expedient to remember that the stipulation of the Ought is the primary intention of the norm-giving. Attention is to be paid furthermore to the three different functions of the permission: limitation of the Ought, cancellation of the Ought in a dynamic process, and permission for the exclusions of an opposite Ought by hierarchically higher permissive norms.[35]

Norm-logical consequences and facts. Norm-logical consequences are often dependent on facts. From universal normative sentences there follows an individualization for elements of the quantification universe, since these universal quantifiers are understood as internal quantifiers. Since the normative system contains conditional norm-sentences (normative rules and rules for norm-generation), many norm-logical conclusions are also based on descriptive premises.

The following types of norm-logical inference rules can be listed:

(a) Inferences on the basis of the relations between normative operators:

$Op \succ Pp$

["From 'p ought to be', there follows 'p is permitted'"]

$Fp \succ P\neg p$

["From 'p is forbidden', there follows '$\neg p$ is permitted'"]

$Op \succ F\neg p$

["From 'p ought to be', there follows '$\neg p$ is forbidden'"]

$Fp \succ O\neg p$

["From 'p is forbidden', there follows '$\neg p$ ought to be'"]

(b) Detachment rule:

$p > Oq, p \succ Oq$

[35] A more detailed discussion of norm-logical inference was attempted by me in the 2nd edition of my "*Rechtslogik*" (The Logic of Law), Duncker & Humblot, Berlin 1989.

["From 'If p, then q ought to be' and 'p', there follows 'q ought to be'"]

(c) Individualization rule:

(x_i is an element of the quantification universe)

$\bigwedge x(OFx) \succ Ofx_i$

["From 'For every x, there obtains: x ought to F', there follows 'x_i ought to F']

(d) Subsumption rule:

$\bigwedge x(Fx > Ogx), Fx_i \succ Ogx_i$

["From 'For every x there obtains: if x satisfies F, then x ought to G' and 'x_i satisfies F', there follows 'x_i ought to G'"]

(e) Rule of norm generation:

Inferences from rules of norm generation are similar to subsumptive inferences, from which they differ in that the conclusion is tied to the content of the generating act. '$A(N)$' designates the fact that a norm-generating act of content N has taken place.

$$\bigwedge A \bigwedge N[A(N) > N], A_i(N_j) \succ N_j$$

The content of the act determines the conclusion. The generating rule and the ascertainment of the act justify the norm generation from a dynamic point of view.

Chapter 8

Is Willing Liberum Arbitrium?

8.1. The concept of the freedom of will and the sources of the problems of the liberum arbitrium indifferentiae

What does freedom of will mean? Why is freedom of will a never-ending problem, so to speak, of ethics, of legal philosophy and of theology?

On a first level of consideration the thesis of the freedom of will says that one can do what one wishes to do. Of course not in any sense of omnipotence, but in the wholly modest sense that one can do or leave undone as one has decided to, to the extent that the content of the volitional decision concerned is something that is realizable and does not exceed the abilities of the agent.[1] In principle we have a personally experienced notion and certainty that we are able to act according to our will. This much can be asserted, even though we occasionally also experience modes of action, or the omission of an

[1] The psychological problem of velleity and that of pathological aboulia can be left out of consideration here.

action, which we *ex post facto* deem to have been in conflict with our conscious decisions.

The actual philosophical problem lies on a second level: can one want freely what one wants? Or, more clearly formulated: are the decision-determining moments subject only to the agent's free decision? Are there any moments at all which lie outside our free decision and determine the activity of our will? It can hardly be reasonably claimed that the decision process is totally independent of all determining moments, independent of the (external) situation and independent of the agent's volition (or opinion), independent of his internal constitution, his wishes and preferences. Volition (or decision) cannot – not even by advocates of indeterminism – be depicted as detached from all external and internal circumstances, as a *prima causa*, so to speak. Even the indeterminist does not regard the process of deciding as something independent of the agents's knowledge and practical orientation; rather, he merely believes that despite this framework of external and internal circumstances the agent still has the decisive scope of decision and action to decide freely between alternatives – let us say between p and $\neg p$. In a somewhat simplified formulation: even though the agent's wishes and values and all utility considerations speak for p, he may nevertheless decide in favor of non-p and act in accordance with $\neg p$. Here one is reminded of *Kant's* conception, which is in principle deterministic, but knows, so to speak, of *one* exception, one that finds expression in the famous thesis "Thou canst, because thou ought to".[2] Here, Kant founds his theory of moral freedom – which he also calls "causality through freedom" –

[2]The widespread interpretation of this sentence as a thesis from which it follows that only that can be a content of Ought which is possible, i.e. which the agent can realize, I regard as erroneous.This sentence was not meant, nor did Kant ever intend, to limit the contents of Ought to the possible, but rather to introduce "causality through freedom". The moral law, immanent as it is to our reason, can be obeyed as a special determinant of our action.
A limitation of the Ought to the possible (i.e. the empirically possible, as distinct from the logically possible) I regard as highly problematical. For one thing, it would exclude as norm contents any ideals which can be fulfilled only

on man's ability to obey the moral law: the categorical imperative. As a noumenal being, man is able to follow a moral determination.[3]

The customary argumentation in favor of the indeterministic view is mainly based on two arguments, and it is motivated by the endeavor to furnish a ground for responsibility, since a great many thinkers and the general popular opinion proceed from the view that responsibility cannot be philosophically construed without presupposing freedom of the will.

The two main arguments for indeterminism are:

(a) Our immediate experience tells us that we can decide and act of our own free will (if no external compulsion is present) and that in the past, too, we could have acted differrently if we had decided differently, i.e. had willed differently. Our willing is thus experienced as a free act, not as a function of determining circumstances. The genesis of our motives, and those moments which have shaped our preferences and thus our manner of deciding, do not, as a rule, lie in the realm of consciousness. In other words: intuitively we experience unrestrained arbitrariness, not a network of determinants which would keep this arbitrariness under control.

(b) Those moments which might qualify as such determinants, hence moments of which we know from experience that they can modify the behavior (or the action) of people, are quite different in nature from those moments, in principle observable (if need be with instruments), which usually occur as causes or boundary conditions in causal laws. Every agent experiences what moments determine his action decisions: they are moments in the nature of information, not physico-chemical states such as the conditioning circumstances of the causal laws of science are. While it is true that in our thinking in

approximately, e.g. the general norm "Thou shalt not steal", for, so sociology teaches us, unlimited compliance with this norm is empirically impossible.

[3]Let us leave open here the question whether this cannot also be (and maybe should be) conceived of more generally as a possibility of normative determination, as ability to act according to norms (even if these should not result from the categorical imperative).

connection with our action, as well as in our justification of actions, we work with reasons for our acting, we do not, however, understand them in a sense which would exclude the *liberum arbitrium.*[4]

The essential motive for indeterministic views does not consist in actual considerations about action-theoretical structure, but in the intention to furnish a philosophical basis for moral and/or legal responsibility as well as for the justification of praise and blame, of reward and punishment. For it is implicitly assumed, or certain reasons – problematical ones, in my opinion – are invoked to support the view, that only under the assumption of a *liberum arbitrium* these basic concepts of ethics and law can be meaningfully defined.

I am of the opinion that the problem of the freedom of will should be analyzed totally independently of any consideration for the problem of responsibility and that the responsibility concept should be discussed only in a second step, with this discussion taking place, namely, on the basis of a clarified view of the problem of the freedom of will. If, in contrast, the analysis of the determinism vs. indeterminism dispute is made to fit the intention to provide a preconceived foundation for the responsibility concept, then one does not only spoil the characteristic of the problem of the will, but one also places the conception of responsibility on wrong foundations, namely on ones created to support one's preconceived opinion.

8.2. Freedom of will from the point of view of the information-theoretically founded action theory

The conceptual basis of this action theory – as well as of the conception of the freedom of will – is the introduction of the concept of scope of

[4]The conception that would trace back causal determination to physiological – hence physico-chemical – processes, so that man's behavior, even if it is the result of an action, has no degrees of freedom, is far removed from common sense; rather, it is a construct which atems from wholly different argumentation structures.

action, plus the thesis that the selection of the action to be realized is determined by an information process which at bottom is of final (as opposed to causal) nature. This final character expresses itself in the fact that for determining one's selection it is always necessary to draw upon pieces of practical information or volitional acts (voluntary decisions). This structure of the action comprises within itself the basic element of the freedom of will: the agent, as an entity capable of action, has a behavioral trajectory which is split up into alternatives, each starting at the moment of observation and projecting into the future.

The agent's behavior that is understood as action is faced with alternatives which – if one wishes to use this terminology – can be termed scopes for free action. Here, however, a few problems still need to be clarified:

(a) Can – particularly with respect to the psychophyscical agent – the real existence of a scope for action be proven? Can it be made plausible that beings capable of action have indeed scopes for possible action at their disposal? It is an indisputable fact of experience that people reflect about their acting and that they take their decisions and regulate their actions as a function of their knowledge and wishes. It can also be empirically ascertained that knowledge – factual information about the situation of the agent and his environment, about causal relationships, about action programs (e.g. recipes for food dishes) and know-how – influences the agent's mode of acting. Hence it can be proven that man's manner of behavior comprises at least some, and different, behavior possibilities, i.e. that scopes for action do indeed exist.

(b) Connected with the empirically founded thesis of the existence of scopes for action is the conception that through an information process – a selection process based on information processing – a decision can be made between the alternatives that are available.

The theory of the freedom of will in accordance with the information-theoretically founded action theory is based on the thesis of the existence of scopes for action and on the thesis of the determination of the action through an information process of an intentional nature.[5]

The scope for action is of tree-like structure.[6] Until the point in time in question it is a linear trajectory which then branches out, thus producing the similarity to a tree. In comparison with the structure of a real tree, however, there is a fundamental difference: the branches can come together again, for one and the same result may be reached along different paths.

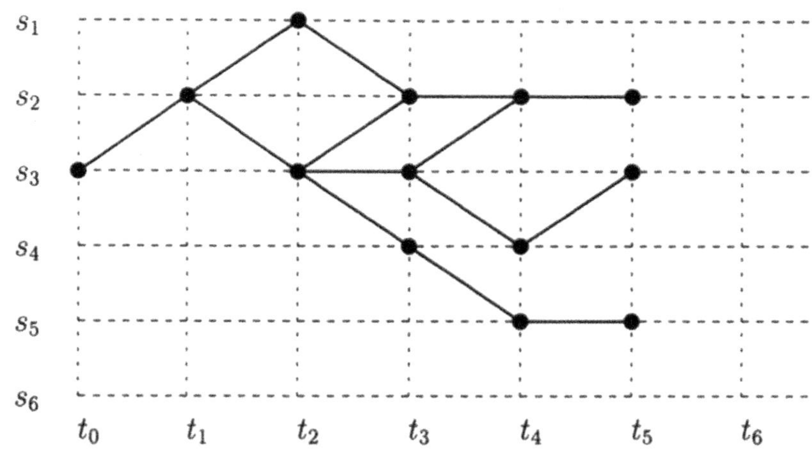

$t_0, t_1, \ldots =$ are points in time
$s_1, s_2, \ldots =$ are states of affairs

[5]The concept of the scope for action plays an essential part in another context of these reflections, namely in the preparation of the action-determining processes. In the argumentation about freedom of will it is only a question of whether a scope for action exists, whereas in the deliberations about action the question at issue is the ascertainment of actual action possibilities as a basis for their relative evaluation and as a preparation for preference-based decisions of choice between the alternative behavior possibilities.

[6]Hence it is related to what *G. H. von Wright* calls the "life-tree". See G. H. von Wright, Handlungslogik. Ein Entwurf (Logic of action. A design), in id., *Handlung, Norm und Institution. Untersuchungen zur deontischen Logik* (Action, Norm and Institution. Investigations into deontic logic), de Greyter, Berlin/New York 1977, p.93 et seq.

Now while we can regard the thesis of the existence of scopes for action as well-founded (both by internal and by external experience), we do not know the tree-like scope itself. For one thing, the agent does not know the future world completely, no more than he knows his own future subjective possibilities [e.g. he does not know what he will learn or unlearn (forget) in the future], and he has no advance knowledge about his future program ideas. The scope for action is not a definitely given reality, but is dependent on the future development – not known in advance in detail – of the subjective knowledge and preference development of the subject of the action.

Nor does the acting subject have complete and unequivocal knowledge of the totality of his preferences. They often reveal themselves only in the selective act.[7]

Now what follows from these considerations for the problems of the freedom of will?

Before I can go into this question I must call attention to a difference to which usually no attention is paid. The claim that the action is determined, that the agent is not, in this sense, a prima causa, that his will and his action are conditioned (although he usually does not perceive these conditioning relationships) is something entirely different from claiming that the conditioning relationships can be recognized and that this recognition will deepen with the progressing development of science, so that, as in other fields of our knowledge, full cognition is possible and to be expected, if not now, then in the future. The question of the recognizability of the action determination is frequently also linked up with the thesis that knowledge about the determination of an action also implies its foreseeability. If I am familiar in detail with the determinants and all circumstances of the action, then, so it is believed, it will also be calculable in advance how the agent will act in concrete situations.

[7]And this not always in an unequivocal way at that. The selective decision in the case of equivalence of the alternatives may be a chance decision, so that the alternative chosen need not have preference (in the sense of strong preference).

As a matter of principle it must be emphasized that the thesis of the determinedness of the action – which is all that determinism claims – is something entirely different from assuming the recognizability of the determination and the foreseeability of how a specific agent will act in a given situation.

The grasping and understanding of what is happening is dominated by the causality principle. Actions are occurrences in the world for which it is to be assumed, according to the causality principle, that we do not grasp them as merely being there, but as having been caused, i.e. as being determined by conditioning (evocative) circumstances. We always meet them with the "Why" question. Hence the question presents itself here of the determinedness of the occurrence we understand as action. Since in general the determination of causality depends on the recognition of laws, this leads to the question whether and in what way laws can be indicated which, together with the ascertainment of relevant circumstances, will permit the causal determination of actions. This, according to the Hempel-Oppenheim conception, i.e. the nomological-deductive explanation scheme, is the indispensable prerequisite for a causal explanation, since the mere regularity of successions of states of affairs does not suffice to justify theses about causal relationships.[8]

Where causal explications on the basis of relevant causal laws are given, the use of these laws will in the following three cases run essentially parallel: as calculation of the future course of behavior trajectories (i.e. as prognoses proceeding from the actual situation),

[8]Cf. C. G. Hempel, P. Oppenheim, Studies in the Logic of Explanation, in: B. A. Brody (ed.), *Readings in the Philosophy of Science*, Prentice Hall 1970, p. 8–27. I disregard here the difficulties that occur if the justifying law is not deterministic, but stochastic. Then, assuming the validity of the law, it is quite possible that the eventual result will not be the most probable, but a less probable one. If one were then to say that this improbable result is justified by this law, this would hardly be acceptable. Strictly speaking, it seems to me to follow from this that stochastic laws actually do not determine the individual case, but only classes of sequences of events of the type concerned.

or in possible cases (even contrafactual analyses are included here[9]), or as retrodictions.

The explanation of the action – even though the action is entirely embedded in the natural occurences in the world, i.e. can be described as a behavioral sequence – cannot be treated along the lines of causal law, i.e. not simply according to the Hempel-Oppenheim explanation scheme. The reason for this is the fact that, wherever actions occur, information plays an essential part in the system that conditions the results of the action.

Pieces of information are not directly observable. The acting of a subject S is determined by an information process. This is the fundamental thesis of the action theory advocated here. The individual, actually action-determining pieces of information which would be the conditions of the application of causal laws are not directly recognizable. The knowledge stored in the memory of the subject S is not known in detail to the outside observer, nor is it present to the subject himself (S does not know, for example, what he has forgotten, and he cannot estimate himself to what extent forgotten things will nevertheless influence his future manner of reacting).[10]

The action-determining information process is – as already shown[11] – always inter alia dependent on position-taking pieces of information. Without them, no selection can be realized. While the agent's practical system can, in rough outlines, be estimated through interpretation, it will never be known in such detail that the action becomes entirely

[9]See N. Rescher, Lawfulness as Mind-dependent, in: id. (ed.), *Essays in Honor of Carl G. Hempel*, D. Reidel, Dordrecht 1969, p.178–197; O. Weinberger, Der nomische Allsatz (The Nomological General Sentence), Grazer Philosophische Studien, vol.4/1977, p.31–41; id., Contrary-to-fact and Fact-Transcendent Conditionals. An attempt to deal with treat the logic of the fact-transcendent and contrary-to-fact conditionals by means of truth-functional logic), in: *Ratio* 16, 1974, p. 15–32.

[10]W. R. Ashby, *An Introduction to Cybernetics*, 8th ed., Methuan, London 1971, p.115, 170 (1st ed. 1956).

[11]Cf. p.87 et seq. of this book.

predictable through calculation – neither to the external observer, nor to the agent himself.

The selection is either determined by a choosing act whose practical constellation the observer can model only by interpretation – which in essence is true also for the agent himself, e.g. when he analytically reflects about his decision *ex post facto* – or it is a result of a teleological-preferential analysis by the agent. Neither the criteria applied in the evaluating assessment, nor their relative weighting are given, but both are required for the justifying determination of the decision.

The pieces of action-determining information are anchored in the subject of the action, but they are not transparent. The action-determining information process can be represented – it can be modeled, so to speak – but the actually effective pieces of information are not given in detail and not ascertainable by observation, so that the prognostic calculation as to how the agent will act cannot be performed.

The essential moment, which, while not disturbing or canceling the causality principle that governs everything happening in the world, brings with it the non-transparency of the action determination and the unpredictability of the contents of the future actions, is the insertion of the information process into the specific happening that is understood as action.

Now it has also become evident how important it is to differentiate between the existence of the determination and its recognizability. The dependence of the action on the information process does not speak against determinism, but is does rule out perfect recognizability of the determination.

Freedom of action in the sense of being in a position to behave according to one's decisions is based on the empirically and introspectively recognized existence of scopes for possible action as well as on the insertion of information processes for the purpose of choosing between action possibilities. The components of this freedom of action are the free activity – a freedom experienced as such – of the recognition of action possibilities and/or action programs, and the information-controlled selection of one alternative from the field of possibilities.

8.3. Excursion on the recognition of causality and on causal explication

Since in the discussion of the philosophical dispute around the freedom of will quite subtle gnoseological problems are relevant, I wish to present here a general reflection about some problems of the recognition of causality, which is also meant to characterize the development of causal thinking.

The primary point of departure for my analysis is the assumption, already mentioned before, of the gnoseological primacy of the practice (see p.82 et seq.). Since action requires not only situational information, but also information about possible effects, i.e. about causal consequences of possible actions, it belongs to the essence of man's cognition of reality that this cognition does not confine itself to ascertaining states of affairs and occurrences, but will also, and at all times, endeavor to investigate factual connections. Our observation of all that happens in the world is dominated by the causality principle in such a way that cause-and-effect relationships and connections in conformity with natural law (i.e. empirically necessary connections) are to be investigated.

This tying of our cognition to the causality principle is connected with the postulated usability of recognized causal relationships for our actions.

In his noteworthy book "Society and Nature. A Sociological Inquiry" (Chicago 1943) *Kelsen* describes the action-related view of all occurrences in the world and their explanation through the animistic (personalistic) approach to the happenings in nature, such as it is found in primitive societies. We need not examine here the sociological and anthropological adequacy of this conception of the mental attitude in primitive cultures, nor is the primary action-relativity, – disregarding here animistic conceptions – essential for the thinking of primitive communities. This relation to possible action also forms the basis of causal thinking in our culture. Presented schematically: The cause of an event is that which we must posit through our actions in order to bring the observed event about. This conception lies at the basis of all causal thinking, even though the causality principle and the gnoseological considerations about the recognition of causality have successively experienced an enormous further development. Connected with the causality principle is the assumption of the regularity of the happenings in nature. In a slogan-like abridgment: identical causes produce identical effects (with differences of time and place not being relevant for assessing this identity). The causal interlinking of phenomena is viewed as constancy of the mode of behavior of systems, which behavior is invariant in the sense that it remains unchanged at every point of the universe and for every time determination.

It is worth noting that this characteristic of cognition is essential also for the applicability of the recognition of causality in action determination. While the experience on which the cognition of the laws of nature bases itself lies always in the past, the applications for action determination lie, in contrast, in the future. Hence the laws of nature are only applicable for action determination as rules that are valid throughout all differences of time. Analogously, with respect to the determinations of space: if nomological knowledge is to be usable for action-determining analyses, it must be valid also for determinations of space that lie outside the space in which the experience was gained.

Causality was understood linearly and, as it were, transitively. If p causes the event q and q the event r, then p was also the cause of r. Cause-and-effect phenomena progress in chain-like fashion. – However, the processes in the world were soon recognized as more complex relationships, namely as the coming into being of effects as a function of other circumstances than the cause alone (as possible action content). An infection as an illness is not only determined by the bacillus with which a body is confronted, but also by a host of circumstances that co-determine the outcome of the disease. In the conditionalistic conception the linear-chainlike causality is transcended – even to the point where the distinction between cause and co-determining circumstances is relativized. There then emerges a picture of causality which is far removed from linear conceptions. One may call it networked causality, or, in line with Russell's concepts, think of it as a rejection of causality plain and simple and as its replacement by mere functional relationships.[12]

I doubt, however, whether this is an adequate way out. In my opinion the relationship between the empirical-nomological recognitions and their usability in action analyses will always continue to exist. And moreover, a merely functionalistic recognition would leave the question of the nomological character of these recognitions and their transfactual applicability unanswered (see below on p.205), where I will have something more to say about the nomological character of the laws of nature as manifesting itself in their particular type of necessity).

In the original, simple – as it were – conception of the causal relationships, the proximity in space and time of cause and effect was, so to speak, an implicit assumption. The Newtonian laws spelled the end of the conception that causes work in their immediate vicinity. The possibility of an *actio in distans* becomes a matter of course for the understanding of causal relationships. It has also become somewhat more difficult to introduce distance in time as a meaningful possibility of causality. I believe that, to put it figuratively, these "dormant causes", too, should be accepted. Engrams, phenomena of memory (not only in a psychological sense), the transformation of structures which will frequently be action-determining only much later, and in a changed way, can be regarded as examples of relatively long past causes with late effects.

[12]B. Russell, On the Notion of Cause, *Proceedings of the Aristotelian Society* XIII, 1912–13.

Entirely new and fundamentally different dimensions of the problem field of determination emerge there where systems are taken into consideration whose behavior is determined (at least) to a great extent by processes of information processing.[13] With repect to agents or subjects of actions the question of determination acquires a wholly different character, and it becomes highly important to differentiate between determining processes on the one hand and the recognizability of the determination through observation on the other hand.

The explanation of actions presupposes that there are subjects of actions who have a peculiar structure that can be schematized in the following way: there is a controlling information system and a controlled system of action (or of the realization of the action) as partial system of the acting subject.

The controlling system – viewed by me here as a system which both determines the decision and guides the realization of the action – can be structurally described by indicating the processing operations it can accomplish. The functioning of the system is dependent on pieces of information supplied as attitudes of the subject (practical information) and as knowledge data.

The volitional decision and the action are evidently determined by two factors: (a) by the structure of the subject, his attitudes, his knowledge and his capabilities, and (b) by external circumstances and influences. On this rough characteristic there will be general agreement. In the course of time, the moments mentioned under (a) are not constant, but are subject to changes brought about by the experiences of life. This view, too, will probably appear generally acceptable, although opinions vary as to whether the decisive basic structure – the character of the subject, as one can put it – remains essentially constant or is molded itself by life, hence is

[13]Problems of ascertainability and predictability occur also in other fields, however, particularly in micro-observation. Such problems, which are connected with Heisenberg's uncertainty principle, need not be discussed here.

subject to profound changes, especially in cases of particularly radical influences.[14]

The controlling system which establishes the will and produces decisions is a system of pieces of information. The latter cannot be directly grasped through observation. They are actually existing facts; they also have material bearers, although this material existence does not constitute the essence of the pieces of information: the material bearers of the information can be replaced through recoding.

Pieces of information often lead a latent existence: they do exist, but will only under certain circumstances produce effects. My familiarity with the English language is knowledge, latent knowledge and potential ability. This ability emerges from its latency when I use the English language as a communication instrument. Just what actual informational contents my knowledge and my linguistic ability have is manifest neither to an external observer, nor to myself.

The action-determining information system is present neither with respect to the knowledge content, nor with respect to the practical

---

[14]The dispute around the immanent constancy of a person's character can be left aside here. It may well be that man's will has, by nature, a specific fundamental attitude and mode of reacting, that his "intelligible character" (as meant by Kant and particularly by Schopenhauer) will prevail in any event, so that his behavioral and volitional mode will remain relatively constant, or that a person's type of character, while not fixed from the very beginning, will become permanently constituted in the first years of his or her life, as probably all psychologists assume today. For our considerations it is decisive that as a rule a certain practical orientation becomes established, but that during its formation in the first years of life, and under suitable circumstances also later, the practical system (the orientation of the will) will be more or less modified by new influences. In any event it is a system which takes in pieces of information and thereby transforms itself.
Analogously, if the subject of the action is not a psychophysical person, but a collective agent or an institution, the following can, *mutatis mutandis*, be said: in such cases, too, a development of the guiding information system in the course of time is to be expected, and even with collectives and institutions there are trends towards a constancy of character (*sit venia verbo*). In the theory of institutions it is emphasized that the guiding ideas in the institutions do have this tendency toward continuance, depite influences motivating to changes.

attitudes (the system of ends, the valuations and preferences, and the effective norms), rather, it is not susceptible to direct grasping through observation. To infer from this that the resulting behavior (my action) has not in any way been caused by anything would be totally unfounded. It is rather a matter here of a determination that for reasons of principle is *non-transparent*; both its origin – often quite remote in time – and the changes brought about by newer inputs and internal transformations (e.g. through forgetting) are non-transparent to the external observer, but equally, in large measure, to the agent himself.

In his action-determining deliberation the agent can become aware of the actual constellation of his practical system, his goals and normative yardsticks, but not always completely so and not always with clear weighting.

The fact of the non-transparancy of the action-determining information systems offers a plausible explanation for the compatibility of the determinedness of the action as a reality of the world with the non-recognizability of the action determination *in concreto* and with the unpredictability of the future actions of individual agents.

The answer to the venerable problem of the freedom of will is expressed in the concept of non-transparent determination.

Causal recognition in the natural sciences is in essence oriented to nomological generality. It is not the mere succession of states of affairs in the individual case that can serve for justifying the causal explanation of this causal course of events; rather this requires the generality of a justifying statement by a law of nature. The attempt to furnish a causal explication of human action is thwarted, among other things, by the unsuccessfulness of all efforts to draw up general causal rules for the process of deciding. For this reason a prognosis of decisions and actions according to causal laws is not realizable.

Even such a simple thing as reproduceability is not assured in the fields of psychology and action determination. Identical input data will encounter, in the case of a repetition, a changed situation of the subject. In the case of recurrence, mental notes may be made, which will not occur e.g. in the case of a one-time exposure to a column of numbers. The system of pieces of practical information, which determines the decision-taking, will already have been changed to some extent when having to decide a second time on the same matter. It has been tried to express this phenomenon by the slogan that man has history, i.e. that, precisely through his experiences, he will forever keep changing. Only a coarse, merely statically founded probability estimate of behavioral processes is possible.

Explanations of action are therefore more appropriately realizable through understanding interpretation than through the customary methods of causal investigation.

8.4. Excursion about the structure of the nomological causal proposition

If one wishes to clearly determine the meaning of the laws of nature – including the purely descriptive laws of society – one must present a structural theory (a logic, as it were) of the nomological causal propositions. This logical-formal question (with methodological implications) can be treated separately from the epistemological question of how one arrives at general causal knowledge and how one justifies causal laws.

Some things are *communis opinio* here, while others are disputed and dependent on the specific conception of the author. My approach, as already mentioned, proceeds from the principle of the primacy of the practice and provides such a structural explication of the nomological causal propositions as appears to me to be required for the use of the knowledge represented by them in the context of the action determination.

It is expedient to the nomological causal propositions the form of general conditional sentences by which a connection between cause (including accompanying circumstances) and effects is expressed. The essential problem of the explication of the nomological sentences is the question whether – or in what respect – the nomological causal proposition differs from a usual general conditional sentence. The particularity of nomological descriptive sentences will have to be sought in the specific type of generality and/or the character of necessity of these sentences.

The logical-structural side of the causal laws finds expression in the question how nomological generality is to be characterized. The purpose of these analyses is to show in what way and why nomological propositions differ from other general conditional propositions.

The answer to this question is primarily being sought by distinguishing between accidental and nomological generality.

If I have exactly three black dogs, then the accidentally general sentence "All my dogs are black" is well-founded. But nothing follows from this about the truth value of this sentence for the case that I am going to buy a fourth dog. The truth of the general sentence "If x is my dog, then x is black" is given only in the situation, "accidentally" given as true, that I possess only black dogs. But it does not express an essential relationship between "being a dog of mine" and "being black".

Now it has been tried to lift the nomological generality out of the merely accidental generality by demanding for it independence of time and space. This explanation of nomological generality I do not regard as sufficient. The expansion of the validity range to all points in time and space does not suffice to define nomological generality, at least not in case we relate the determination of time and place to our empirical basis. The nomological causal proposition expresses an assertion which does not possess validity for the present, the past and the future, nor for all places that satisfy the subsumption conditions, but rather also to possible occurrences and behavioral sequences, as well as to dispositions and contrafactual matters. Only if we stipulate the unlimited validity of the relationship as a characteristic transcending experience will we arrive at the concept of nomological generality. This means, however, that we conceive of this relationship as one of essence, or in other words: stipulate it to be a necessary one.

Thus, the characteristic feature of the nomological general proposition is not an expansion of the observation field of our empirical research, but rather the decision to ascribe to the sentence the character of necessity (or in another terminology: of essence). If we attribute necessity to the sentence, then – because of the recognition of essence – this relationship will be valid for all times and places.

I find it important to point out here that certain epistemological concepts and trains of thought of both everyday and scientific life are closely connected with the problems of nomological generality. Besides depending on the structrual problems of the causal laws, disposition statements and their justification are also dependent on the conception of the nomological universal sentences. Furthermore there are the problems of the contrafactual conditionals, which – as probably has been generally realized by now – are not useless trivialities, but essential elements of analytical thinking. We are dealing here with retrospective reflections in the form of the question "What would have happened if (or if not) ...?". Retrospective reflections not only promote self-criticism, they are also elements of attempts "to learn from history".

Although oriented to the future, action-determining reflections are based on fact-transcending possibility analyses. The action deliberation – and the action programs and action decisions it engenders – lead to the agent's designing, on the basis of nomological sentences, possibilities how he can act. The causal sequences of events are handled as existing possibilities whose truth is independent of whether such a possibility will actually be realized. The deliberation moves within a network of fact-transcending relationships whose justification is supported by recognitions that are fact-transcendent and hence independent of actual realization.

Causal laws are human achievements serving to describe relations of reality and to make them calculable, but these laws are not identical with the real relationships in the world. Cognition may be more or less adequate, and as experience and research progress further it may be defined more exactly and/or be revised. It is in this view that the essential characteristic of cognition lies: it is construction, justified, tried and tested, and not disproved conjecture (assumption), to speak in Popperian terms.

With *N. Rescher* I am of the opinion that lawfulness consists in the attribution of empirical necessity such as we ascribe to a generalization, thus distinguishing it from generalizations of merely accidental nature.[15]

Rescher explicates the nomological generalization in contrasting it to the merely accidental one in the following way: The simple generalization "All X are Y" is interpreted, if understood as a nomological one, as "All X are Y and moreover: if z (not an X) were an X, then z would be a Y". On the basis of this interpretation of nomological generalization Rescher shows that the nomological sentence, unlike the merely accidental one, is not contraposable (op.cit. p.181 et seq.). He states furthermore: (I) "Lawfulness is a matter of imputation (of the imputing of this epistemological property to a generalization)", and (II) "Lawfulness does not lie in the content of the generalization, but in how it will be used",[16] so that from this point of view a specific theory of the nomological generalization is not necessary at all.

By "hypothetical force", in Rescher's terminology, we are to understand that the sentence is valid also for merely assumed cases – including contrafactual ones – or that we are prepared to apply it over and beyond the field of experience and that of the real facts.

I do not consider the choice of the term "hypothetical force" a propitious one. Nevertheless the author's point is clear: nomological generalizations are attributed validity over and beyond the range of

[15] N. Rescher, "Lawfulness as Mind-dependent", in: *Essays in Honor of Carl G. Hempel*, ed. by N. Rescher, D. Reidel, Dordrecht 1969, p.178–197.

[16] "*Lawfulness is a matter of imputation*: when an empirical generalization is designated as a law, this epistemological status is imputed to it." "Lawfulness is not a matter of what the generalization says, but a matter of how it is to be used. By being prepared to put it to certain kinds of uses in modal and hypothetical contexts, it is we the users who accord to a generalization its lawful status, thus endowing it with nomological necessity and hypothetical force." (op.cit. p.185).

the empirical basis on which this recognition is founded. I express this as follows: they have fact-transcendent validity.

The nomological necessity and the hypothetical force (fact-transcendency) extend in essential fashion beyond what can be ascertained through observation and experiment. Laws are, therefore, not logically derivable from their observational basis; they are imputations which must be well-founded, namely through conformity with the facts and coherence of the system with the entire body of knowledge of the given branch of science. The laws (laws of nature) are not discovered, but created. They do not only express regularities, but moreover nomological necessity, and they claim hypothetical force – or, as I would put it, fact-transcendent validity.

From his analyses, Rescher derives two highly important philosophical consequences: (a) The possible does not exist in reality. We might say: it is not a particular mode of being, no ontic status, but a mental creation. (b) From the structure of the nomological recognition as assertions with hypothetical force, Rescher arrives at a stand on *Hume's* and *Kant's* critique of the cognition of laws. One cannot, he says, come to a stop at Hume's recognition that experience itself provides no recognition of the nomological necessity. One had to agree here with Kant to the extent that the nomological element was introduced by the recognizing human being into the assertions of the law. As the source of lawfulness Kant regards the inherent way in which the human mind functions. Lawfulness, however, was not lying in the immutable structure of the recognizing subject, but was a consequence of the application of conceptual schemes employed by us for explanatory purposes, and of transfactual imputation.

With Rescher's epistemological conception I can agree to a great extent, but on the question of modalities I would like to add a few remarks. I cannot agree with his opinion that the nomological element consists only in one's being prepared to apply the generalization – if it is understood nomologically – also fact-transcendingly. Rather, I am convinced that the nomological generalization must be given such a structure as expresses the fact-transcendency and thus justifies this fact-transcending application. The nomological generalization must be given such a structure as expresses its necessity (or its fact-transcendency). Applying the ordinary generalization also fact-transcendingly is not sufficient. The conviction of the language user (researcher, thinker) that this causal relationship is valid with nomological necessity must find expression in the structure of the sentence.

Possibility as a preliminary stage of being, as "semi-being", so to speak, is a reminiscence of an animistic or creationist conception and should be eliminated from modern philosophical thinking. From an empirical point of view it makes no sense to speak of a reduced ontic status in comparison with being. I am of the opinion that modal thinking is not a description of graduated existence of things or states of affairs, but is rather to be regarded as a well-justifiable construction that plays an essential part in the world-view of acting beings.[17]

From a certain point of view, namely in considering the problems of determinism, there exists a time-dependent inequality of the modal determination; the factuality of the past is to be understood as determined past events. Only contrafactually can one reflect on what would have happened if ... (or if not ...). It is only from the present moment on that the behavioral tree is split up into different future possibilities.

Here, too, the possible is not to be understood as something of a semi-being nature, i.e. not as a reduced ontic status, not as a preliminary stage preceding real being.

Does it make sense to speak of possibility without a framework, of possibility in an absolute sense, as it were? I doubt it. When speaking of possibilities one must also say just what is possible, i.e. give a description of the possible, or a characteristic of its contents. The slogan "Anything is possible" of lottery companies makes sense only against the background of a certain determination of the quantification range of "anything". When we speak of possible worlds, we do so under

[17]For a different opinion, see: N. Hartmann, *Möglichkeit und Wirklichkeit* (Possibility and Reality), de Gruyter, Berlin 1966, p.5.

the – explicit or tacit – assumption that a possible world is a complex of states of affairs which can logically be represented as a consistent conjunction of descriptions of states of affairs.

We cannot think up possibility from the nothing, construct what is possible, entirely without any assumptions, without a framework in which the alternative possibilities are embedded. Only in the case that, in a subject field, necessary matters such as indispensable structural elements are distinguished from other elements which may be different, i.e. are regarded as variable, that modal statements ("it is possible ...," "it is necessary ...," ...) become meaningful.

The structural frameworks may be logical forms or, instead, frameworks of a certain subject field. If one passes over, through abstraction, from the sentence "Socrates is a philosopher" to the structural scheme of the class membership formula "$x \in X$", then "Socrates" will be replaced here by a variable to whose range of values Socrates belongs as an element. The variable is an empty space that can be filled with names of values, or, as one usually puts it, the "variable can assume values". Socrates is dropped only as an element at a certain place (as value of the variable); not dropped, however, is the place in the structure occupied by the name "Socrates". All this applies analogously to the class variable "X", which replaces the class of the philosophers.

Every sentence obtained from "$x \in X$" by replacing "x" by an individual name and "X" by a class name is a logically possible case of a class membership proposition.

Possibilities can, in my opinion, be meaningfully spoken of if and only if:

1. structural frameworks are given, which frameworks contain places for variation ;

2. possibilities are to be indicated, i.e. if a possibility field is to be determined, then it is necessary that

3. the corresponding value ranges can be indicated for the places for variation. If this is the case, then a field of possibilities – let us

call them "logically permissible" or in short "logical possibilities" – can be constructed by purely combinatorial analysis.

Now as to the method of determining logical possibilities. Logically possible is everything which in the range considered can be construed by assigning to each place for variation of the skeleton one value from the variability range concerned. If the value ranges of the places for variation are indicated by characteristic features (as intensionally understood properties), then a rule can be formulated enabling one to recognize whether a given structure constitutes an element of the possibility field. But it is not possible to indicate nominatim the totality of all possibilities (nor, of course, their number). If, however, the permissible values are enumerable, then it is a relatively simple combinatory task to indicate all possibilities and calculate their number.

The combinatorily determined possibilities – termed by me logical possibilities (i.e. possible within the given framework of necessities) – are not all, and not always, possible in actual fact. Certain ones of these possibilities are excluded by laws of the field or by relationships stipulated for the range, or by the theory valid in the range. Then there remains a field of actual possibilities.

The essence of the nomological proposition lies in its validity over and beyond unlimited generality. Only a nomological assertion can be used as justification basis of fact-transcending assertions. Justifications in the field of assumptions, contrafactual claims or of disposition statements require sentences that express a fact-transcendent necessity.

Persuasive is Rescher's view that the cognition of law is man-made in the sense that it is not logically determined by experience alone and that a nomological sentence says more than is logically derivable from empirical data. However, I feel somewhat closer to Kant than to Rescher. Not only the stipulation of transfactuality compels us to regard the recognition of law as structured by the immanent principles of the collection of experience; rather, the manner of collecting is necessarily nomological (with stochastic lawfulness also being included here), a causal structuring motivated by and tested through facts. Nomological sentences expressing causal structures form, in equal measure, the basis of the explanation of actual events, the analysis of assumed possibilities and the justification of contrafactual assertions.

Now, however, as to my objections: the special features of a proposition of law is not seen by Rescher in a structural peculiarity of such sentences, but in the observer's preparedness, with which he meets the unlimited generalization, to apply this generalization also hypothetically – or in my terminology: with fact-transcendent validity. ("For lawfulness lies in the eyes of the beholder, since the lawfulness of a generalization consists in its being regarded and treated and classified and used in a certain way."[18] The fact that Rescher starts out with an explication of the nomological descriptive sentence which he terms structurally different from the usual generalization, and that he demonstrates in detail the logical difference between both sentences – namely that the contraposition applies to one of them, but not to the other – might be judged to be an inner contradiction in his view. Rescher's concluding thesis that lawfulness consists only in the preparedness with which the generalization is encountered to accord it wider application I regard as problematical. If one changes only the manner of application of the generalization, but not the logical structure of the sentence that is to express the nomological generality, then the following difficulties arise: (a) if one equates the nomological generalization structurally with the ordinary one, then there is no reason to be seen why the latter, and not the former, should be transposable; (b) an application of the generalization transcending the realm of reality would be unjustified if the generalization has only the usual structure.

Unlike, Rescher I am of the opinion that the proposition of law must hence be given such a logical form as makes its nomological necessity find expression in the structure and the theory belonging to it. I find it logically impermissible to perceive the nomological necessity only in the pragmatic moment of the language user's being prepared

[18]N. Rescher, op.cit., p.191.

to apply the generalization also in a hypothetical context. For the question must be asked: what permits us to apply a proposition having validity in a certain universe (e.g. in reality or in a certain field of experience) also beyond this field if the structure and meaning of the proposition do not indicate that it is valid for this expanded field?

There is no doubt that the range of the variables, or the quantification range, must be determined if the meaning of a generalization is to be clear. If the range has been so determined that it coincides with reality (or a part of reality), then an application of the sentence to something non-factual, e.g. to something merely assumed or contrafactual, logically means a non-sequitur.

Rescher is correct to the extent that the decision to assert a nomological proposition is not a mere ascertainment of facts, but a stipulation motivated by empirical facts and relations to the scientific system. From a methodological and epistemological point of view the law is "man-made". Logically, however, the statement of law must be conceived of as structure which gives expression to the stronger binding ties (corresponding to the nomological necessity) and justifies an expanded application beyond the range of experience or reality. Hand in hand with the decision to regard the relationship represented by the generalization as a nomological one valid also for assumptions, contrafactual assumptions, etc. – in brief: as fact-transcending –, a generalization must find application whose structure represents the fact-transcendent meaning and applicability of the sentence concerned.

8.5. Fact-transcendence of the recognition of causality as a rational basis of disposition propositions and contrafactual conditionals

Disposition propositions occur in everyday linguistic practice just as much as in a scientific context. One is not always clearly aware of this peculiarity of these propositions. When something is termed water-soluble, brittle, or a good conductor of electric current, then these are predications about dispositions, just as when someone is called intelligent or gifted with a good memory. As different as these statements may be, they have one feature in common: they are not provable by observations made at the moment of their being asserted. The assertion "This crystal is soluble in water" is not tied to any actual process of the dissolution of the crystal in water. The sentence may be true and well-founded even if the crystal never comes into contact with water at all or ever will. The justifying foundation of the disposition statements is not actual experience, but knowledge about fact-transcendent properties of the object concerned. The same applies analogously to all disposition predications, which otherwise may differ widely. Some are statistical characteristics, e.g. not he is "intelligent" who always and everywhere finds intelligent solutions, but he who does so quite frequently.

Contrafactual conditionals – be they individual or general – are essentially different from truth-functional conditionals ('$p \rightarrow q$'). Their antecedent is untrue, but they themselves are sometimes true and sometimes untrue, whereas the truth-functional conditional '$p \rightarrow q$' with untrue antecedent is always true. It is therefore generally recognized that contrafactual conditionals are essentially different from conditionals in propositional logic.

One might think that the condition of contrafactual conditionals lies always in the past, for only then would it be proven that it was not satisfied. However, this assumption is out of place. It makes good sense to make contrafactual assumptions for the present or ones lying in the future. "If I were rich I would not work any more, but only go on interesting journeys" [I know myself well enough to know that this contrafactual sentence is not true.] "If I would throw a china vase out of the window tomorrow it would break" is contrafactual (e.g. because I do not possess any such vase at all).

The basis of the justification of disposition propositions and of contrafactual conditionals lies equally in fact-transcendent recognitions. In my opinion, therefore, the contrafactual conditionals may be regarded as special cases of fact-transcendent sentences. What must be explained now, and what adequate proposals are required for, is the structure of the nomological fact-transcendent conditional sentence. The characteristic feature of these sentences is the fact that they are not only valid for the real world – such as it is, was and will be – but also for a possibility field, a class of possible worlds that can be conceived of (or constituted) by varying the constituents of the real world, with the limitation, however, that in all these worlds of the possibility field the relation "If p, then q", whose nomological transcendence is at issue here, must be valid.

It must be emphasized in particular here that the construing or constructing of possibility fields does not presuppose any possibility concept. Instead of "possibility fields" I might simply have spoken of a domain superordinated about the reality R which is gained according to specific rules as a system of alternatives to R. Hence this presentation is not a circular one.

Our possibility concept and the constitution or construction of possibility fields about ranges of states of affairs provide us with the means to deal with the problems of fact-transcendent propositions and develop the theory of their justification.

How can the difference between accidental and nomological general propositions be logically explained; or, put more clearly: how can the logical structure of the general-nomological proposition be set off against that of the ordinary one (or one with a limited range) in such a way that such predictions and contrafactual assertions can be justified by nomological general propositions, but not by accidental ones?

Accidental general propositions do not change their logical character at all when the field is widened. If, in the aforecited example of my three black dogs, mention is made of three dogs from among all dogs in Austria, all dogs of the present world, or all dogs of the past, present and future, the corresponding general proposition will nevertheless remain limited to one single field, even if this field should be the universe of everything existing. Any assertion which with respect to a somehow given class makes a claim of a general nature does so only with the claim to truth of factuality, not with the strength of an essential recognition, not as a nomological statement and not with fact-transcendent validity. *De facto* a statement is justified only within the empirical field, since e.g. about all dogs of the past, present and future I can make only nomologically justified statements, unable as I am to have any direct empirical knowledge about each of these dogs individually.

Only if the general proposition assumes a fundamentally different structure can a statement with experience- and fact-transcendent validity be made. The nomological general proposition does not refer to a specific reference class of reality, neither merely to my household, nor to Austria or the universe, but to a system of alternative worlds such as can be constituted by a field of possibilities about a factual domain.

Let the real domain about which a field of possibilities is being constituted be called 'R', and let '$[M/R]$' be the designation of a field of possibilities about R defined in accordance with the gnoseological situation.

The fact-transcendent general proposition (rule) can be written in the following way:

$$(x)(Fx[M/R] \rightarrow Gx)$$

This can be read as follows:
"For every x of every alternative A_1 of the field of possibilities $[M/R]$ about R the following holds: If x (in A_1) has the property F, then x (in A_1) has the property G." '$[\ /\ ] \rightarrow$' can be understood as a conditional functor that espresses a stronger relationship than the functor of the material implication (of the conditional of propositional logic) '$\rightarrow$'. The material implication might be written as '$[R] \rightarrow$', with R indicating the given reference field. The functor '$[\ /\ ] \rightarrow$' of the field of possibilities has two empty places which serve for the indication of the basic field and of the manner of constitution of the field of possibilities.

A sentence of this form can be used for expressing a nomological relationship if the field of possibilities is adequately determined, namely in such a way that the invariant structures represented in the nomological statement will remain in existence in all alternatives of the field of possibilities, with the places of variation being so determined that all actual or only imaginable determining conditions of the law occur as alternatives. Through the transition from the general proposition about *one* field to an assertion about a system of alternatives which in the framework of a structural skeleton form a class of possible objects (or possible worlds), this statement, the fact-transcendent conditional sentence, acquires the character of an intensional relationship, or, put more precisely: of an extensionally explicated intensional relationship.

If, for example, the claim "All ravens are black" is represented as a sentence about reality in the form

$$(x)[Ra(x) \rightarrow Bl(x)],$$

then it is noted that in the universe of real objects (or, as the case may be, of all objects of the present, past and future) there exists no object x possessing the property Ra, but not the property Bl. If, however, it is said with respect to the field of possibilities, i.e. to all the possible worlds that are alternatives to this real universe that, if in any one of these alternative worlds an x has the property Ra, this x will also have the property Bl, then an essential relationship between these properties is thereby asserted. Precisely this is the meaning of assertions in the form of nomological general propositions.

The nomological general proposition gives expression to the fact that the asserted relationship – in our example: that there are no non-black ravens – is not only presented as an empirical fact, but is also viewed as a relationship of essence. What it means that the affirmed relationship is viewed as one of essence can be explicated in the following manner: This relationship is not only valid for the given empirical field, but has also both experience-transcendent and fact-transcending validity, and it forms the framework of the alternative worlds of the field of possibilities above the empirical world, or above reality.

Hence the field of possibilities of a nomological proposition is so defined that there exists a system of alternatives above reality, in all of which the asserted relationship is valid.

The affirmed nomological relationship, or relationship of essence, forms the defining framework of the field of possibilities, and to the variable places permissible values of conditions are assigned.

If the nomological general proposition is explicated logically as a general fact-transcending conditional sentence, then its meaning is evidently dependent on the determination of the field of possibilities.

The nomological general proposition will then acquire the form

$$(x)(Fx)[M_{F,G}/R] \rightarrow Gx),$$

in which the indexes appended to M indicate that the constitution of the field of possibilities is to be accomplished in such a way that the relationship between the property F and the property G will remain valid in all alternatives.

Through stipulating certain limiting conditions – which may also be limitations of time or space and which I name 'α' – it is possible to represent the so-called quasi-laws in the form:

$$(x)(Fx)[M_{F,G;\,\alpha}/R] \rightarrow Gx)$$

Here the index 'α' gives expression to the fact that only such alternative worlds are taken into consideration in which, besides the predicted relationship, the conditions α are satisfied as well.[19]

Now we are faced with the task of considering the fact-transcendent sentences – and in particular the nomological propositions – from a justification-theoretical point of view.

---

[19]In the practice, the exact logical analysis encounters here the considerable difficulty that in the so-called quasi-laws the limiting conditions are not explicitly known and can only be indicated in the form of *ceteris paribus* clauses and the like.

When a nomological proposition is related to all of reality, its validity range is expanded over and beyond the data supporting it empirically, since for the empirical proof of the validity of a nomological sentence one cannot draw upon all facts, but only upon empirical data. In the real field R, too, a general proposition means going beyond the limits of the empirical basis. This transition from the field of experience to reality as such is necessary if recognition is to play the part it is entitled to from an anthropological point of view. The validity of the sentence in R depends on whether the generalization is justified by a sufficiently tested theory. If this is the case, i.e. if the theoretically-founded generalization appears to be justified, then it is equally permissible to relate the generalization, as recognition, to the totality of all facts as to corresponding fields of possibilities above the realm of reality, including contrafactual alternatives. The reason for the validity and the strength of the justification are the same in all cases, and they are based on the fact that the generalization is understood as a recognition of relationships of essence.

The nomological proposition is applied with equal force to the reality beyond the field of the experience supporting it – thus e.g. to future facts – as for the analysis of mere possibilities or contrafactual relationships.

If the validity of a nomological proposition is regarded as problematical, then one will examine the theory it forms part of and enquire after its adequacy within the framework of this theory and the degree to which is has been tested; but if it is applied as a law, then it will form the framework for the determination of both the empirically necessary and the possible; it forms the basis for the explanation of events, for prognoses and for retrodiction.

On the basis of my view of the nomological proposition and of my opinion that nomological proposition have experience-transcending validity only because we have arrived at the conviction that they express knowledge of essence, so that, for the same reason, they also have fact-transcendent validity, it can be explained in a simple manner when individual states of affairs can be characterized as necessary, and furthermore how dispositional and contrafactual propositions can be understood and justified.

A sentence about an individual state of affairs – e.g. that the toy-balloon burst when it was pierced with a needle – is necessary true if and only if (and precisely because) it is a specification of a corresponding nomological general proposition. It is a consequence of *Hume's* recognitions about causality that neither succession in time, nor coincidence in space, nor rule-like parallels in the course of similar phenomena prove causal connections. Rather, the recognition of causality of individual events is likewise justified by nomological knowledge.

Dispositional assertions are justified if and only if they correspond to a relationship of essence, i.e. if with respect to the object whose dispositional property is indicated the corresponding nomological proposition is valid. The latter forms the justification of the dispositional statement. "Sugar is soluble in water" is true if and only if it is valid by force of law (i.e. with fact-transcendent validity): under the conditions as assumed, sugar will always dissolve in water. "John Doe is intelligent" is justified if it can be claimed with fact-transcendent validity that John Doe will in all probability solve certain tasks that can be drawn upon as intelligence criteria.

Contrafactual conditional sentences can be presented, with good reason, as true or false if and only if the affirmed relationship has transcendent validity.

The justification of contrafactual conditional sentences rests undoubtedly on the validity of fact-transcendent sentences. "If I had dropped this lump of sugar into water it would have dissolved" can be claimed with good reason (even if the sugar was burnt), because the corresponding nomological proposition is true. But one must not equate the contrafactual sentence with the nomological one justifying it. One can meaningfully pronounce contrafactual conditional sentences without being able to prove them. "If I had studied one more day for my examination I would have passed it" is meaningful even though I cannot prove it. But I understand what would be necessary to prove the sentence.[20]

8.6. *Remark on Chisholm's Problem*[21]

The proposed structural scheme of the fact-transcendent conditional sentence supplies us with a means to carry out a rational and clarifying analysis of contrafactual conditional sentences in everyday language. Chisholm's ascertainment of the *duplex interpretatio* of sentences of the type "If Apollo were a man, then ..." is a good relevant example. The ambiguity can be eliminated by constituting the field of possibilities differently. In one of the two possible reconstructions of the sentence "If Apollo were a man, ..." the contrafactual sentence "If Apollo were a man, he would be mortal" is justifiable as being true (namely: if the field of possibilities is so determined that the alternative attributes of Apollo vary, but the concept 'being human' remains constant); but in the other one this would instead be true of the contrafactual sentence "If Apollo were a man, there would be at least one immortal human being". In this case the properties of Apollo would be retained in all alternatives, but the characteristic features of the concept "being human" would vary.

8.7. *Possible social influences on action, and the dispute around the freedom of will*

The assumption, as a matter of principle, of the (non-transparent) determination of action constitutes a basis for the meaningfulness of the various forms of social influences exerted on action. [Under the

[20] An analysis of the contrafactual conditional sentences as special cases of fact-transcendent sentences was presented by me in the article "Contrafactuality and Fact-transcendence", in: *Ratio*, vol.16, no.1/1974, p.15–32 (especially p.30 seq.).

[21] See R. M. Chisholm, The Contrary-to-Fact Conditional, *Mind* 55(1964), p.289–307.

assumption of strict indeterminacy such efforts would make no sense, since trying to influence a *prima causa* would be a futile endeavor.] Education, norm-giving, the presentation of examples, praise and blame, reward and punishment are all meaningful measures, although we know beforehand that there is no certainty, but only a certain probability that they will be effective.

Giving shape to reality in the social field will, in my opinion, only be meaningful within the framework of a deterministic view, coupled with the clear realization that in so doing one is trying to exert an influence on largely non-transparent realities and structures.[22]

A special question, and one hard to analyze, of action determination is the relationship between conscious, partially-conscious and unconscious moments in the action-determining information process. The consciousness accompanying the decision and action processes varies. It is hard to determine just what of the action-determining information process the psychophysical agent becomes aware of, and in what measure. Yet for the action-explaining motive interpretation this circumstance of the degree of the awareness seems to be of minor importance.

8.8. Norm-giving in the deterministic worldview

There is no doubt that norm-giving is meaningful even in the spirit of a deterministic philosophy and that the function of social norm systems can be understood from this point of view. The existence of institutionalized norm systems is a sociological fact; norms work as determination factors of human action. The functioning of norms presupposes in no way an indeterminism, neither in a conception as *prima causa*, nor as an explication fiction (as meant by Vaihinger). The fact of the free action as a resultant of information-determined

[22]The moral-philosophical problems of how or in how far education and paternalistic measures are compatible with moral autonomy may be left out of consideration here. Education and other forms of social influence on other persons is a fact and – in my opinion – an inescapable social reality.

decision processes is a sufficient basis for the possibility to regard norms as action-determining elements. Both from a subjective point of view, where the Ought is accepted either freely or through various forms of social pressure, and in sociological observation, the Ought appears as a possible factor in action determination. For the observer can ojectively ascertain, through observation, effects of the norms on the behavior of people and on the constitution of social institutions.

The effects of norm-giving are not "absolute", i.e. the action of the addressees is not determined exclusively by the stipulated duties, but in various and often complex ways. Norm-giving creates fixed – if not always rigidly determined – forms of behavior and action. Norms given will in various ways become determinants of action, e.g. through the effect of examples set by other people behaving in conformity with the norms, through the motivating effect of praise in the case of fulfillment and blame in that of non-fulfillment of the given Ought, while in many fields – especially in that of law – there are special institutions for bringing about behavior according to the norms through penalties or rewards.

The existence of norm systems has an essential influence on our actions also in that they determine the expectations we have as to the behavior and actions of our fellow-men and partners. With regard to this problem, two remarks are important. (I) A person's action is in many cases interaction with other people, or at least, through various relationships, dependent on the behavior and actions of others. (II) How we act, what we decide in favor of depends in great measure of the expectations with which we approach our partners, opponents or other people. These expectations are partly prognoses, partly demands. The institutionalized norm system is an essential element by which the expectations – both as prognosis and as demand – are determined. This role of the norm-giving must not be so imagined, however, as if the thing to be expected were always precisely the fulfillment of the Ought. The influence of the Ought on what is to be expected is highly differentiated, but the normative situation is always one of the things to be taken into consideration when one wonders what one can expect of others.[23]

8.9. Responsibility in the deterministic world-view

The problem of responsibility has its place in the field of action, of the accomplishment of certain results by actions. For the assessment of the responsibility it is always a relevant question what an agent to whom responsibility is attributed has accomplished, can accomplish or could have accomplished if he had or had not acted in a certain fashion.

The relation between the accomplishment and the attribution of responsibility is not, however, a direct and immediate one. One may, under certain circumstances, not bear any responsibility for one's doings and omissions, e.g. if one is not *compos mentis* or has been acting under absolute coercion, and one can be responsible for events not brought about by oneself, or be held liable for events one did not bring about.

Therefore the real situation of the responsibility as stipulated by a norm system can be described most adequately by proceeding from the consideration that responsibility is a normative attribution and not a factual relationship given by nature.

It goes without saying that responsibility as a normative attribution is independent of one's stand on the determinism problem. Responsibility is meaningful and determinable as a consequence of normative stipulation, also in the perspective of the determinist. Problems could result only from the following two questions: (a) the question of the effectiveness of the attribution of responsibility, and (b) the

[23] *N. Luhmann* has tried to reduce the norm itself to a special kind of expectation. With this problematical conception I have variously taken issue elsewhere. See in particular O. Weinberger, Luhmann's Approach to Ethics, Jurisprudence and Legal Sociology, in: *ARSP*, 1996, p.543–52.

the question of the moral justification of normative attribution of responsibility from a deterministic point of view.

Just how one assesses the effectiveness of attribution as motivation to action depends more on one's conception of action, namely whether one regards action only as an expansion of reflex reactions, or as the result of action-determining pieces of information, or – as seems reasonable to me – as a combination of both moments, than of one's stand on the determinism problem.

The justification of the norm-giving proceeds along two lines: it is based on the recognition of the effectiveness of norms (and here the determinist's position is somewhat stronger than that of the indeterminists), or as a result of a moral weighing.

One might object that, if man's action is a result of the effect of determining factors – though possibly non-transparent ones – then the agent cannot help behaving as he does. To call him to account would lack moral justification: merit, guilt, praise or blame should be attached, not to the agent, but to the determinants of his action. Now this would be a flagrant misinterpretation of determinism.

The action determinants include in any event also internal factors, the character of the agent, so to speak, and this determining factor has a broad field of effects, since every other factor is taken in through the filter of the agent's personal manner of reacting. These personality characteristics themselves, however, are no absolute constants, but rather results of the process of life, or as it might be put: results of one's external fate as well as of one's actually realized form of life, or one's learning and practicing, one's achievements or failures.

Thus in the normal case it appears to be justifiable to attribute the responsibility for results of actions to the agent, all the more so since experience teaches us that man is capable of realizing accepted and fixed intentions regardless of their actual utility.[24]

---

[24]This may have highly negative social consequences as well. Cf. O. Weinberger, Angst vor dem menschlichen Wahn (Fear of Human Illusion), in: A Grabner-Haider, O. Weinberger, K. Weinke (eds.), *Fanatismus und Massenwahn*(Fanaticism and Mass Hysteria), Graz 1987, p. 4–34.

The consideration of a non-transparent determination possibly dating back to a distant past does cause, however, a certain "softening" of the moral and/or legal judgment: under certain circumstances one will be prepared to take exculpatory circumstances from the agent's past life and pathological or quasi-pathological determinants into consideration.

Chapter 9

Action and Institution

The core of the action theory advocated by me is constituted by the finding or invention of action alternatives and programs as well as by their teleological weighing in an optimization process in accordance with the ends and preferences of the practical system assigned to the agent. However, an action theory which aspires to grasp the complex reality of action must consider yet another component and another system of action-determining elements, namely the existence of institutions as frameworks of the action. The theory of the institutions, the explication of this phenomenon of the basis, both ideal and concrete, of action and human interaction, forms the second supporting leg of a realistic action theory, besides the structural theory of the action-determining processes of information processing.

9.1. Anthropological basis of the institutions

Human life is embedded in institutions. The behavior of people, when compared with other living beings, is marked by extraordinary scopes of freedom and great plasticity. True, there are – as with other living beings – heredity-coordinated behavior patterns, but in the case of man they are modifiable to a high degree, and their determining role is in large measure replaced by institutions. There are institutions of highly different types, and it is difficult, perhaps even impossible, to give a clear and unequivocal definition of this concept. It strikes me as adequate to regard the term "institution" as the designation of a family concept (in a Wittgensteinian sense), which excludes a strict definition in the usual sense. Instead of giving a strict definition I will now try to discuss the nature of institutions and their function as frameworks of action.

Institutions are man-made, facts of individual and social life which form frameworks of individual action and of interaction.

It is a characteristic anthropological feature of cultural man that he creates institutions and – viewed from another perspective – shapes his life in the framework of institutions. It can be said that homo sapiens both contributes, of necessity, to the generation of institutions and, equally necessarily, realizes his life in institutional frameworks.

Through institutions, types of action are established. One does not do "just something"; rather, one realizes actions that are determined, as to their type, by institutions. In writing, reading, working, praying, engaging in a certain type of sports, etc., I realize actions of an institutionally typified kind.

In individual behavior and action, too, an important relationship between action according to one's own preference and the institutional facts manifests itself. The individual modes of action are in most cases socially inspired, and their realization is often dependent on existing institutions. What trouble will one not go to in order to follow fashion trends! If there were no network of roads, I could not make any excursions by car.

There is also the possibility, however, to stipulate for oneself patterns of conduct that do not conform to any existing social patterns. I may e.g. think up a certain game, lay down rules for it and abide by this pattern of conduct as long as I care to. Such stipulations can be viewed as rudiments of institutions which secondarily may also become established socially.

Where action is in some way interaction, be it positive cooperation toward common ends, be it competition or the settlement of a conflict, an institutional framework for the action will always be necessary. And it is a fact, well proven by social experience, that forms of interaction do become established, i.e. that interactions do acquire an institutional character.

Quite generally it may be said that institutions are elements of the context of the action, relating as they do to both individual and/or interactional action, and they constitute that social reality in which individual matters and social ones meet and mutually influence one another.[1]

The question now presents itself just how the various institutions are to be ontologically characterized in detail. This problem field I wish to illustrate by contrasting *Hauriou's* classical theory of institutions with my own neo-institutionalist view.

9.2. The classical conception of the institutions according to Maurice Hauriou

Hauriou's theory is built up as one of law, this in such a way that the fundamental reality are the institutions which for their realization generate law. A more or less systematic presentation of his theory is given by the author in the monograph "Die Theorie der Institution und der Gründung" (The Theory of the Institution and of its Founding), oddly subtitled "Essay über den sozialen Vitalismus" (Essay on Social Vitalism).[2] The institutions are, to him, the actual realities of the law.

[1]This is not contradicted by the aforementioned fact that action typification may also occur, under certain circumstances, in strictly individual life without leading to societal generalization or social institutionalization.
If one realizes that the individual person may also contribute to the establishment of social practices, then one will include these preliminary stages of institutionalization, too, into the theory of institutionalization. Then, of course, a question will remain open which is hard to clarify, namely under what circumstances individual practices can become social institutions.

[2]M. Hauriou, *Die Theorie der Institution und der Gründung. Essay über den Sozialen Vitalismus* (The Theory of the Institution and of its Founding. Essay

The law, as an institution, is simultaneously something social-real and something spiritual, an ideally determined entity, as becomes evident in the fact that the *idée directrice* constitutes the central concept of this theory.

The concept 'Institution' is defined by Hauriou as follows: "(A)n institution is an idea of the work or of the enterprise which finds realization and legal status in a social environment. In order that this idea may become a reality in the concrete world of facts, a power will take shape by which it is equipped with organs. Among the members of the social group participating in the spreading of the idea, there will come about, under the supreme guidance of the organs, manifestations of community which follow certain rules."[3] In this view, the subjective elements in this process are the creative power and action, while the objective elements are the legal norm, the social environment, and the public order as an organization possessing duration and continuity.[4]

Institutions are founded, this in such a way that "the founding of the institutions possesses legal character and (...), from this point of view, the foundations of the legal duration are of a legal nature themselves, too." ... "Institutions come into being, live and die according to the rules of law. They come into being through founding processes which furnish them their legal basis and thereby ensure their continued existence. They live both in the objective and in the subjective sense by virtue of repeated legal acts by government and administration that are decreed according to a prescribed procedure. Finally they die on the grounds of legal ordinances providing for their dissolution or abolishment."[5]

Thus, institutions are social entities of a relative duration and of a spiritual structure as expressed in the guiding idea, and they manifest themselves through law and through legal rules; in this

about Social Vitalism), in: R. Schnur (ed.), Die Theorie der Institution (The Theory of the Institution), Schriften zur Rechtstheorie 5, Berlin 1965, p.27–66.

[3] M. Hauriou, op.cit., p.34.

[4] M. Hauriou, op.cit., p.33.

[5] M. Hauriou, op.cit., p.34 et seq.

process the legal norms play a secondary part: "It is the institutions which create the legal norms, and not the legal norms which create the institutions."[6] The actual (primary) objective element is not the legal system, but the institution.

Hauriou distinguishes two kinds of institutions: "institutions-choses" (hence literally: institutions of things) and personal institutions ("institutions-personnes" (hence literally: institutions of persons), but centers his attention on the latter institutions.

Hauriou's concerns are: (a) to show where in society creative power resides, and (b) to reveal its dependence on spiritual elements and to explicate the processes of the founding and of the "life" of institutions.

Question (a) is answered by Hauriou in unequivocal fashion. Primarily it is power which, resting on guiding ideas, creates institutions, guides society and constitutes the source of law. "This, however, is precisely where the problem lies: what matters is to know just where in society creative power resides: whether, namely, the legal norms created the institutions, or whether it is not rather the institutions which by virtue of the power of leadership inherent in them create the legal norms. It is this enquiry after initiative and creation which makes the system of the objective legal norms come to failure. To allow for the creation of the social institutions by the legal norms would mean indirectly to concede their creation by the social environment, which, on its part, allegedly produces itself the legal norm. Herein lies all too palpable a fallacy. To the social environment can be ascribed only a moment of inertia which will convey itself, in amplified form, to any individual initiative where such initiative is adopted by the environment, or, alternatively, the environment will approve a disturbing obstacle where the initiative is rejected by it. But it neither has, out of itself, an initiative of its own, nor has it any creative power. Thus it is out of the question that from it any legal norm, creative in its own right, will come forth which we may assume to precede the institution."[7]

---

[6] M. Hauriou, op.cit., p.65.

[7] M. Hauriou, op.cit., p.32.

The guiding idea, or the idea of the work to be realized, not only constitutes the connecting link with vitalistic ideas[8], it is also the most characterstic feature of the theory of institutions. We need not go into the relation between Hauriou's theory and vitalism in biology, since this question does not touch upon the essence of Hauriou's doctrine.

To Hauriou, the guiding idea is the moment which creates the institution as a functioning and relatively stable social reality and which to this end installs power. The organized power serving the guiding idea is justified by it, and it is the source of the awareness of community in society. The power which serves the guiding idea constitutes the creative element in society. The concept of the guiding idea designates the spiritual element in the establishment of institutions. While in principle it is of a direction-giving and teleological nature, it must not be equated with the goals in the usual sense. There is something mystical about the guiding idea (cf. the quotation in footnote 8 above). To Hauriou, guiding ideas are not mere functions of social volition and expressions of social constellations and objectives, but something vitally and spiritually existing. "In reality one cannot create ideas at all, one can only stumble upon them."[9]

Constituents of the institutions of the association type are, besides the idea of the work to be accomplished, the organized power in their service and the manifestation of community within a social group. "Every institution of the association type is marked, as we know, by three elements: 1. the idea of the work to be accomplished in a social group; 2. the organized power serving this idea for the purpose of realizing it; 3. the manifestations of community taking place within

[8] "By this, Claude Bernard's 'idée directrice' (guiding idea) is undoubtedly understood in a vitalistic sense, and this assuredly will resound all the way to the biologists, too. It is particularly among them, however, that vitalism has its adherents, and finally it also remains a fact: projected onto the social plane, the guiding idea appears as objective in the factually existing phenomenon of the union or association; it is this guiding idea which influences the members, and it is its mysterious effect which sets masses in motion." M. Hauriou, op.cit., p.47.

[9] M. Hauriou, op.cit., p.39.

the social group with a view to the idea and its realization."[10] Not only the members of the group upholding the institution submit to the power and organization in their manifestation of community, the executive power itself, too, succumbs to the authority of the guiding idea. In the phenomenon of the institution, the power-based organization experiences an upward moral revaluation.[11]

Collective persons come into being in a *three-stage movement successively comprising incorporation, embodiment and personification*; from this, there arises a *personnalité morale* on whose basis a legal entity – a legal person – can be introduced. It is only the sociological factuality of the collective persons which forms the basis for the possibility of legally introducing such legal persons.[12]

Not quite clearly developed is Hauriou's theory of Natural Law. His thinking reflects a Thomistic influence,[13] but I do not clearly see just how far this influence goes. "The *law* is a kind of program directed simultaneously at the realization of an orderly social system and of justice."[14] The Natural Law keeps developing further and further, but it is not changeable in itself; it is individualistic and anti-socialistic, and it is an ideal conception in which the law is to be both the creator of the social system and of justice, hence *ars boni et aequi* and at the same time *ars stabili et securi*.[15]

The essential features of Hauriou's institution theory can be put on record as follows (disregarding his metaphysical and vitalistic theses):

---

[10] M. Hauriou, op.cit., p.35 et seq.

[11] M. Hauriou, op.cit., p.42 et seq.

[12] Cf. J. Delos, La Théorie de l'Institution (Institution Theory), *Archives de Philosophie du droit et de sociologie juridique* (Archives of Legal Philosophy and Juridical Sociology) 1931, p.119 et seq.

[13] G. Renard, *La Théorie de l'Institution. Essai d'ontologie juridique* (Institution Theory. An essay in legal ontology), Paris 1930, p.XIII.

[14] M. Hariou, Sozialordnung, Gerechtigkeit und Recht (Social order, justice and law), in: R. Schnur (ed.), *Die Theorie der Institution* (Institution Theory), op.cit., p.67–95; p.91.

[15] M. Hauriou, op.cit., p.95.

(a) Institutions have a spiritual core which forms the basis of the institution and is expressed as guiding idea – as determination of the work to be accomplished.

(b) The guiding idea is the primary element which brings about the founding of the institution. The human substratum of the institution, the persons administrating or operating it, identify themselves with the guiding idea and bring about the accomplishment of the work striven for.

(c) For the accomplishment of the work the institution generates norms and, if necessary, the required organization. In any event, to Hauriou it is not the norms which create institutions; rather, the opposite is true: the institutions are the sources of law, for the norms are employed as instruments for the realization of the guiding ideas.

(d) Institutions have their autonomous existence; the guiding ideas form the justification of a power which is binding both on those vested with power and on the subordinated members of the institutions.

(e) Institutions of things are contrasted to personal ones. The former, too, have a substratum of persons.

9.3. The normativistic ontology of the institutions

MacCormick' and my theory of the institutions is not an offspring of the classical theory, but rather came into being independently of the latter.[16] First and foremost it was the need to explain the validity of

[16]See: N. MacCormick, O. Weinberger, *Grundlagen des Institutionalistischen Rechtspositivismus* (Foundations of institutionalistic legal positivism), Duncker & Humblot, Berlin 1985 [English version: id., *An Institutional Theory of Law. New Approaches to Legal Positivism*, D. Reidel, Dordrecht et al. 1986; Italian version: id., *Il diritto come istituzione*, Dott. A. Giuffrè editore, Milan 1990; French version: id., *Pour une théorie institutionelle du droit. Nouvelle approche du positivisme juridique*, Brussels, Paris 1992]; O. Weinberger, *Recht, Institution und Rechtspolitik. Grundlagen der Rechtstheorie und Sozialphilosophie*, Steiner, Wiesbaden 1987 [English version: id., *Law, Institution and Legal Politics. Fundamental*

systems of social norms as a reality which primarily called this theory into being.[17]

It therefore takes no wonder that normativist institutionalism (neo-institutionalism for short) is built up wholly differently from Hauriou's theory. Nevertheless there are striking conformities in several important questions.

1. Every institution has an ideal core, which as regards its meaning is of a practical nature, consisting as it does of norms, ends, values and preferences. This core cannot be directly observed, but only understood. Here there is a certain affinity with the classical theory of institutions: in both theories it is emphasized that institutions always have an ideal core that determines the nature and the function of the institution. In Hauriou's view this core is formed by the guiding ideas, in my theory by the core of pieces of practical information. Here, however, there is an important difference to be found as well: in Hauriou's view, the guiding ideas, as source of the institutions, are realities that have been found to exist, while norms are only aids for the accomplishment of the task imposed by the guiding idea. For this reason, norms, in comparison with the guiding ideas and the institutions generated through them, are only something secondary. In the neo-institutionalistic theory, on the other hand, the ideal core consists itself of norms and other practical pieces of information. This core is constitutive for the institution. Though it undergoes further development through the actual functioning of the institutions, it would be pointless to regard the existence of the institution as the primarily given reality. Rather, the existence of the institution

---

Problems of Legal Theory and Social Philosophy, Kluwer, Dordrecht et al. 1991]; id., *Norm und Institution. Eine Einführung in die Theorie des Rechts* (Norm and Institution. An introduction to the theory of law), Manz, Vienna 1988 [Czech version, Masarykova univerzita, Brno 1995].

[17] In my personal case: particularly in confrontation with the basic norm theory of the Pure Theory of Law, which I considered unsatisfactory. Justifying the validity (or existence) of the legal system through a hypothetical assumption is absurd, since the recognition of facts can, as a matter of principle, only be justified by experience, never through hypothetical stipulation.

and of the corresponding practical system are inseparable elements of the institutional reality and of the action context of human society. Likewise normatively built up are the structure of the institution and the organization serving it – the latter mainly through norms of competency.

2. Institutions are the site of the interplay of individual action and community life, even though both, the individual and society, maintain a relative independence.

Man's living and acting is marked by the relationship between the individual action of the subject on the one hand and the communities on the other hand. The individual's behavior is dependent on communitarian relationships: his individual behavior is molded by inherited, acquired or otherwise internalized patterns, which, however, does not rule out his freedom to creatively modify and shape his modes of behavior. Every form of community action, be it an interplay of actions by two or more persons in the same, in opposite or in mixed directions, or a collective action by corporate bodies (institutionalized non-psychophysical persons), is a resultant from the personal behavior and the actions of individuals in institutionalized frameworks. The interplay between individual and community – understood in an action context – is the place of the institutions: institutions make this interplay possible, and institutions are the result of these individual/social relations and interactions.

3. Institutions are complex entities: they consist of observable processes, including institutional objects, and pieces of practical information that cannot be directly observed, but only by an understand mind.

This complexity is characteristic – if in differentiated fashion – of our milieu of life: it is in large measure of an institutinal nature, and it is action context which can be recognized only in this complexity of observable reality and comprehended meaning, and through grasping the institutional functions.

4. Besides their core of norms and other pieces of practical information the institutions have both a personal and a material

substratum. Human beings, individuals and/or collectives take part in institutions, they administrate and operate the institutions and appear as their agents and organs. Through institutions, roles are defined and ascribed to persons. We look at our fellow-men through the spectacles of the institutions and at social life as a play with an institutionally determined casting of parts.

The material substratum is formed by objects and products that are created and used with a view to their institutionally determined functions. Money (coins, banknotes), traffic signs, games (chessboard and chessmen), or a football are examples of institutional objects. They cannot be adequately characterized by mere physical-descriptive statements. In order to know what a banknote is it is not sufficient to exactly describe the colorfully printed piece of paper, one must also know the function of these institutional objects, their role in life and the associated normative regularization.

5. Our apparatus of concepts concerning everyday life is to a high extent characterized by institutional features, in addition to purely descriptive ones. In this connection we are hardly aware that when I e.g. present someone as my son, reference is being made to an institutional relationship.

It is precisely the density of the institutional relationships in which we take hold of our environment that leads us to the point where, on the basis of analytical reflections, we distinguish between brute facts and institutional ones.[18] Although many a physical ascertainment, e.g. the measurement of the temperature, depends of institutionalized stipulations (about the definition of the freezing-point and the temperature scale), it contributes to the clarification of our knowledge and to our orientation in the world to distinguish between those facts or ascertainments which occur as simple facts, as

[18]Cf. G. E. M. Anscombe, On Brute Facts, *Analysis* 18. 3. 1958, p.69–72; furthermore J. R. Searle, *Speech Acts. An Essay in the Philosophy of Language*, Wiggershaus, Cambridge 1969.

objectified descriptions of reality – i.e. as brute facts – and those facts which are conceived of in essential fashion as institutional facts.[19]

6. Institutions have a certain "life of their own". They are realities sui generis. What does this life consist of? That is difficult to determine generally and precisely. On the one hand it is a matter of an institutionalization process. Institutions always mean a certain type of stabilization, of creation of patterns, standards and/or forms of life that possess a certain relative permanence, though not by any means constancy. They are orientations of actions, an essential factor for the constitution of action potentialities of the individual person, of his standards of ends and values as well as of his forms of action, just as they are elements of social reality and the basis of all types of community action. In accordance with my conception of action, the practice of action-determining information-processing requires at least a partial stabilization of action patterns and value assessments. The institutions are the points where these fixations come about in a certain interlinking of individual matter and communitarian ones.

The institutionalization and predominance of the guiding idea of the institution frequently make for a certain moment of inertia of the institutions, causing them to hardly ever abandon, as a rule these primary innermost attitudes. In ideology and politics this means that the current outward appearance and the manner of behavior of the institution at any given moment frequently are mere tactics and that the basic guiding motive – even if temporarily repressed – will always re-assert itself as basic idea. It occurs not infrequently that institutionalized forms – e.g. legal bodies – continue to exist even though they no longer serve any meaningful purpose. The opposite

[19]Although the determination of the temperature of an object depends even in actual fact on the institutionalistic stipulation of the freezing-point and the temperature scale, this dependency is not an essential one; hence the ascertainment of the temperature is not a recognition of an institutional fact, but a brute-fact datum which under different institutional stipulations of measures could be realized in equivalent fashion. For the recognition of the nature of a banknote as an institutional object, however, the institutionalized normative and functional determination is essential.

phenomenon also occurs, however: a radical change of the guiding ideas and of the function of the institution. Institutions go through an internal development. An institution may e.g. grow, the circle of persons involved may expand; a change of the situation in which an institution exists may lead to its modification; quantitative changes in the institution may necessitate changes in its organization, etc. The function of the institution's central idea may change as a result of external or internal developments. An enterprise may be founded for the sole purpose of making profit by satisfying economic needs, but under certain circumstances the enterprise may become a major social or power factor. The institution's "life of its own" excludes a petrification of its central idea.

7. Institutions have as a rule a certain organizational structure. The organization means a presence of personal and material elements between which functional relationships exist. E.g. a university as an organized body consists of buildings, pieces of furniture, instruments, books, a staff of teachers, officials, etc., with these things and persons being bound to one another through interaction relationships and united to form an orderly system, all of which come into view as behavior regularities and Ought relationships. Organization is hence an institutional fact. Everything integrated into the organization acquires institutional significance, and the processes taking place with the elements of the organization are understandable only by virtue of the institutionalized relationships within the orderly system mentioned above. Frequently, too, an interlinkage and hierarchization of institutions will come to pass, leading to wholly new social realities. These developments are an interlocking of new situations and purposeful foundings. The unfolding of the institutions is both: spontaneous development and purposefully justified organization.[20] I believe, however, that there is no exact dividing line between these two determi-

[20]To connect this with the reflections of F. A. v. Hayek, cf. F. A. von Hayek, *Law, Legislation and Liberty. A new statement of the liberal principles of justice and political economy* (3 vols.), vol.1 "Rules and Order", Routledge & Kegan Paul, London 1973.

nants of the development, for that which, from a historical point of view, appears to the observer as a spontaneous result of the development is, in an actual situation, interspersed time and time again with analyses of purpose and weighings of a rationally-evaluating nature.

8. The theories about the relationships of the individual and of society are usually classified according to whether they regard the social phenomena predominantly as resulting somehow from a summation of individual persons, or, on the contrary, explain the nature of the individuals from the influences of society. Neo-institutionalism opts for neither approach. The institution has its 'life of its own'; its attitude in the practice can be shaped by individual subjects, by exponents of ideas and through the activity of communication installations. But it is not – as liberalistic theories usually demand that it should be – a summation of the objectives and preferences of the individual participants in the institution. Rather, by and large the inverse relationship is valid: the ideal core of the institution comprises individuals who identify themselves with the institution, which can come to pass for a wide variety of reasons, certainly not always and not exclusively out of personal interest, for personal advantage or for an expected subjective-egoistic benefit. According to the institutionalistic conception, the institution is also a factor which shapes the individual, although, varying with the circumstances, in a highly differentiated way. In the neo-institutionalist view, the relationship between society and individual is a complex cyclic process which cannot be explained by mere observation from the one or from the other side.

9.4. Attempt at a classification of institutions

As I asserted already before, institutions form a family concept. This has the result that a perfect classification is hardly achievable. A clear-cut classification is rendered difficult by two circumstances: (a) by the existence of "preliminary forms" of institutions, which forms, while having an analogous function as frameworks of action, have not –

or not yet – been institutionalized; (b) by a difference between German and English terminology. In the German language, one usually speaks of "Rechtsinstitute" ("legal institutes" in the romanistic terminology), such as e.g. property, marriage, mortgage, etc., whereas in English one speaks of institutions.

Quite generally, not only from my point of view, it is demanded that types of institutions should be distinguished. But about the question just what types of institutions exist, or what a typology of institutions should look like there is no generally accepted opinion. The typology proposed in the following should not be understood as an essential component of my theory, but only as a proposal for an approximate orientation.

A typological distinction between *normative institutions* and *real institutions* may be placed at the top of our typology. Normative institutions such as property, matrimony, testament, contract, etc. are conceptual building stones of the legal system.

There are various possibilities for determining units of the contents of norms systems, in particular of the legal system. The normativistic theories concentrate on the determination of

(a) the elements of the contents of the law as modes of behavior which – under complexes of conditions – are prescribed or prohibited, and

(b) the authorization, subject to certain conditions, to generate norms.

According to the institutionalistic conception, certain complexes of normative stipulations form a certain whole, which is usually designated by a specific term and is constituted by objective connections. This whole is a more or less detached or relatively isolatable element of social reality.

The normativistic view according to which prescriptions of behavior form the decisive building-stones of the contents of a legal system is not in conflict, in my opinion, with the view that the legal system is a complex of normative rules. For the construction of the legal system as a system of institutions forming its building-stones perceives only additional connections in social reality and recognizes the necessity of combining separate legal regulations to functionally connected complexes of norms, since it is only in this conception that a juridical and social-functional justification of the law – from, of course, an institutionalistic perspective – can be given.

One may take the view that the introduction of concept names for legal institutions is superfluous and that the assumption of the existence of certain ideal entities – such as 'property', 'matrimony' – merely feigns the existence of such special entities, whereas in reality only certain normative relations (duties, claims, authorizations) exist which a person has vis-à-vis another person or other persons.[21] Now it would theoretically be conceivable to completely characterize the totality of possible human behavior and the legal positions by behavior and power-conferring norms. *De facto*, however, thinking and justification in law is determined by reflections about institutions as the building-stones of the legal systems. A norm-giving which would take all possible situations into account and would stipulate the legal consequences for every possible situation is practically impossible; morover, it is only from an institutional point of view that the particularities arising from unusual constellations of facts can be so analyzed that justified normative conclusions will be won also for these special cases. In other words: the possibility of a reduction to behavior and power-conferring norms is brought to nought by the impossibility of completely grasping and normatively determining the totality of all possible situations.

Constructive juridical thinking always leans on certain objective units that are normatively introduced with reference to social realities. The social basis of matrimony e.g. is formed by certain factual constellations: the relations between man and woman, the relations between the generations (parents/children, education, transfer of property, etc.) which permit – and in a way compel – the introduction of marriage as an institution. How this is done normatively is a process of life practice that must cope with a host of actual circum-

[21]Cf. A. Ross, Tu-tu, *Harvard Law Review* 70, (1956/57), p.812–825.

stances of life. Only from an institutionalistic point of view can the legal-political analysis be understood, and only in that way can it be rationally carried out (namely if and when society and jurisprudence arrive at systematic *de lege ferenda* reflections.)

Legally, the institution – e.g. matrimony, property, legal persons, mortgage, etc. – is determined by the corresponding normative rules, and actually it is exactly that which these rules stipulate. But we will understand the institutions only as a socially relevant complex if we view them as functional units which form building-stones for the content of the legal system. Only on the basis of an institutionalistic approach can it e.g. be said that the institution 'property' will remain in existence even if certain rights or duties connected with property are changed. The basic functional determination of the institution is also the basis on which it is possible to speak of *one* institution in various shapes in various legal systems. This is an important circumstance which makes the comparison of law systems possible and which also has effects at many a point in international private law.

With respect to most normative institutions – but I am not sure whether to all – it is expedient to introduce such a typification of the rules determining them as was proposed by MacCormick: *institutive rules* which specify the conditions for the coming into being of individual cases of the institution concerned; *consequential rules* which stipulate the normative consequences of the existing individual cases of the institution – frequently with additional circumstances being taken into account – ; and finally *terminative rules* for the real instance of the institution.[22]

Such a subdivision of the rules permits the introduction of conceptual building-stones of the legal system, as well as the view that through certain amendments of some rules determining the institution the latter is not abolished as a whole, but only changed, and in particular adapted to the developments in society. Logically the *normative*

[22]Cf. D. N. MacCormick, Law as Institutional Fact), in: id., O. Weinberger, *An Institutional Theory of Law. New Approaches of Legal Positivism*, D. Reidel, Dordrecht et al, p.49–76.

changing of the institution can of course also be reconstructed as a succession of complexes of norms, but for practical juridical thinking the presentation on the basis of institutionalistic conceptions is easier to handle.

The neo-institutionalist theory of law looks at the normative institutions from an action-theoretical point of view. It emphasizes that by virtue of the institutions not only legal relations, legal obligations, claims and action possibilities come into being, but that other psychological and social consequences in the evaluation field likewise come about. The institutions open up scopes for action, they rouse expectations concerning the behavior of one's fellowmen and they have consequences for the relations – including the extralegal ones – between the members of society. I therefore consider it essential that the recognition of law should not be limited to the understanding of normative relations – hence of the legal consequences of facts and actions –, but should also include the consideration of other consequences (e.g. economic effects, expectations, duties, moral evaluations, etc.). Actually we will only then understand the existence and functioning of the law if we know both the legal consequences and the other – psychical and/or social – effects of modes of behavior.

A real instance of an institution consists of norm and observable fact: of Ought, human behavior, and objects which in the framework of the institution have certain roles or functions. A concrete marriage consists of a pair of humans; in this institution one is not just a man or a woman, but husband and wife, and specific relationships are constituted to be things, particularly to be components of the joint property of the spouses.

In some institutions the moment of the material and organizational substratum comes more prominently into view, in other ones less prominently so: institutions such as tribunals, schools, corporate bodies, etc. are creations of man, or as one might say: a kind of artefacts, with a material, organizational and functional substratum. Their organization and functioning as well as their social tasks are determined by norms (behavioral norms, competence norms) and by stipulated ends.

The institutions just discussed, in which organization and material artefacts play a central part, as well as corporate bodies and institutions of things[23], are looked at by me first and foremost from an action-theoretical point of view. The organization appears in this perspective not only as a structure, possibly of a hierarchical and functional nature, and not only as a regularity of behavior, but also as something determined by norms and ends.

In the institutionalistic conception the person in a general juridical sense is viewed not only as a point of the normative accounting, as a bearer of rights and duties, but also as the subject of actions, as a unit to which a system of ends is assigned and which in a certain way is competent to generate legal acts which, when performed by organs, are regarded as acts of the person concerned.

In the case of so-called natural persons this appears to us as a matter of course: they are human beings and as such capable of action. But in what sense can other – not psychophysical – persons be said to act or to be capable of action?

Be it noted, to begin with, that in the case of human individuals, too, their competence to perform legal acts is not always given as a manifest fact. The *nasciturus*, the infant, those ailing in a certain way are human individuals who *de facto* are not, or only to a highly limited extent, factually or legally capable of action. Thus, properly speaking, a certain normative decision comes into play in each case which determines the legal relevance of the natural capability of action. Even in the case of subjects who physically are undoubtedly fully capable of action this relevance may be juridically limited or excluded (in Roman law e.g. in the case of persons under *patria potestas*).

For all 'institutionalized' persons (i.e. those having been given the character of an institution) there is a certain regularization of their forms of action which takes the institution's own system of ends

[23]Cf. Hauriou's well-known subdivision of the institutions into institutions-personnes and institutions-choses, as referred to in the aforegoing.

into account. With all non-psychophysical subjects there occurs in principle always an acting by means of organs. Here the institutions of persons and those of things (e.g. a foundation) have the fact in common that they have their own system of ends (or at least a skeleton of it) which differs from the system of ends of the person acting as organ.

Non-psychophysical persons are possible, and existent as a social reality, for the reason that man is a community creature and acts communitarily.

Community action may either be cooperative action of some kind, or it is collective action.

Cooperative action, as is well known, varies with the structure of the relative orientation of the participating subjects to their respective ends; invariably, however – may the ends envisaged by the participants otherwise diverge, or their interests even conflict – there is a common end, namely to engage in this cooperative undertaking.

The borderlines between certain types of co-operative and collective action do not seem to be sharply drawn. We will speak of collective action if there exists a body structured in a certain way with an internal organization and organs for the performance of the actions that are attributed to this body. This existence of the collective person is a network of material elements. individual persons, normative rules for the prescribed behavior, and of orientations as to ends and values. This network exists as an institutional fact.

According to the formal-finalistic action theory advocated by me[24], man is able to act as an organ of a corporate body (of a collective subject of action) for the reason that the guiding of the action is an information process that can be rationally modeled and because the individual human person is not only capable of processing his subjective ends and values in his own, personal action, but also of processing communitarian ends and values of collective action, and of realizing the corresponding acts in the name of a collective or a corporate body. *The formal conception of the action-determining*

[24]Cf. chapters 4 and 5 of the present book.

information-processes makes a rationalized and intersubjectively understandable representation of the selection processes and of their justification possible, and this forms the precondition for acting in the name of someone else or as an organ of an institution.

This relationship can exist by and for itself as a sociological fact: in certain situations, man forms collectives and acts as their organ (i.e. in the name of the collective and according to its ends). In the modern legal culture, the formation of institutional persons, their organization and the attribution of the acts of the organs as acts of the collective have been regulated by law, i.e. they will be legally recognized if and only if the corresponding authorization norms are satisfied.[25]

In every case - hence even if we are dealing with legally not regulated collective subjects – the organization and the functioning of the body are dependent on – at least implicitly existing – regulatory systems which normatively establish the framework and the forms of the action of the collective.

9.5. Methodological implications of neo-institutionalism

The neo-institutionalistic conception, which was developed in conscious opposition to Kelsen's and his school's Purity Postulate, has, in addition to the two fundamental theoretical consequences – namely the replacement of the problematical basic norm theory by the neo-institutionalistic validity theory and the revision of the theory of legal dynamics – important consequences for the possibility of developing

[25] This, however, is not to say by any means that from a sociological point of view collective action exists only within a general juridical framework. Viewed sociologically, collectives can exist independently of whether the law pays attention to them and accords them the status of a corporate body. They are always based, however, on certain normative systems of rules, be they possibly even of an extralegal nature.

functional and political analyses of law and of the social institutions.

The validity of the legal norm. The thesis that a certain norm or a system of norms is valid is undoubtedly a (true or false) assertion about a fact. To justify a fact – of whatever type – solely by an assumption, by a hypothetical stipulation such as is constituted by the basic norm is unjustified and contradicts the most fundamental principle of the empirical sciences, namely that ascertainments of facts must be supported by empirical data.[26]

In the normativist-institutionalistic view, the validity of a system of social norms consists in that an institution (e.g. in the case of law: the institution 'state') functions, realizes its organization and makes its decisions on the basis of this system of norms. The existence of the institution and that of the corresponding system of norms (i.e. its validity) are inseparably intertwined facts. The assertion that a legal norm is valid is based on two moments: on the understanding of the norm, and on that of the recognition, based on observation, of the institutionalized effect of the norm in the institution.

Institutionalistic versus pure conception of legal dynamics. In the spirit of his Purity Postulate, *Kelsen* explains legal dynamics by saying

[26]If Kelsen, in order to justify his approach, remarks that no scientific discipline can do without axiomatic suppositions, this is not correct to such an extent that it would justify the ascertainment of a fact by a mere assumption. There are axiomatic stipulations which lay down the basic conditions for empirical cognition. But the justification of the existence of facts is always based, in the final instance, on empirical data. This is clearly shown by the methodology of working with axiomatic systems. The axiomatic system is determined by stipulation and stipulated derivation rules. And, as is well known, the axiomatics can, according to *Carnap's* tolerance principle, be built-up in a great variety of ways. It is possible e.g. to present a system of axioms of a euclidian geometry, but also of a non-euclidian one. The system of axioms – even if logically perfectly structured – does not say anything yet about the space in which we live. Only experience will tell us whether and to what extent the system of axioms adequately describes the space of our world. And this fundamental empirical principle that assertions of fact cannot be justified without empirical proof is valid quite generally.

that the higher (better: superordinated, or justifying) norm is the true reason for the validity (*conditio per quam*) of the justified norm. Subsumption facts or the fact of the realization of norm-generating acts are in his eyes only a secondary circumstance (*conditio sine qua non*), but not a basis of norm dynamics, not a reason for the generation of a secondary norm.[27]

If we have two sentences such as are necessary for gaining a conclusion, then there is no logically acceptable reason for regarding one of these two premises as the reason (*conditio per quam*), but the other one only as a necessary (secondary) condition. Only the stubborn insistence on the Purity Postulate leads to the reduction of the role of the actual occurrences in the dynamic process so that law dynamics can be depicted as a process only in the field of norms.

[27] "From the fact that something *is* it cannot follow that something *ought to be*, just as it cannot follow that something *ought to be* from the fact that something *is*. The reason for the validity of a norm can only be the validity of another norm. A norm which constitutes the reason for the validity of another norm is figuratively termed the higher norm in relation to a lower one." ... "Yet in the syllogism whose major premise is the Ought-sentence: One ought to obey God's (or His Son's) commandments (which sentence expresses the higher norm), and whose conclusion is the Ought-sentence: One ought to obey the Ten Commandments, or the commandment to love one's enemies (which sentence expresses the lower norm), an essential term is constituted, as minor premise, by the sentence: God has ordained the Ten Commandments (or: the Son of God has commanded us to love our enemies), which sentence ascertains an Is fact. Major and minor premise are both conditions of the conclusion. But only the major premise, which is an Ought-sentence, is a *conditio per quam* in relation to the conclusion, which is likewise an Ought-sentence; which means that the norm expressed in the major premise is the reason for the validity of the norm expressed in the conclusion. The Is sentence acting as minor premise is only a *conditio sine qua non* in relation to the conclusion; which means ... that the Is fact ascertained in the minor premise is not the reason for the validity of the norm expressed in the conclusion." H. Kelsen, *Reine Rechtslehre* (Pure Theory of Law), 2nd ed., 1960, p.196 et seq. Kelsen misinterprets the principle that Ought does not follow from Is. Correctly understood, it merely says that without an Ought premise (or without a practical premise) no Ought conclusion is possible. It says nothing, however, as to whether sometimes, for deduction purposes, descriptive premises need not be resorted to as well. E.g. in the case of subsumptive inferences this is always the case.

Neo-institutionalism, in contrast, emphasizes precisely the interplay of norm and actual events in the legal-dynamic processes. Moreover the neo-institutionalist theory distinguishes between two different types of facts that bring about law dynamics. Either we are dealing with facts which because of their occurrence "automatically" bring about a change of the normative situation, e.g. the attainment of a certain age by a citizen, with the normative consequence of his becoming entitled to vote.[28] Of a different type is the generation of a norm based on an authorization to perform norm-generating acts. Here the fact needs to be ascertained that such an authorizing act has taken place, and its content must be understood.[29]

The rejection of Kelsen's Purity Postulate. The Purity Postulate as the taking of a scientific stand on the cognition of law is justified by the Pure Theory of Law with the lofty goal of the objectivity of research and by its non-valuational character, with pure cognition being termed apolitical, free of political tendencies that would interfere with objectivity. Considering that legal scholars often act as apologists of the ruling political system, the stipulated objective of working objectively and apolitically appears tempting. It is incontestable, however, that law has to do with values, that it articulates a valuating point of view. Then what is the meaning of "looking at the law unburdened by values"? This must not be understood in the way usually brought about by the Purity Postulate, namely in that one dispenses with grasping the value-oriented points of view innate in the law; rather, one should try, on the contrary, to understand these value-oriented points of view of the legal system examined and to

---

[28]See A. Procházka, Normative Theorie und Rechtserzeugung (Normative theory and the generation of law), in: V. Kubeš/O. Weinberger (eds.), *Die Brünner rechtstheoretische Schule (Normative Theorie)* [The Brno law-theoretical school (normative theory)], Manz, Vienna 1980, p.304–323. In cases of the aforecited type the author speaks of "automatic norm generation".

[29]Cf. chapter 7, p.180 et seq., p.188, where I explained the structure of the empowering norm, as well as the genesis of law generation through authorized acts.

present them objectively, without, however, identifying oneself with them or rejecting them. In brief: the value-free consideration of valuable objects certainly does not mean that one disregards these value-moments, but rather that one tries to understand them without judging them evaluatingly.

Hence the idea of value-free consideration does not justify by any means a Purity Postulate as a demand to dispense with value-moments. What remains standing, of course, is the distinction, emphasized time and time again by the advocates of the Pure Theory of Law, between the cognition of law (i.e. the ascertainment of what is valid law), and the generating of law, i.e. the legal generating of a valid norm. Going into the argumentation – of great interest to neo-institutionalism – basic to the generating of law does not blur the difference between norm-cognition and norm-generation.

Remark

In the parlance of Austrian jurists the Pure Theory of Law has become so influential that by the term "juridical" one understands only normative-understanding and interpreting consideration, under exclusion of the questions of the argumentative and sociological genesis of the norm, of its functional assessment, and of the consideration of the social effects of the normative determination. If we do not submit to Kelsen's thinking there is no objective reason why juridical analysis should not examine the question what social moments and justifications determine the contents of law and what social effects a certain norm will have. I entirely fail to see why such essential questions should be of no concern to jurists.

In reality the limitation of the juridical view by the Purity Postulate brings about the elimination of juridical social analysis and the possibility of social critique. Hence it is some sort of political ideology, at least de facto, though possibly not by design.

Legal-norm theory. Complex considerations of neo-institutionalism versus the theory of the legal sentence. For the methodology of the legal sciences and for understanding sociology, neo-institutionalism brings a turning-away from the atomistic approach. The study of the legal sentence produced important insights into the logical structures in which normative contents can be represented. Forming as it does the basis for the logical analysis of law and of other systems of norms, the analysis of the structures of the norm-sentence has undoubtedly been of great importance for the development of analytical jurisprudence.[30]

In the development of the theory of the structure of the legal sentence there have been two stages: in the first stage one endeavored

[30]This can be asserted despite certain erratic developments. The most important influence on this development of European jurisprudence was probably exerted by *Kelsen*. His investigations started out with the "*Hauptprobleme der Staatsrechtslehre entwickelt aus der Lehre vom Rechtssatz*" (*Main Problems of Constitutional Law as Developed from the Theory of the Legal Sentence*), 1911, continued with the "*Reine Rechtslehre*" (*Pure Theory of Law*), first edition 1934, second, enlarged edition 1960, and ended with the posthumously published and not completed "*Allgemeine Theorie der Normen*" (*General Theory of Norms*), 1989. These investigations were always directed at logical structures and were most influential, even though frequently based on problematical foundations, and they culminated finally in a norm-logical skepticism actually implying the negation of the possibility of a logical analysis of law. For if one claims that there exist no logical relationships and no valid norm-logical inferences – which is the fundamental thesis of Kelsen's "General Theory of Norms" – then the "Logic of Law" and the intention of analytical jurisprudence are at bottom illusory undertakings. For a critique of Kelsen's "logic" of law, see O. Weinberger, *Normentheorie als Grundlage der Jurisprudenz und Ethik. Eine Auseinandersetzung mit Hans Kelsens Theorie der Normen* (*Theory of Norms as Basis of Jurisprudence and Ethics. A Critique of Hans Kelsen's Theory of Norms*), Duncker & Humblot, Berlin 1981; *id.*, Kelsens These von der Unanwendbarkeit logischer Regeln auf Normen (Kelsen's Thesis of the Non-Applicability of Logical Rules to Norms), in: *Die Reine Rechtslehre in wissenschaftlicher Diskussion. Referate und Diskussion des Internationalen Symposiums zum 100. Geburtstag von Hans Kelsen* (The Pure Theory of Law Scientifically Discussed. Proceedings of the International Symposium on the occasion of Hans Kelsen's 100th birthday) Vienna 1982, p.108–121; *id.*, Logic and the Pure theory of Law, in: R. Tur, T. Twining (eds.), *Essays on Kelsen*, chap.8, p.187–199; id., Der normenlogische Skeptizismus (Norm-logical skepticism), in: *Rechtstheorie*, 17/1986, p.13–81.

to present a universally valid uniform structure of law, i.e. one sought to prove that the form of the legal sentence is suitable for the representation of all legal contents and all mental operations conducted with the law, while in the second stage one became aware that major differentiations of the structure of the legal sentence are necessary. Distinctions were made above all between principle and norm, and between norms of behavior and power-conferring norms.[31]

Normative institutionalism appreciates these structure-theoretical investigations and emphasizes the importance of these efforts for a rational-analytical jurisprudence,[32] while simultaneously, however, directing its attention at the moments of the connections of meaning and functionality existing between complexes of norms.

An interest in the logical structure of norms leading to the elaboration of a theory of the forms of justification and proof in the normative field is in no way in conflict with efforts to understand functional complexes of norms, nor with arguing on the level of such functional relationships.

For the field of the normative institutions (or legal institutes), *D. N. MacCormick* – as already mentioned above – has described *one* aspect of these complex relationships by distinguishing between three functional types of norms: through *institutive norms* it is determined how instances of these institutions come into being, through *consequential norms* the legal consequences of the institutions thus coming into being are established, and through *terminative norms*, finally, the dissolution (or the other form of termination) of the institution is defined.

[31]See O. Weinberger, *Rechtslogik* (Logic of Law), 2nd ed., Duncker & Humblot, Berlin 1989, p.6.

[32]I myself have devoted many papers to these problems, for I regard the formal and logical relationships as preconditions for institutional and functional analyses. It is precisely an adequate understanding of logical relationships which makes us recognize that this is not the whole of the methodological problems. To one who strives first and foremost for "purity", however, the whole of rational analysis will remain closed.

The approach of neo-institutionalism, which goes beyond the theory of the legal sentence, has several sources. The following strike me as the most important ones:

(a) The norm can be regarded as a teleologically justified stipulation. Its meaningfulness and adequacy can be argumentatively examined from teleological points of view.[33]

(b) The stipulation of the Ought frequently occurs stepwise: on the one hand through different degrees of abstractness – cf. the different roles of principles and behavioral norms[34] –, on the other hand through the chain of norm-giving bodies, which perform norm-generating acts that lead to the stepwise concretization of the contents of the Ought. (Cf. the relation between a law and an executory order for its implementation.)

(c) If institutions are regarded as results of the realization of certain guiding ideas one will obtain an interesting perspective for argumentation which in my opinion contributes as much to one's understanding as to the justification of the norms one stipulates in the system.[35]

---

[33] Here, various ways of asking questions are possible: the argumentation will either be governed by the objectives set by the very system of norms being examined, or the examination can be conducted from the point of view of other systems of ends and values. (This happens e.g. if a legal system is evaluated from the point of view of a pre-assumed religious system or a political conception.) Cf. R. von Jhering, *Der Zweck im Recht* (The End as Pursued in Law), vol.1, 2nd ed., Breitkopf & Härtel, Leipzig 1884. K. Engliš, Kritik der Normativen Theorie (A Critique of the Normative Theory), in: V. Kubeš, O. Weinberger (eds.), *Die Brünner rechtstheoretische Schule* (The Brno School of Legal Theory), Manz, Vienna 1980, p.176–193 (especially p.185 et seq.)

[34] Attention is invited here to the analyses by *Dworkin*, who clearly demonstrated the logical difference between deciding on the basis of behavioral norms, and justifying decisions with the aid of principles. (R. Dworkin, *Taking Rights Seriously*, 2nd ed., Harvard, Harvard University Press 1978.)

[35] The argumentation with guiding ideas is not, in my opinion, sharply separated from the teleological consideration (this in deviation from M. Hauriou).

(d) A peculiar perspective of the argumentation is the functional analysis of the normative system. It always forms a certain connection between, on the one hand, this system as an Ought and a program, and on the other hand, the realization of that which the Ought prescribes and of the organization serving the stipulated end.[36]

(e) In the institutionalist view it is not called for to strive for uniformity of institutional structures, e.g. to introduce always collective decision structures (supposedly being the only democratic ones). The structure of the institution and its organizsation must be shaped appropriately with a view to the task to be accomplished.

The progressive role of the functional analyses. The functionalist approach goes in reality beyond an explicit reference to the guiding ideas and an 'efficiency test' testing from this point of view. Attention is also given to the sociopolitical effects of norms, measures and organizations. Effects and side-effects are discussed. The field of the effects and reactions is as a rule wider than the proposed basic intention as expressed in the guiding ideas. Frequently, consequences not considered before will come to pass. The functionalistic approach will focus time and time again on new aspects of social reality, open up paths for critique and engender ideas for reshaping matters. In this way it

[36]The term 'functional analysis' is understood differently in different contexts: in the understanding variety of sociology as explanation of the contents of institutions as well as of the co-operation of institutions and individuals. Meaning is explained out of functional relationships, in which connection various explication models can be applied – e.g. after *Habermas* the craftsman model, the stage model and the cybernetic model [J. Habermas, *Zur Logik der Sozialwissenschaften* (On the Logic of the Social Sciences), Suhrkamp, Tübingen 1967.] With *Luhmann*, the functionalist approach is so understood that equal effects of different moments are regarded as equivalent. If e.g. the stability of an institution is taken into view, he considers it irrelevant, from a functionalistic point of view whether stability, is achieved by consensus, violence or other moments. I shall understand the functionality of institutions, of their norms and organization as a test of their effectiveness from the point of view of the guiding ideas.

becomes the driving force of social dynamics with an open program and with emergent features.

Functional analysis as an element of critique. In political and ideological argumentation, slogans and simple theses, presented as self-evident, play an important part and, as I see it, often a deceptive one. If for a clarification one employs, in addition to conceptual-analytical reflections, also functional analyses, one will gain the distance required for critique, and elements of objectivity will be introduced into this – otherwise so subjectively determined – field.

I would like to illustrate this with a few examples which show the interplay taking place here between conceptual and functional analyses. If one pleads for the political ideal of freedom, of free self-determination of people – an ideal probably found attractive by everyone – one will not find it hard to find agreement for the view that everyone should determine his life-plan as he wishes and should realize it with as little hindrance as possible. And therefore the postulate of maximum freedom for all, as far as it is compatible with the same freedom for everyone else, seems to be generally acceptable. And yet a concept-analytical consideration shows that this liberalistic ideal (e.g. as formulated by Kant) is wholly indeterminate. As soon as freedom is viewed in the context of social relations, there is no freedom pure and simple, no licentiousness for one's own wishing and willing, but only different freedoms, dimensions of being free in relation to other freedoms. Between the various types of freedom there are relationships, and one type can work out in the factual social context as limitation of some other freedom. Absolute economic freedom may e.g. under the actual conditions of life imply major curtailments of freedom for the have-nots. Though having formally the same freedoms, the other one has no possibility to make use of them (for lack of property). Freedom is rightly demanded not only for the individual, but also for communities. – One freedom postulate generally accepted in democratic systems is the freedom of religion, and with it the right to freely exercise religious rites. But is such a blanket authority for religions really acceptable as an ideal of freedom, considering the well-known fact that some of these religious systems impose most rigorous limitations of freedom: e.g. the death penalty for drop-outs from the religious community, the clamoring for a holy war, for the annihilation of dissenters? – Although the global demand for maximization of freedoms may remain justified insofar as uncalled-for curtailments of freedom and disposition ought to be avoided, the freedom postulate does not define the political program, since in the latter it is precisely the decision between different freedoms and their relative weighting which is at issue. Under the undifferentiated slogan of freedom, inacceptable limitations of freedom may well come about, as the example of religious freedom shows.

And one other example of great interest in our time: one demands freedom of information in every form. What comes out is often systematic indoctrination and spiritual-moral coercion, e.g. in the form of marketing methods in election propaganda.[37]

One of the best-known slogans of political theory is Adam Smith's thesis of the invisible hand which lets the individual's striving for profit serve the well-being and progress of the general public. This dictum by Smith is an intelligent and, for a certain field, correct simile. It expresses for the field in which it is valid a functionalistic relationship, namely the actual effects of the intentional behavior of individuals on the social level, with this social effect being an emergent event which did not form part of the contents of the intention leading to the action. Nevertheless this thesis must not be used as a universally valid rule: i.e. one must be aware of the limits of the functional relationship and make it clear that it would be wrong to conclude that a striving for personal profit will always benefit society as a whole and that this slogan, as a political program, embodies the solution of all social problems. There are social problems which are not solved at all by the invisible hand, or at least are not carried toward an optimum situation, e.g. environmental problems. Moreover it seems to me that today wholly different elements have assumed a major role for

[37]See chapter 10.

characterizing the economic processes: organizations reducing competition, power factors in economic life, economic criminality (mafia), armament and war, and the transformation of the social information system.

Neither sociological individualism, nor holism. Neo-institutionalism does not fit into the scheme which divides sociological theories into individualistic and holistic ones, with the latter explaining the behavior of individuals as functions of the effect of social moments on the individual, while the former try on the other hand to explain the social phenomena and institutions as phenomena out of the character and the action of the individual (i.e. the personal) elements of the communities. Neo-institutionalism chooses a third way: the institutions are viewed as independent entities with an ideal texture of their own; the constructive role of the individuals (i.e. of the personal elements of the institution) in the construction of the institutions, as well as the determination of the subjects and of their manner of behavior by institutions become partial moments of the institutional reality.

The differentiatedness of the institutions. There is such a great variety of institutions – constituted as they are for different tasks and, as it were: in different spirits – that it is neither meaningful nor reasonable to postulate identical organizational forms for them. On the contrary: if organizations are to be efficient, they must be tailored to their respective tasks and thus must differ from one another. If some theoreticians of democracy define collective ruling as democratic and contrast it to the monocratic form of decision-making, this does not appear adequate, since this manner of defining implicitly calls for collective forms of decision-making everywhere. If the institutions are to be effective, their organization and manner of decision-making must be adapted to the "work" (as meant by *Hauriou*). Hence monocratic decision-making is sometimes quite expedient and can e.g. by checks and balances (i.e. functional balances of the structures) be subjected to the democratic ideals.

Chapter 10

The Democracy Problem from a Neo-Institutionalistic Point of View

Just what democracy is can on the one hand be explained by an approximative elementary characterization, or else one may try to present explicative theories which, although far more definite and concrete, in reality pin down only partial aspects of this structure of society. Probably the most incisive presentation of the general tenor of the democratic systems is furnished by *Lincoln's formula*: "Democracy is government of the people, by the people and for the people". Society and the state are not a dominion of a ruling dynasty, a church or some other institution, but a field of popular self-government. The objection that Lincoln's formula is nebulous and far removed from any recipes for its realization is undoubtedly justified, but the formula does not aspire to be or do anything of the sort; it offers no instructions for political action, but merely articulates ideas and ends to be pursued by a political program. The many and manifold partial theoretical descriptions contribute to an understanding of democratic reality, and some of them have even had a non-negligible influence on the practice of political action. The palette of these theories is rich indeed, varying as it does from the opinion that democracy is pseudo-autonomy to *Habermas's* conception of discursive democracy.

10.1. Against romantic conceptions of democracy

A great many theories of democracy have been developed against a background of romantic views, exemplified by theses of the type "Vox populi, vox Dei", "The people cannot err" or by the philosophical conception of the philosophy of discourse, according to which processes of discourse ensure the path to the true and to the correct.

Neo-institutionalism does not look at democracy from a romantic point of view. The belief is erroneous that the people know and need to know just what, in the people's interest, are the optimal solutions to political problems. It is meaningful and necessary to analyze interests, to view them in their functional relationships, and to weigh them in the corresponding cognitive framework. The solutions to social problems cannot be proposed by the popular masses; rather, they are products of individual personalities or specialized groups. The evaluation of social measures depends on pieces of information, analyses of consequences, and value-experiences which as a rule are not accessible to the mass of the people. Furthermore, the value orientations of the masses are to a high degree susceptible to manipulation. Popular masses can even be made to enthusiastically opt for total war, although hunger, millions of dead, and other consequences of war hardly correspond to the well-founded interests of the people. The romantic conception of democracy rests on the wholly implausible assumption that, while the individual has to decide on the basis of pieces of information and systematic analyses, collective decisions will, in contrast, hit upon the right thing "purely instinctively". The heuristic and critical function of discursive processes for democratic life can hardly be contested, but the assumption that such processes – e.g. in combination with a majority consensus – will produce rational and optimal decisions is a piece of democratic romanticism which neo-institutionalism rejects.

10.2. Some explanatory models of democracy

Kelsen and *Weyr* are of the opinion that, while democracy cannot ensure the autonomy of every individual, it does mean a minimization of collective curtailments of the individual citizen's autonomy. For, they say, democracy is committed to the idea of freedom, and the majority principle guarantees the closest possible approximation to the freedom of all. However, a majority decision may under certain circumstances entail, in substance, greater curtailments than the rejected alternative. If the votes are divided over various conflicting opinions, the alternative gaining a majority may not optimally express the wishes of the individual voters. While the majority principle does not guarantee an optimal approximation to what the individual citizens want, it is, however, acceptable and unavoidable as *ultima ratio* of collective will-formation.

Such formation of a collective will is always dependent on previously established norms which regulate this process and legitimize its result as a valid decision of the collective will.[1] Norms must be stipulated in advance to determine the circle of persons entitled to vote and for the voting procedure. In the case of elections the important things are first and foremost the nomination of the candidates and the stipulation of norms for the balloting process. Perfect adjustment to the voters' will can only approximately be achieved. In the case of votes about non-personal issues there are even far greater complications: a) one can only vote about such alternatives as are presented; b) by voting one cannot invent possible alternatives; c) the decision about one point changes the relative evaluation of other points of the

[1] O. Weinberger, Abstimmunslogik und Demokratie (Voting Logic and Democracy), in: B. Sutter et al. (eds.), *Reform des Rechts* (Reform of Law; Festschrift on the Occasion of the 200th Anniversary of the Faculty of Law, University of Graz, Austria), Graz, Austria, 1979, p.505–623.

complex that must be decided about; d) the sequence of the questions to be decided about by voting changes the preferences entertained for the subsequent ones, and hence the outcome of the vote; e) individual preferences cannot be unequivocally transformed into a collective system of preferences corresponding to the majority – as shown by the *Arrow paradox*;[2] f) in the political practice a deception is frequently provoked concerning the actually existing relationships, namely by the nature and formulation of the questions, particularly by the combination of seveal questions to a whole.

A highly influential model of democracy is *Schumpeter's* model of competing elites. Schumpeter's model proceeds from a realistic view of the political-parties democracy.[3] Factual control is always exercised by elites, which in a competitive struggle for electors' votes vie for predominance. The voter's will comes into play by the fact of his vote's deciding about the power of the competing elites. Party propaganda becomes the goal and the essential content of everyday political life. The effort to capture the voters' favor frequently assumes dubious forms: personality cult, manipulation, granting of socially unjustified favors and the employment of marketing-like propaganda. The struggle for electoral votes is undoubtedly a piece of democratic reality, but certainly only a partial aspect of democracy in action. The model underestimates functional moments and the constructive force of the guiding ideas. The pragmatic consequences of *Schumpeter's* theory are often problematical. It is correct that the elites are democratically legitimated if they and their program are accepted by the voter; it is wrong, on the other hand, to regard precisely that political program as correct which will net one electors' votes. Such an attitude leads to our present-day democracy becoming pathological. *Schumpeter's* view brings about a profound demoralization of the political practice and tends to make broad strata of the population

---

[2]K. J. Arrow, *Social Choice and Individual Values*, Yale Univ. Press, New Haven, 6th ed., 1973 (1st ed. 1951).

[3]J. A. Schumpeter, *Kapitalismus, Sozialismus und Demokratie* (Capitalism, Socialism and Democracy), 3rd ed., Munich 1972 (1st ed. 1946).

sick and tired of democracy. The belief in *Schumpeter's* model often leads to a policy of partiality and of candies for voters as well as to boundless political propaganda. *Schumpeter's* theory overlooks essential moments of spiritual identification with the institutions and leads to something much criticized: populism.

The problems of democracy have been closely related from two sides to economics: by bourgeois economism and by Marxism. *Downs*[4] and other thinkers try to explain the behavior of people in a democracy as an economic weighing process: the relations of the ruling to the electorate and the behavior of the voter are interpreted as profit maximization. While this makes sense as a partial observation, such a conception is not a realistic presentation of an overall politicological view. It simply is not true that people can only be won over to measures which cater to their personal interests. Money and economic utility considerations are resorted to to explain the motivation of people and are made the exclusive yardstick of correct action. Democratic-humanistic ideals are underestimated as social forces; social values and the reality of the quest for social justice and of solidary behavior are left out of consideration, although no adequate understanding of social reality is possible without taking these moments into account. Nor is *Downs's* assumption coming true that the economic motivation of democratic behavior will lead to economic equalization.

In the Marxist view, it is the production conditions which are the prime determining factor for the structures of society, the social relations, and the evolution of society and culture. Spiritual and cultural matters, norms, values, etc. are functionally connected with the material world as its superstructure and are explainable from economic moments. This basic view is being linked with the thesis that the problems of democracy are to be subordinated to the idea of the class struggle and that a corresponding reshaping of economic relations is a precondition for effective democracy. This thesis of the

---

[4]H. Downs, *Ökonomische Theorie der Demokratie* (Economic Theory of Democracy), Mohr, Tübingen 1968 (original: 1957).

ultimately determinant role of the economic basis is wrong,[5] because there exists no such thing as a material basis independent of ideal moments such as knowledge, know-how, inventions, value conceptions and orientations to ends. The forms of production are always co-determined by normative regulatory and organizational forms, and a separate characterization of the economic factors as supposedly independent ultimate reasons for everything happening in society is not possible at all.[6] The only thing this theory is right about is the fact that economic problems – the social determination of people's economic positions – are of essential relevance for democratic life. But it is not only a bipolar class-struggle structure which is decisive here: likewise of importance are differentiated functional relationships within the social institutions as well as other problems inherent in the power constellations.

Marxism as the "official philosophy" of the socialist countries – but not every Marxist – adheres (or adhered) in the practice to the view that the postulate of living in democratic forms has to yield to the demands of the class struggle, which is waged as and calls for a dictatorship of the proletariat. The searching plurality of opinions is repressed, in central points even eliminated, something which, in my opinion, is hardly conducive to the cause – namely the unfolding of socialism – of these systems themselves.

The democratic society is a complex of groups with highly differentiated interests. These groups are by no means disjunct classes;

---

[5] "According to the materialistic view of history, the determining moment in history is, in the final instance, the production and reproduction of actual life." (F. Engels, Letter to Conrad Schmidt of 5 August 1890.)

[6] Cf. O. Weinberger, Rechtstheorie jenseits von Idealismus, Realismus und Materialismus. Ein Plädoyer für den normativistischen Institutionalismus (Legal Theory Beyond Idealism, Realism and Materialism. A Plea for Normativistic Institutionalism), paper read at the International Colloquium on "Materialism and Idealism in Legal Thought" in Weimar, GDR, 2nd April 1986), in: K. A. Mollnau (ed.), Materialismus und Idealismus im Rechtsdenken.Geschichte und Gegenwart (Materialism and Idealism in Legal Thinking. History and Present), *ARSP*,special issue 31, 1987, p.16–26.

rather, an individual will frequently belong at the same time to several interest groups: he will e.g. be a member of a professional group (as e.g. a civil servant, mechanic, farmer, etc.), of a social group (as an unskilled worker, entrepreneur, scientist, etc.), of a church, a national or ethnic group, etc.

In a modern democracy there exist corresponding interest organizations whose task it is to articulate group interests and bring them to bear. The democratic system is viewed as a complex of such interest organizations, and the process of bringing these interests to bear and of elaborating realizable compromise solutions is regarded as a component of such democratic practice. A workable balance or an adjusting compromise between the interest-defined pressure-groups is regarded by some political scientists as a structural characteristic of modern democracy. The pressure-group theory describes one aspect of present-day democratic life and explains important formative processes, but it does not furnish an overall picture of the democratic system.

10.3. Democratic will-formation and the guiding ideas of democracy

Democracy is at the same time

(a) *a form of government* – self-determination of the people through processes of collective will-formation,

(b) an *ideology* that can be represented as an open system of principles, value standards, values adopted, and preferences,

(c) *a broad system of social discourses* that are conducted by functionally different strata of society and that should proceed under open-society conditions.

As is well known, processes of democratic will-formation can lead to decisions which run contrary to important material principles of democracy. Democratic processes may be corrupted by propaganda, ideological indoctrination, or ideological slogans. Dictatorships are sometimes installed democratically or through manipulated, seemingly democratic processes. Principles touching upon the very substance of democracy may be destroyed by democratic process. An example: if the given interests are suitably shaped, i.e. tend to call for it – e.g. in the case of threatening unemployment – discriminatory measures are occasionally taken against individual groups (e.g. against foreign workers, or against non-members of political parties or of labor unions).

A democratic system can therefore only then function as such if, in addition to the rules by which processes of democratic will-formation are introduced in the first place, a system of postulates concerning the contents of democracy is likewise recognized and effective in society, and if there exist in this society democratic customs as well as a feeling for the value of democratic ideals.

In the spirit of the institutionalistic conception, the system of the postulates defining the contents of democracy may be regarded as guiding ideas of democracy which constitute the spiritual and moral core of this form of life. These postulates must not be simply set aside by formal process. They can and should, however, be subjected to social discussions and be developed further in discursive processes of will-formation. The material principles of democracy, or, in institutionalistic terms: the guiding ideas of democracy, are not strict rules prescribing one's behavior, but rather conceptions of ends to be pursued and regulatory ideas developed in concrete analyses. They point the way for evaluating the organization and for assessing the functionality of the institutions. An adequate consideration of the material principles will be ensured if and only if democracy is understood as consultation, discussion and critique, rather than only as a struggle for majorities.

The postulates as to the contents of democracy include *principles of the human-rights type* as well as those principles which are required for the social formation of an open society.

Since neo-institutionalism regards man as an agent, an acting person, all those factors appear to it as principles essentially touching upon the substance of democracy which determine man's possibilities of action. These action possibilities are determined by economic and social-structural moments. Therefore the discussion of *equality* and of *social mobility* belongs in any event to the basic problems of the democratic postulates. There will be no issue with *formal equality* as a principle of justice, whereas material equality is unrealistic and therefore not a practicable political objective.[7] The *objective of social adjustment* is, however, at least until a decent form of life commensurate with human dignity has been ensured, a fundamental requirement of democratic life. Over and beyond all this I wish to emphasize two further material principles: (a) the principle of *equal opportunity* in the formal sense, but also with the tendency of striving for genuine equality of opportunity; (b) if society is to be stable and life in it worth living, then it must be so structured as to offer, in principle, everyone the possibility to improve his or her living conditions. Democracy must never acquisce in the existence of hopeless situations such as they are found in some societies even alongside a high level of prosperity. *Man is a being capable of action, but also entitled to opportunities for action and possibilities for improvement.* The guiding ideas of democracy hence also comprise principles of social justice. *Democracy is a community striving for justice.*

I regard it as a characteristic feature of many undemocratic ideologies that they have a tendency to subordinate all life to one single goal; their thinking is marked by a singleness of purpose, with the goal being the Kingdom of God, the glory of the nation, socialism (or, put differently: the dictatorship of the proletariat), free enterprise, etc.[8] But the *conditio humana* and the nature of human choosing

[7]O. Weinberger, Gleichheitspostulate. Eine strukturtheoretische und rechtspolitische Betrachtung (Equality Postulates. A structure-theoretical and legal-political investigation), in *ÖZöR* (Österreichische Zeitschrift für öffentliches Recht = Austrian Public-Law Journal), 25/1974, p.23–38.

[8]Cf. O. Weinberger, Monofinale Ideologien. Die moderne Gesellschaft zwischen Offenheit und Fundamentalismus, in: K. Weinke et al. (eds.), *Bedrohte Demokratie*, Graz 1995, p.223–237.

and evaluating are of a different structure: a persons's ends, values and principles cannot – unless reason and prudence are abandoned – be reduced to a single, absolute basic principle. Man lives under a plurality of ends and values which must be heeded in a balanced way, and every principle, in my opinion, has its limits and can be subjected to a relative weighing against other principles.[9]

Viewing the material principles of democracy as guiding ideas of the institution 'democratic state' does not yet ensure the elimination of the immanent dilemma of every democracy, namely the factual conflict between the autonomy of the popular will and the guaranteeing of the principles concerning the substance of democracy. The danger that exists as a matter of principle, namely that through a formally unimpeachable democratic decision certain principles concerning the substance of democracy (e.g. certain tolerance principles, such as religious freedom) will be abolished, continues to exist.

Democracy is forever endangered, and these dangers cannot be excluded by the proposed theoretical construction. All that follows from the theory is the memento to give priority to the protection of the material principles, to institutionalize the discursive unfolding of the guiding ideas, and to think up measures through which, with popular autonomy nevertheless being maintained, democracy will function in the framework of the guiding ideas. This is absolutely possible (even though not absolutely ensured), for we know that guiding ideas have a highly determinative role in the life of institutions.

The structure of the institutions must be so determined functionally that it satisfies both the guiding idea of the work to be accomplished, i.e. the institution's social role, and the general democratic guiding ideas. In determining the structure of the institution the following criteria need first and foremost to be observed: a) an adequate distribution of competences, through which efficient control and

[9]Thus I plead for a morality of optimization in a plurality of viewpoints and values. (This is by no means the *communis opinio* of the ethicists.) There is no single absolute principle of the good; all principles can under certain circumstances be outvoted by others.

a democratic limitation of power must be ensured; b) the effectiveness of a system of internal and external checks as an indispensable element of action guidance; c) the motivating effect of the structures on the behavior of the participating persons.

The institutionalistic thesis of the differentiatedness of the institutions has the effect that no uniform organization form is regarded as democratic; rather, it is demanded that such forms be chosen which promise that the institutions will be effective in the spirit of their guiding ideas.

Transparency is always an essential postulate with respect to public life in a democracy. (All the more must personal privacy be protected.) Transparency of political events is a precondition both of the possibility of public opinion formation and of all checking processes.

From an action-theoretical point of view, checking is an essential component of every action program and of every organization of effective institutions.

Now it forms part of the essence of action that the result of the acts performed in its course may deviate from the intended result. Deviations from the goal of the action have two sources: (I) uncontrolledly varying influences of the environment, and (II) imprecision or faultiness of the performance of the action. – Deviations from the goal are unavoidable and cannot always be blamed on the agent. Cause for blame does exist, however, if the agent proceeds without sufficient control, be it self-control by the agent himself, or socially organized supervision such as must accompany every social action.

The theory of control is aware of the possibility of deviation in action and of the need for checks. It works therefore with feedback programs. However, feedback programs cannot always be applied, since sufficient knowledge of the possible deviations and of their causes is frequently lacking. Checks and corrections are always necessary, however.

In the field of social action the control problem assumes a complex character. It is only through their organs that bodies corporate and other administrators or operators of community action are able to act at all. The acts attributed to such administrators or operators of social action are realized by individual human beings or by collegial organs. The human being acting as an organ performs an action deliberation in the spirit (i.e. in conformity with the ends) of the subject as whose organ he is acting. The interests of the institution in whose name a functionary acts, and his own interests as a member of the institution or as an individual human being will in part overlap, but in part they will also differ from or even conflict with one another. Such a conflict between the interests of the functionary and those of the institution on whose behalf he is acting may lead to a malfunctioning of the organization and to deviatory actions of its organ.

It is frequently said that in dictatorships there is more dishonesty, corruption and abuse of political functions than in a democracy, and that the chances of their being uncovered are greater in the democracies, since here the functionaries are subject to control by the opposition, as well as by the general public. It must not be overlooked, however, that in the political-party democracies factors occur which work in the opposite direction: (a) Every political party strives to present a clean record, which fact makes for an unquestionable tendency to cover up malfunctions of and lapses by the party's own functionaries. (b) Between the functionaries of political parties (or of labor unions, or of chambers of any kind) there exist – probably necessarily so – certain ties of collegiality. They must develop feelings of and behavior marked by solidarity. Hence it is absolutely understandable that we find mutual benevolence here. But this must remain within limits if democracy is not to go to ruin. The limit lies there where functions are abused for personal enrichment.

The essence of control or checking in a democracy can be characterized as follows:

(i) Checking is to be regarded as an immanent component of reasonable action both in individual and in social life practice.

(ii) Every social organization is to be designed as an action system equipped with control mechanisms.

(iii) In the case of social institutions, both internal and external political checks are required.

(iv) Various control methods may be considered. Transparency and checking must be anchored in the organization itself. Division of labor, adequate competence determination and the stipulation of certain incompatibilities[10] are necessary for the proper functioning of control and for limitation of power.

(v) The political control exercised must examine:

(a) The effectiveness of the organization and its functionality from the point of view of the relevant guiding ideas,

(b) the adequacy and well-balancedness of the goals set,

(c) the interpersonal relations in the institution under the aspect of fair assignment of roles, and furthermore:

(d) whether the structure of the organization and the positions of the persons in the institution are acceptable from the point of view of a democratic worldview, and

(e) the question must be asked whether the functions and competences are not applied abusively and whether the functionaries do not abuse their power primarily in furthering their own interests.

(vi) Democratic control is not merely hierarchical checking of subordinated levels by higher ones, but neither is it only critique from "below" vis-à-vis the 'powers that be'; rather it is both! It must be built up as a networked system in which, besides the political factors

[10] Such incompatibility of functions cannot always be formally stipulated in the political practice. For democratic functionaries and officials it should be a matter of honor to avoid the coincidence of functions that elude democratic and economic checking.

and organizations, science and the mass media as well as, at least potentially, every individual can also participate.

10.4. The idea of a discursive democracy. Democracy as an open society

Various currents in the development of modern democracy, and particularly the awareness that it is only in combination with rational opinion-forming processes that mere voting procedures will produce meaningful social decisions, have let to the discursive conception of democracy. Worth mentioning is here *T. G. Masaryk's* "Democracy is discussion" – interestingly supplemented by his memento "Vulgus vult decipi", answered by him with "ergo ne decipiatur".[11]

More recently, *Habermas* has come out in favor of a discursive theory of democracy.[12] This theory is based on Habermas's discourse philosophy, in which consensus in (ideal, domination-free and – approximately – in real) discourse is the criterion of rationality and correctness[13], and on a – somewhat problematical – theory of the legitimacy of law. It is not surprising, therefore, that the discourse theory

[11]Cf. O. Weinberger, Skizze einer funktionalistischen Theorie der Demokratie (Outline of a functionalist theory of democracy), in: J. Novák (ed.), On Masaryk. Texts in English and German, Studien zur österreichischen Philosophie (Studies on Austrian Philosophy)/3, Amsterdam 1988, reprinted in: O. Weinberger, *Moral und Vernunft. Beiträge zu Ethik, Gerechtigkeitstheorie und Normenlogik* (Morality and Reason. Contributions to Ethics, Theory of Justice, and Logic of Norms), Böhlau, Vienna et al. 1992, p.274–298.

[12]See J. Habermas, *Faktizität und Geltung. Beiträge zur Diskurstheorie des Rechts und des demokratischen Rechtsstaates* (Facticity and Validity. Contributions to the Discourse Theory of Law and of the Democratic Law-abiding State), Frankfurt a.M. 1992; O. Weinberger, Habermas on Democracy and Justice. Limits of a Sound Conception, in: *Ratio Juris*, vol.7, 1994, p.239–52.

[13]O. Weinberger, Der Streit um die praktische Vernunft (The Dispute about Practical Rationality), in: *ARSP*, special issue 51/1993, p.30–46; id., Basic Puzzles of Discourse Philosophy, in: *Ratio Juris*, Vol.9/1996, p.172–81.

of democracy, while plausible in itself, is linked up in this author's writings with quite problematical theses.

It sounds quite appealing – and democratic – when *Habermas* writes: "Certainly it is in the democratic process of legislation that legitimacy has its source" (p.117), but I do not know whether it is expedient to regard as illegitimate all law not generated in a democratic law-generating process. "If, however, discourses ... constitute the place where a rational will can take shape, then the legitimacy of law is based, in the final instance, on a communicative arrangement: as participants in rational discourses, those under a common legal system must be able to examine whether a disputed norm will or can find the consent of all those possibly affected by it!" (p.134) Here the problematical view – as I find it – of discourse philosophy that rationality is conceptually anchored in discourses becomes evident. The argumentation is moreover encumbered by the unclarity of the class "all those possibly affected". This class can hardly be called clearly determinable, but there is no doubt that many of 'those affected' will not be able to participate in the discourse (e.g. children, or future generations that are frequently affected by our decisions). If "will find consent" is toned down to "can find consent", the thesis becomes wholy unclear.

I also find it odd when the author says: "A legal system can only be legitimate if it does not conflict with moral principles" (p.137). Among the moral principles *Habermas* also counts human rights. However, he says, morality is not superordinated to law in a hierarchical sense. But since he regards morality as stronger than law in that the latter must not run contrary to the former, we actually do have morality taking hierarchical precedence here of law.

Habermas bases his democracy theory on the following theses:

1. Practical questions can be decided impartially (p.140). This, in my opinion, is problematical, since these decisions depend on value standards and preferences which are not given objectively, i.e. not given independently of attitudes and of factions within political parties.

2. "Those and only those action norms are valid to which all those possible affected can give their consent as participants in rational discourses" (p.138). The class of those potentially affected cannot be clearly delimited and will in any event frequently be different from that of the participants in the discourse. Moral solidarity is called for also toward those not capable of discourse. The Judeo-Christian morality emphasizes particularly the protection of widows and orphans, of the weak and disabled, in fact of all persons who would not be able to assert themelves in a discourse. Here the ethics of discourse fails. There is no reason why it should always be possible to achieve universal consensus.

3. "As 'rational discourse' one should consider *every* attempt to reach an understanding about problematical claims, provided the attempt is undertaken under communication conditions which permit the free discussion of topics and contributions, pieces of information and reasons within a public space established through illocutionary obligations." (p.138 et seq.). The assumption of an "illocutionary obligation" – in particular the preparedness to discursively defend every thesis – is not a necessary principle of communication. Forms of discourse imply neither an adequate rational analysis, nor the use of fruitful methods of research and argumentation. Discussion does not guarantee rationality (understood in a non-*Habermasian* sense).[14]

4. In morality discourses the argumentation assumes the form of the universalization rule (p.140). On the one hand, universalization is not unequivocally determinative, and on the other hand it is not sufficient to support all moral argumentations.[15]

5. Morality principles operate on the level of an *internal* state of a certain operational game, democracy principles, on the other hand, on the level of an *external* discursive shaping of opinions and wills (p.142). This distinction is similar to the traditional separation of

[14]For a critical view of illocutionary obligations, cf. also N. Rescher, *Pluralism. Against the Demand of Consensus*, Oxford Univ. Press, Oxford 1993.

[15]Cf. O. Weinberger, *Norm und Institution* (Norm and Institution), Manz, Vienna 1988, p.228 et seq.

morality and law; I do not regard this differentiation by *Habermas* as informative.

6. "Taking a morality of reason as their yardstick, individual persons test the validity of norms under the assumption that they are factually adhered to by everyone." (p.148). Such unrealistic assumptions – found also with other authors – are, in my opinion, neither necessary nor useful.

7. Private and public autonomy of the citizens are to be brought to bear with equal importance being attached to both. Habermas claims to have developed a discourse-theoretical autonomy concept which makes the internal connection between human rights and sovereignty of the people apparent (p.151). I regard Habermas's suggestions of an internal connection between human rights and sovereignty of the people as an unjustified and unfruitful assertion.

I concur with *Habermas's* opinion that social discourses and their adequate organization form an essential element of the democratic system and can even be regarded as a defining characteristic feature of democracy. I reject the view, however, that discourses as such constitute sufficient proof of the legitimacy and correctness of social decisions and standpoints.

Not making such assumptions about discourses as criteria of rationality and correctness as the philosophy of discourse does, I turn my chief attention instead to the study of the social conditions of the open society and to those moments which, particularly in our time, obstruct in the political practice the democratic discourse and destroy its rational-critical function in the same way as they thwart the democratic formation of a genuine political will. Rather than stipulating (like *Habermas*) only the unrealistic postulate of freedom from domination, I turn my critical attention instead to all eristic tricks and to the immensely effective indoctrination potentials which in modern democracies sap the genuine discourse processes of their progressive effect. I contrast *Habermas's* illusionary discourse optimism with a realistic-critical attitude. I, too, am in favor of discursive democracy and try to make it effective by fighting against the political indoctrination strategies which today pervert the democratic processes and create, instead of an open society, an indoctrination system.[16]

My view of discursive democracy emphasizes – partly in contrast to Habermas – the following moments:

1. Discourses have heuristic, critical and checking functions.

2. They provide democratic legitimation because they can end in consensus, but they are not proof of objective correctness. What has been legitimized by consensus or by decisions by supreme authority possesses validity at the moment, but not thereby alone objective validity as such.

3. What is decisive is that structures and procedures are created that conform to the ideals of the open society. They include, besides transparency in public matters, the existence of independent and free platforms for discussions, the separation of state and ideological institutions – such as, in particular, political parties and churches – as well as a general striving for objective and rational argumentation. Also, a truly active discussion climate must be created.

4. Scientists and philosophers – not only journalists – must have a voice in the social discourse, without anyone assuming that this will be the scientific, i.e., as it were, the correct opinion. Objective criticism and anti-eristic efforts must emanate from citizens whose profession it is to investigate and critically examine.

5. Democracy is to be viewed as a system which is able to a high degree to tolerate and put up with different opinions. It is a dynamic ideology in which social dynamics is based equally on a search for consensus and on critical analyses and dissent.

---

[16] O. Weinberger, *Habermas on Democracy and Justice. Limits of a sound conception*, op.cit.; id., Demokratieprobleme in der Informationsgesellschaft (Problems of Democracy in the Information Society, in H. Konrad et al. (eds.), *Staat = fad* (The State. A Dull Thing), Graz 1995, p.179–196; id., Zwei Hauptprobleme der modernen Demokratie (Two Major Problems of Modern Democracy), *JRP* 1995, p.1–9; id. Zur Theorie der politischen Argumentation (On the Theory of Political Argumentation), in: *Rechtstheorie* (Legal theory), vol.26(1995), p.163–4; id., Information and Human Liberty, IVR World Congress 1995 in Bologna, IVR Proceedings, in: *Ratio Juris*, Vol.9/1996, p.248–57.

10.5. Theory of political argumentation. Chances and dangers of the information society

Proceeding from a realistic approach to political argumentation, neo-institutionalism tries to develop the argumentation theory further and to highlight in a critical way the manner in which convictions are created in the modern democracy.

At least since *Aristotle* and the Stoics there have been systematic reflections about the furnishing of justification and proof for general structure-theoretical reasons. These considerations moved in two directions: the study of proof and proving led to the foundation of logic and to the theory of the systematic structure of the sciences, while reflections about the processes of justification and intersubjective persuasion led to the development of rhetoric and of its special branch: eristics.

The central question was the theory of proof and that of the construction of scientific systems, but already in antiquity the Greeks also developed practical instructions for successful argumentation by lawyers and politicians. In the field of pragmatic persuasion, a doctrine – eristics – was developed for teaching how, in a disputation, the weaker position can be made the stronger, i.e. the more convincing one.

In the modern development of the social sciences and the humanities, a great many thinkers became aware that not everything can be strictly proven, but that, instead, at many points of theoretical and practical reflection it is not so much strict proof, but rather justification in the form of 'making plausible' which carries weight. It is characteristic of these argumentation theories that they regard argumentation as an interpersonal process, hence as one coming exclusively within the field of linguistic pragmatics. With this I cannot concur. *The central question in argumentation theory is the relation between the objective validity of argumentations and the pragmatics of interpersonal persuasion.* Therefore the argumentation theory cannot be exclusively dealt with in the field of the pragmatics of persuasion;

rather, consideration must also and always be given to the objective structures of the subject field being treated and to what in this field has to be regarded as sound reasons. It is only under this condition that the sincerity of the quest for truth in and the social value of a discourse can be properly judged.

Two aspects of argumentation must, as a matter of principle, be distinguished:
1. the objective justification of theses and/or practical attitutes by means of sound reasons, and 2. the pragmatic processes of intersubjective persuasion.

It is only through distinguishing between these two aspects of argumentation that one can arrive at a practicable argumentation theory that can also say something about the validity of arguments and face up to the task, not only of ascertaining the formation of convictions through interpersonal processes, but also of examining the problem of whether these processes approximate objectively solid results.

If the argumentation theory is to make a meaningful contribution to the analysis of argumentation in social philosophy and in politics, then it is necessary to distinguish sound reasons from the persuasive acceptance-promoting strength of the argumentations. It is only if one pays attention to the double-faced character of argumentation: on the one side its objective validity and on the other side its persuasive effect, that one can arrive at a workable argumentation theory. In our consideration of political argumentations we are not only interested in the persuasive, conviction-creating effects, but invariably also in the question whether the argumentations and discourses lead to a social optimization of the knowledge level and of the decisions.

The question just what reasons are objectively sound is of course a highly complex one, and the answer will likewise be complex, for it will vary with the field of observation. It strikes me even as problematical whether an exhaustive answer can be given to this question at all. Since we have no complete catalog of possible problems and problem fields at our disposal, it will not be possible either to exhaustively represent a priori the processes of valid justification in the various possible fields. The methodology of each problem field determines just what in that field will serve as objectively valid justification. And this, too, may depend on the theoretical conception. But never can the determination of the objectively sound reasons be replaced by the ascertainment that a certain audience recognizes certain assertions as convincing reasons for a thesis.

A critical argumentation theory is blocked up from the very beginning if, in *Habermasian* fashion, one equates the quality of reasons with their pragmatic persuasive strength for an audience; and an evaluation of social discourses and opinion-forming processes as to their spiritual and enlightening importance would be rendered totally impossible by such identification. If one would not distinguish between sound reasons and persuasive effect, there would be no difference between the propagandistic activity of illusion-ridden fanatics, who – sometimes successfully – argue in support of witchcraft, racial supremacy or Holy War, and the well-justified ascertainment of historical facts, of economic inter-relationships or of prognoses (e.g. about tomorrow's weather or the threatening population explosion).

The ideal image of proof is the mathematical and logical proof. When I prove mathematically that $\sqrt{2}$ is not a rational number this thesis has been strictly proven. (Even logical proof need not be indisputable: it is possible e.g. to regard the adequacy of the logical system as problematical.) Not everyone will come to invent an appropriate method of proof, and even if proof is presented by one's partner in a dialogue, one need not recognize the validity of the proof. The objective validity of the proof and of the objective reasons given do not depend of their being accepted by the audience.

Not every thesis of an argumentation is strictly provable in a given situation. Nevertheless, purely objective reasons can be given to justify the thesis, e.g. by proving its content to be highly plausible. Thus the objective justification given will not always be strict proof, but it will always be based on sound reasons, such as experience, probability, coherence with other ascertained facts, and the like.

Wholly different is the type of argumentation we will arrive at when we consider argumentation as a process of persuasion between speaker and audience. Those and only those arguments will then be efficient which promote the acceptance of the thesis by the audience. Seen from this point of view, the arguments will not only have a relationship with the given topic, but also with the audience. Even objectively invalid arguments can create convictions, e.g. arguments *ex autoritate* or deceptive statements. Usually, objectively sound reasons will also be pragmatically good arguments.

In *searching argumentation* the partners in discourse will strive first and foremost at gaining true convictions and correct practical attitudes. This may be the case in a dialogue or in the address of a speaker before an audience.

In practice there are a great many situations in which the argumentation is not of purely searching nature, but where the person presenting the argument, because of his specific role, has been preassigned the task of coming out in favor of a given thesis, of a preassigned point of view, or of the interests of a person or group. In such a case, arguments will be sought that are likely to support the thesis and convince the listener of the truth or validity of the preconceived opinion.

For lack of a better term I call this interest-controlled or "advocatory" argumentation, but in doing so I neither wish to imply that the argumentation of lawyers is always of this nature, nor that this manner of arguing is realized exclusively by lawyers. This mode of thinking and argumentation occurs very frequently e.g. in argumentations by political parties or by advocates of specific interests.

In this advocatory manner of argumentation, self-critical reflections are avoided and counter-arguments evaded. One is only interested in making one's thesis prevail and in propagating it – often even regardless of whether it is true or false, correct or incorrect. The addressee of advocatory argumentation is not an equal partner in an intellectual search, but a mass of people whom the speaker seeks to influence and mold.

The borderlines between searching and interest-controlled argumentation are not sharp. Even if one has the task of defending certain interests and forcing them through, objectivity may be advantageous under certain circumstances and will often permit the finding of acceptable compromise solutions.

There are many possibilities to instill convictions by means of deceptive arguments, as is amply proven by advertising in business, which also proves that the borderlines between objective information, one-sided presentation, and deception are fluid.

Our age is rightly called the age of the information society. The volume of the information accessible to every individual has grown immensely, but so has the flood of information closing in on us – whether we like it or not. Now the question must be asked what influence these facts have on the idea of discursive democracy and its practical realization. I regard the effects of these facts as highly ambivalent.

The dissemination of information – on a social scale mainly realized by the mass media – is a precondition for rational democratic will-formation. However, the flood of data to which the citizen is exposed does not always consist of useful information for his practice of living and for his making rational decisions in his own interest, but rather amounts to a high extent on an exertion of influence in the interest of the sender – the advertiser, the political propagandist, or agitator.

Viewed politically[17], indoctrination practices and marketing methods are becoming so widespread in party-political life – and regrettably sometimes also in propaganda by the government – that balloting and voting results are more and more tending to reflect the effects of indoctrination rather than being expressions of the will of the citizens, hence of decisions "from the grassroots".

[17]We can leave the field of advertising in business out of consideration here, although it is, in a certain way, likeweise politically relevant, e.g. by its being imposed on the citizen in quite significant measure, particularly on TV upon the viewer, whose time it disposes of and whom it manipulates in his attitudes.

Political propaganda has a vast field at its disposal for the application of eristic – more or less deceptive – arguments. Mostly they are "half-truths", i.e. remarks calling attention to unimportant moments, and passing over the important aspects.

In view of the complexity of social and economic relationships, different interpretations are possible of the causes of social situations (e.g. of unemployment); and in the same way can the effects of proposed measures be prognosticated differently. The presentation of the motives for proposed measures is not only highly hypothetical (as every motive interpretation is), it can also be distorted on purpose.

I am of the opinion that this development constitutes an acute and serious threat to democracy, causing it to degenerate to an advertising strategy.

This view is often opposed with arguments propagating the idea of the mature citizen who is capable of choosing freely despite marketing propaganda and indoctrination. This defense of irrational propaganda and emotional indoctrination is false and consciously deceptive.

Man's deciding is not only rational-critical choosing, but a complex of emotional reactions and rationally evaluating considerations of preference. A defense of political marketing-like methods is consciously deceptive already for the reason that they are applied precisely because one counts on their extra-rational effect on the citizen.

For the following reasons, the citizen's critical attitude and maturity are only partially effective as means against marketing-like propaganda in politics.

1. Nobody, not even the most critical of thinkers, can escape the influence of communicative indoctrination. We are forced to absorb pieces of information whose effects we cannot escape. Having heard a hundred times that "Cats would buy Whiskas", one cannot help knowing that "Whiskas" is the name of a cat food, or feeling that it seems to be a good cat food. Acquaintance is created, and consciously forgetting is not possible.

2. It is not immediately evident from communications received whether they are true or not true. The addressee of political pro-

paganda or indoctrination has no possibility to verify all that propaganda claims, nor to subject a thesis to a critical discourse.

3. The relationships on which political decisions are based are complex and dependent on a variety of parameters. Usually it is a simple matter to present, as arguments, such half-truths as speak for the view the propagator wishes to make plausible. Only open social discourses can work as correctives, but in marketing-like propaganda they are excluded.

4. It is thought that the plurality of the information sources that become accessible in the information society will automatically lead to correction and optimization of opinions. This optimism strikes me as unfounded. If all or most information sources are tainted by the same systematic error, and if no objective check is interposed (cf. point 2), then the desired effect will not come about.

5. The electorate is not composed of critical and mature citizens, but is a conglomerate of people with different spiritual constitutions and different interests. The emotional marketing methods employed in political propaganda will therefore, at least with a large part of the citizenry, not fail to hit their mark, and they mean therefore a substantial shifting of the voting results.

I do not know whether there are any really effective instruments against political indoctrination. These methods should be morally proscribed. Platforms for open discourse should be created, and guidelines for critically resisting eristic methods ('anti-eristics', as it were) should be developed.

Most democracy theories have only pleaded for consensus processes and more or less demanded at least a basic consensus. In my opinion we should also create a culture of dissent, for spiritual and progressive political life is based on a dialectics of a search for consensus and of critical dissent.

Appendix

Homage to Georg Henrik von Wright

Precisely the fact that in this book I have frequently criticized von Wright's theses and have been trying to present a norm-logical and action theory which in various respects can be regarded as an alternative to von Wright's theory induces me to emphasize, in this appendix, not only the extraordinary merits of this thinker for the development of the philosophical analysis of action-related thinking and of the field of practical philosophy; I also wish to explicitly call attention to the highly important conformities existing between our respective objectives and attitudes in our research, while furthermore it will be my concern to show where our respective approaches differ and from this divergence between our methodological conceptions to explain the differences between our research results.

In my eyes there is no doubt that no other modern philosopher has achieved so much for the development of logical and methodological analysis in practical philosophy (in the broadest sense), nor has set so much into motion spiritually, as this author has. All of us who are interested in this field of practical philosophy have learned a great deal from him and – even more important in my eyes – have been stimulated to reflect about problems of logical and philosophical analysis in the field of the practice (i.e. of the action-related disciplines). For all this we owe him highest recognition and profound thanks.

I do not intend to present and to evaluate at this place the entire philosophical achievements of this famous author. Instead, I shall confine myself to his works in the domain which approximately since 1951 has been his central topic: the philosophy of the practice, and the logic and rational-analytical methodology of the practical fields. And here I feel a profound affinity of von Wright's philosophical interests with my own endeavors. My personal reflections, my critical analyses and my contributions pursued (albeit with modest strength) exactly the same goal: to bring the logical-philosophical theory ahead – as far as possible – in the field of the practice.[1] On the whole – except for a brief period[2] – von Wright proceeded from the independence of action-related thinking and emphasized the explanation of action in an intentionalistic conception. In the fields of the logic of norms (deontic logic), axiology and action theory he has presented an abundance of ingenious analyses and systematic treatises which, more than the works of any other thinker, have contributed to making such investigations and corresponding logical systems an established discipline of logical and philosophical research.

In view of our pursuit of identical research interests and of certain common basic tendencies in our attitudes on practical philosophy the question deserves to be asked why we nevertheless have arrived at such different views in some essential questions of the logic of norms and of action theory.

---

[1]My interest in this direction was not primarily awakened by von Wright, but by the recognition that the structure-theory of law presupposes the clarification of the underlying logical questions. In addition, the desire probably also played a part to be able to treat moral problems with the means of rational analysis. I was interested in particular in the structure of justifications, without expecting that the value problems of ethics could be solved by logical analyses. I have been a non-cognitivist all my life.

[2]I am referring here to the works from the period that von Wright – evidently under the suggestive influence of Kelsen's theory from his latest period – doubted the possibility of a logic of norms. Cf. in particular his address at the 1983 Helsinki World Congress of the IVR on "Is and Ought" (published in: E. Bulygin et al. (eds.), *Man, Law and Modern Forms of Life*, D. Reidel, Dordrecht/Boston/Lancaster 1985, p.263–281), and the article "Bedingungsnormen – ein Prüfstein für die Normenlogik" (Conditional Norms – A Touchstone for the Logic of Norms) in the festschrift in my honor 1984.

I believe that the chief difference between our respective approaches is to be found in our different views on the role of language in philosophical investigation, while furthermore there is the influence, apparently a quite radical one, Ludwig Wittgenstein has had on his pupil and friend von Wright.

If my interpretation is right, von Wright deviates in his views from Wittgenstein in that he regards philosophical problems not only as linguistic ones, but also, at least sometimes, as genuine material problems. In addition he is closer to logical positivism – without trying to make philosophy a specific branch of science – and he strives for attaining systematic rational reconstructions (the construction of specific logical systems). Philosophy is the explanation of our conceptual intuitions, says von Wright in his Intellectual Autobiography in the Schilp-Hahn volume "The Philosophy of George Henrik von Wright" (1987).[3]

My standpoint with regard to Wittgenstein and his conception about philosophizing – and indirectly with regard to von Wright's approach – is expressed in my address at the Wittgenstein symposiun, which I will now cite below, together with an appendix added subsequently.[4]

[3]This view does not strike me as wholly unproblematical inasmuch as our intuition (and the evidence connected with it) is partly a result of rational reconstruction. Intuition by and for itself cannot be grasped, so to speak. It becomes apparent, in my opinion, only from the analysis of the problem situation and from the subsequent constructive or reconstructive thinking.

[4]O. Weinberger, Tiefengrammatik und Problemsituation. Eine Untersuchung über den Charakter der philosophischen Analyse (Depth Grammar and Problem Situation. An Investigation into the Nature of Philosophical Analysis), in: *Proceedings of the 2nd International Wittgenstein Symposium 1977, "Wittgenstein und sein Einfluß auf die gegenwärtige Philosophie"* (Wittgenstein and his influence on present-day philosophy), Vienna 1978, p.290–297.

1. *Philosophical analysis and philosophical cognition*

What is philosophy? A system of assertions expressing specific insights, or an intellectual activity of a special kind? In the spirit of Wittgenstein it can be said that it is mainly a matter here of seeing and analyzing philosophically, i.e. that emphasis should be put on the activity of philosophizing. ['Philosophy is not a theory, but an activity.' TLP (Tractatus Logico-Philosophicus) 4.112] While I would agree that philosophy is above all investigating activity, the nature of philosophy can in my opinion only then be grasped correctly if one understands by 'philosophy' both: the activity of philosophizing as well as the systems of theses or recognitions resulting from such philosophizing.

The activity of philosophizing is traditionally called 'philosophical reflection'. The terms 'philosophizing', 'philosophical reflection' and 'philosophical analysis' desginate one and the same activity. Objects of philosophical analysis are intellectual and other human activities as well as their products. Through philosophical reflection, philosophical theses are gained which in relation to the analyzed activity are to be regarded as meta-propositions.

If the question is asked just what philosophizing is, just how philosophical analyses are conducted and just on what basis philosophical theses are justified, then one is moving, with regard to the analyzed object, on a meta-level of the second grade. Then one will be dealing with the theory of philosophizing, which I call 'metaphilosophy'.

It is important to pay attention to this stratification into analyzed activity – philosophical reflection – metaphilosophy, since one may be successful to varying degrees, on each level. It is possible to correctly perform the analyzed activity, while describing it incorrectly in one's reflection, and vice versa: one can perform the activity badly, but reflect upon it correctly and in this reflection even develop adequate methods for performing these activities. This applies analogously to the relation between philosophizing and metaphilosophy. One may present sound philosophical analyses, while inadequately describing the character of this philosophical analysis, with the reverse likewise being possible: one may know correct methods of philosophizing, but perform poor philosophical analyses.

No modern-age philosopher has influenced philosophical analysis more profoundly than Ludwig Wittgenstein. His main achievement lies in the perseverance and subtility of his investigations, which are exemplary. No less influential was his metaphilosophy. I contend, however, that his theses about the nature of philosophizing (I) do not conform to what he did himself, and (II) do not represent adequately what philosophy is and what it means.

2. *Countertheses against Wittgenstein's metaphilosophy*

I contrast Wittgenstein's metaphilosophical conceptions with the following countertheses:

1. his opinion that philosophy is merely a clarifying linguistic analysis with my contention that philosophy has its own specific material problems;
2. his view that philosophical analysis, as an investigation using the tools of depth-grammar, is a method of looking at language which I contrast with the epistemological and structural analysis of problem situations as a method having as its object, not primarily linguistic, but material relationships;
3. his postulate 'back to natural language' I contrast with my thesis that calling attention to the natural language does not offer a valid philosophical argument and that only an analytical-reconstructive treatment of problem situations provides philosophical conceptions and justifications;
4. his rejection of philosophical problems as mere obsession by language I contrast with my thesis that there are genuine philosophical

problems which are not merely empty plays with words, but which can, rather, be understood and analyzed on the basis of specific philosophical language-games.

3. Does philosophy deal with linguistic problems or with material ones?

If one proceeds from the positivistic view that cognition is nothing else but a well-ordered grasping of reality, then one will assign to every scientific discipline an object which – or whose partial aspects – it has to study. However, the various classes of real objects and the classes of aspects of real objects are each subject fields of the cognition of specific branches of science. Then there will be no specific object of philosophical cognition left. Thus, philosophy is left only with the secondary role of clarifying scientific concepts and theses as well as with the task of striking a balance of scientific research.

This view is in my opinion misplaced. (I) The sciences do not simply divide up the totality of real objects; rather, the field of scientific problems and research is defined by man's reflections as he looks at certain aspects and relationships of reality. (II) The sciences strive for nomological recognitions with fact-transcendent validity; hence, science is not mere registration of reality. (III) Undoubtedly, philosophical analysis also is charged with the role of conceptual clarification and interdisciplinary understanding, but one goes astray if one leaves the constructive role of philosophical reflection out of consideration. The role of philosophy is first and foremost to determine the questions to be asked by the sciences, to discuss the methods, and to understand the plurality of the scientific systems as a totality, as a system of systems. Thus philosophy has not merely a secondary and auxiliary function to fulfill for the sciences, but rather has guiding and constitutive tasks.

The positivist view outlined and criticized above certainly does not conform to Wittgenstein's theory. Nevertheless it seems to me that a certain echo of these conceptions – in particular of the neopositivist view that philosophy has a clarifying task rather than the task of gaining philosophical recognitions – can be found in Wittgenstein's writings. (Compare TLP 6.53, where philosophizing is presented only as protection of the borders of the expressible, i.e. of the propositions of the natural sciences against the surpassing of the linguistic possibilities in metaphysical theses. Furthermore: 'The purpose of philosophy is the logical clarification of thoughts.' ... 'The result of philosophy does not consist in philosophical propositions, but in propositions becoming clear.' – TLP 4.112) I believe that Wittgenstein's stand on this matter did not substantially change since then, as the following passages from the 'Philosophische Untersuchungen' (PU = Philosophical Investigations) seem to prove: "123. A philosophical problem has the form ... 'I don't know my way about'", "133. ... For the clarity we are aiming at is indeed complete clarity. But this simply means that the philosophical problems should completely disappear." (Problems of contents could not disappear, they would need solving.) "119. The results of philosophy are the uncovering of one or another piece of plain nonsense and of bumps that the understanding has got by running its head against the limits of language."

Wittgenstein interprets philosophizing as work in the domain of language, not as a search for contents-related and methodological conceptions (cf. PU 109: "... Philosophy is a battle against the bewitchment of our intelligence by means of language.").

Although Wittgenstein emphasizes that philosophizing is linguistic analysis, it should not be overlooked that actually he is not an advocate of this narrow linguistic conception of philosophizing, since, to him, language as a form of life is always to be understood in connection with the universe of the material and vital relationships. For the importance of Wittgenstein's language philosophy lies precisely in the fact that he analyzes language in the interplay of speech acts, intersubjective communication and real life situations. But once one has accepted this philosophy one must not stop there and merely call attention to these pragmatic elements; rather, one will then have to determine just what roles the various constitutive factors of the language-game are entitled to, in other words: one will then face the task of recognizing just what is linguistic convention and what depends of linguistic structures, just how epistemological critique intervenes in the analysis and how the conditions of intersubjective communication are to be judged.

For the following reasons, Wittgenstein's conception of philosophizing does not strike me as adequate:

1. Despite his demand for comprehensive linguistic analysis he does not succeed in clearly isolating the determining moments; in particular, linguistic conventions, the real structures of the field studied, knowledge critique and communication analysis are not clearly separated.
2. Wittgenstein understands his argumentation as depth-grammatical analysis, hence as a linguistic investigation, although his arguments proceed from contents-related analyses of the problem situation. The transition from the superficial structure to the depth-structure of linguistic utterances can evidently only be accomplished and justified through structural analyses of the real problem field.
3. Wittgenstein underestimates the creative role of philosophical investigations and does not express explicitly that in philosophical analyses one is dealing with the fundamental factual problems of the sciences, which form the structure of the scientific systems.
4. He regards philosophizing only as a therapeutical undertaking directed against the bewitchment of our intelligence by means of language (PU 109). In this endeavor, philosophy had the task of leading the words back from their metaphysical to their everyday usage (op.cit. 116). Philosophy was bound to the factual use of the language ("124 Philosophy may in no way interfere with the actual use of the language; it can in the end only describe it.")

While I regard the thesis as valid that every science and every philosophical investigation is language-dependent and that the question of communicability will always form an essential aspect of any scientific problem field, I nevertheless view the task of philosophical investigation as a material problem rather than merely as a linguistic one. This view leads to the question, however, just on what philosophical argumentation leans. I shall outline an answer to this question in section 4 below.

The essential difference between the linguistic conception and my view – with Wittgenstein occupying, in a sense, an intermediate position in that he recommends linguistic analysis, but performs what should rather be termed material analyses – will now be illustrated by me with the aid of a few examples.

a) When studying, as a linguistically oriented researcher, the problem of modalities, one will investigate the linguistic means for expressing modal assertions; one will then be satisfied with a theory which indicates a class of modal operators, stipulates definitorily their mutual relations and specifies the formation and deduction rules for modal propositions. If, however, one regards philosophy as critical and epistemological material analyses, one will not content oneself with the determination of the linguistic relationships. Rather, one will, on the one hand, determine the epistemological conditions for the use of modal propositions and, on the other hand, base the logic of modalities on a theory, such as e.g. the ideal construction of possible worlds.

b) A language-analytically oriented philosopher will e.g. treat the problem of the freedom of will in such a way as if it were a matter of finding an answer to the question 'What does it mean (or: What does one mean) when one says "The person A is acting freely"?' If, however, the problem of determinism is regarded as a philosophical-material question, then one will investigate the structure of the action seen as an information-processing decision process and will engage in knowledge-critical reflections about acting and about the conditions under which the behavior of persons can be interpreted as action. From such analyses and theories there will result certain answers to the given material problems, and not merely insights into habits of speech.

c) In my view of philosophical analysis, knowledge propositions – that is how I call sentences of the type 'A knows that p', 'It is known that p', symbolically '$K(p)$' – will no longer be determined by more or less plausible stipulations, such as e.g. the proposition '$K(p) \to (p)$'; rather, one will analyze situations of the application of such knowledge propositions and will test the epistemological conditions of the validity of such sentences. Only on the basis of such reflections can it be critically examined whether '$K(p) \to (p)$' is to be recognized as a fundamental proposition. (Compare my study "Wissensaussage und die Unmöglichkeit ihrer Objektivierung. Kann der Satz 'p' durch den Satz 'S weiß, daß p' begründet werden?" (Knowledge proposition and the impossibility of its objectification. Can the proposition 'p' be justified by the proposition 'S knows that p'?), *Grazer Philosophische Studien* (Graz Philosophical Studies), vol.1/1975, p.101–120.)

d) As a not solely linguistically oriented philosopher one will not construct a logic of norms simply as a more or less plausible language-game, but will rather try to base it on a theory that can be derived from the epistemological structure of the normative fields.

4. The source of philosophical argumentation

A philosophical theory is characterized first and foremost by the method of argumentation it employs.

Ordinary Langauage Philosophy, which can find support in various quotations from Wittgenstein about philosophizing, I wish to contrast with a conception that does not take a cue from Wittgenstein's metaphilosophical theses, but from the manner in which he philosophizes in actual fact. I call this view 'problem-situation analysis'.

In my opinion, calling attention to generally accepted (or: good) usage of language is not a valid argument in philosophical investigations. Linguistic problems, questions as to the meaning of certain expressions ('What does one mean when one says ...?') may in certain cases play a heuristic role and call attention to philosophical problems, but such problems do not, in my opinion, spring from the language or from the manner in which it is used, but rather from problem situations that should be subjected to critical epistemic analysis.

Wittgenstein's analysis amounts in the end to contrasting the superficial structure of linguistic utterances to a presentation in accordance with depth grammar. The superficial structure is revealed by the linguistic utterance as presented to us in speech acts. The depth-grammatical structure is a result of the analysis, or, as I would say: is a linguistic reconstruction of the utterance on the basis of the analysis. Wittgenstein's contrasting of depth grammar to superficial grammar actually excludes in principle that language itself could be regarded as a criterion of correctness, for this role should be played by the linguistic utterances in the form in which they confront us, i.e. with their superficial structure. This superficial structure, however, is regarded as deceptive, which is precisely why the depth structure is investigated.

How can an argumentation be built up which justifies the transition from the external superficial structure to the depth-grammatical structure? Evidently this can only come to pass by including into one's considerations also aspects which – though connected with the language and the speech acts – are not components of the speech (the linguistic utterance) itself. Arguments are – as I would like to describe it – the problem situations into which the linguistic utterances are embedded. Wittgenstein's conception thus rightly says that language can only then be analyzed and understood if the speech acts are seen in connection with life- and communication-situations. It must be added here, however, that the analysis and the argumentation by which the depth structure is determined are critical epistemological and communication-theoretical reflections as well as a structural consideration of the problem situation.

By 'problem situation' I mean primarily the thought-historical circumstances which give rise to a problem and provide motivation for reflections, scientific investigations or possibly even the coming into being of new scientific discipline. Thus understood, a problem situation also includes the means available for the study and the solution of the given problem, be they technical means, or insights constituting an advance stage or serving as instruments of the analysis, or social-organizational research conditions. The problem situation in such a thought-historical sense offers us a certain examination result and confronts us with a task – which initially will as a rule be only imprecisely determined.

These starting points for our investigations may be of quite different nature. In any event, however, they will furnish a pre-assigned framework for our considerations. We live in a structured field of experiences and opinions, be they trivial theories of everyday life, scientific systems, or religious orientations. The problem arises either from practical (e.g. technical, economic, social) or scientific needs and tasks, or doubts may have arisen for one reason or another as to the correctness of established theories, thus necessitating attempts to devise new theoretical constructions for grasping the relationships of the given field, or, finally, a new approach may be invented.

While it is possible to distinguish various ways in which scientific and philosophical problems can come into being, these are only ideal-typical characterizations, between which there are no sharp dividing lines. A few examples of thought-historical problem situations:

a) When Wittgenstein was facing the task of considering language not only as an instrument for the presentation of states of affairs, but also as an instrument for interpersonal communication which one must learn to play, he had, in order to solve the problem situation, to elaborate new language conceptions. This newly emerging problem led to Wittgenstein's philosophy of his later period, which dealt with questions that were of another type than those investigated in his 'Tractatus' and for which therefore the purely descriptive language presented there was not sufficient.

b) At one time in history a technique had to be developed to fire most effectively at manoeuvering aircraft. This was the task and primary problem situation from which cybernetics has come forth. This example is particularly instructive, because it shows that problem situations will especially in those cases have far-reaching scientific and philosophical consequences where they stimulate the finding of new theoretical approaches. In this case it was a matter of placing the analyses of pieces of information alongside the consideration of material-energetic processes and of elaborating a theory of target-oriented missile-guidance processes.

c) The justification problem in ethics and legal theory, coupled with the recognition that the logic of descriptive language cannot be applied here, has led to the coming into being of the logic of norms.

However, the thought-historical problem situation determines only the basis and direction of one's considerations, while the actual object of the philosophical analysis is the problem situation in a structural and epistemological sense.

It is impossible to present a general description of a problem-situation analysis or universally applicable instructions for such analyses. The determination of the approach to be used in problem-situation analysis would have to proceed from a typology of all problem situations. It seems difficult to elaborate a fitting typology, and even impossible to gain the conviction that a proposed typology is complete. Here, in any event, only rudimentary work can be done. For the great variety of possible analyses, in any event, such distinctions have been resorted to as e.g. the separation of formal and material problems, or the semantic distinction between descriptive and practical sentences (norm-sentences, value-sentences). Suggestions as to how one should proceed in a problem-situation analysis would have to be differentiated according to this typology. Under no circumstances, however, do these instructions form an adequate replacement for the required insight as to how the essential structures of the problem field can be found out. Aspects of critical epistemology and communication theory must always be taken into consideration simultaneously.

A closer characterization of problem-situation analysis is not possible within the framework of this article, for this can be meaningfully accomplished only with the aid of a voluminous stock of examples, such as I assume to be furnished in rich measure by Wittgenstein's philosophical anlyses. Be it noted, however, that I do not interpret his language-game analyses as language analyses, but as structural analyses of the problem field. It is not merely a matter here of a difference between the terms 'language-game analysis' and 'problem-situation analysis', but of fundamentally different metaphilosophical conceptions, as may be made clear by the following comparison of the common and different features of both views.

Both views have in common that typical situations are analyzed structurally, epistemologically and communication-theoretically. A further common feature is the view that in principle different conceptual (linguistic) frameworks may be built up, but that a useful framework for a specific life-situation or task will depend in essential respects on the structure of the given field and on the given task. In both conceptions of philosophical analysis, linguistic and non-linguistic aspects are investigated in their mutual interrelationships. In both conceptions the determination of the meanings of terms and complex linguistic utterances is tied, in full mutual agreement, to the characteristics of the relevant problem field, rather than being derived *in toto* from ordinary or scientific language.

Not clear to me is the question whether Wittgenstein believes that, varying with how the given problem field is viewed, language-games can always be reconstructed [cf. PG (= Philosophische Gedanken = Philosophical Thoughts) 140; PU (= Philosophische Untersuchungen = Philosophical Investigations) 492, 569; Z (= Zettel = Notations Slip) 320], or, on the other hand, that language-games are sociologically and culturally conditioned frameworks that cannot be changed and must not be changed by the searching philosopher (cf. PU 124). As one sees, supporting passages from Wittgenstein's texts can be found for both mutually conflicting views. Wittgenstein's tendency to interpret philosophical problems as an abuse of language strikes me as being based on the sociologizing conception.

If one interprets Wittgenstein's theory in such a way as to proceed from his 'Philosophische Untersuchungen' (Philosophical Investigations) 124 ('Philosophy may in no way interfere with the actual use of language it can in the and only deccribe it.'), then there exists a striking difference between Wittgenstein's theory and my view of problem-situation analysis.

The possibility of argumentation through invoking 'natural' or 'good' speech usage, as well as postulates of the type 'Back to ordinary language!' are ruled out from the point of view of problem-situation analysis, for the structures that can be found in the problem field are criteria for the adequacy of the language-game; it would be wrong to draw upon the language, such as it has been factually institutionalized, as a yardstick for the permissibility of approaches. True, it is possible to say that, in a given field, structures do not exist by and for themselves, but are rather constituted by the approach and the language used. The possibilities of establishing structures in a problem field are in the nature of setting-up language-games and depend in essential respects on the properties of the given field. But the thesis that the structures in the problem field are established by the approach and the language-game must under no circumstances be interpreted in such a way as if the socially existing language system – the ordinary language – were the yardstick and limit of possible philosophical considerations.

There occurs a major shifting of weight when instead of 'language-games' one starts speaking of 'problem-situation analyses'. One's central attention is then shifted from speaking about things to the question of the structure of these things and to epistemic critique. By this it is made clear that philosophical analysis is always concerned primarily with relationships of substance and never merely with linguistic phenomena.

Viewing philosophizing as problem-situation analysis is related in the following ways to other philosophical conceptions:

(I) The relationship to empiricism: the empirical basis is taken into account in the field of preliminary orientation and practical validation testing. Furthermore there is a valid requirement that epistemic critique must explicitly bring out the empirical basis and the possibility of making the theoretical conception useable by empirical operations. (II) This view comprises a pronounced moment of a conventionalistic nature, for the network of concepts (language-game) is presented in the form of stipulations. (III) Essential features are taken over from the criticistic school of thought. The analysis seeks an answer to the question just how experience is possible in the studied field, with this possibility being understood both structurally and epistemologically. Unlike the criticistic approach, which assumes one and only one structure existing a priori, my conception allows for competing frameworks. (IV) There also is a certain relationship with ordinary language, which is viewed fundamentally different, however, from the way Ordinary Language Philosophy looks at it. Ordinary language, while not being an argument, is on the one hand assigned a heuristic function, while on the other hand it is respected as the basis of which the pragmatic usability of the construction in the process of interpersonal understanding depends.

5. Are there genuine philosophical problems?

In the 'Tractatus' phase of his thinking, Wittgenstein regarded the traditional philosophical basic problems as not rationally tractable, because they cannot be expressed in the language of his 'Tractatus'. ('Actually the correct method of philosophy would be: to say nothing except what can be said, hence propositions of the natural sciences' – TLP 6.53. 'What one cannot speak about, one must remain silent about.' – TLP 7). Later he defends the view that philosophical problems come into being precisely because language, created as it was for use in normal practical communication and working perfectly as it does in this role, is being used in alienated fashion. To Wittgenstein, the traditional philosophical problems are, in their totality, not justified and urgent questions, but rather products of inadequate use of language.

If one does not regard the efforts for a clarification of fundamental philosophical questions only as pathological speculation, but feels at least some of these problems to be genuine tasks, then one will seek another conception. Such a conception can, in my opinion, remain wholly in the spirit of Wittgenstein and actually will conform better to his basic positions than a sweepingly negative attitude towards the philosophical problem tradition which – actually without convincing analyses – he proclaimed himself. If, throughout the range from astonishment to the formulation of fundamental problems of science and of epistemic discussion of methods, there exist life-situations in which we perform intellectual work while also conducting exchanges of opinions with our fellow-men, then philosophical reflections – perhaps not all, but many of them, – can be understood as thoroughly meaningful argumentation on the basis of specific language-games.

This is the view I would like to advocate, for such questions as the induction problem, the explanation of the fact-transcendence of cognition, the determinism problem, the criticistic enquiries after the structural possibilities of experience, etc. strike me as inevitable, and everyday language – because of the peculiarity of the reflections involved – usually does not provide an adequate instrument for philosophical reflecting.

It has been pointed out (e.g. by Prof. Anscombe) that actually it is not possible to philosophize in the Wittgensteinian way, hence to continue his philosophy. Is this merely the case because of the wholly special nature and greatness of his thinking and his personality? I do not think that this is the sole reason.

1. It is necessary to pass beyond Wittgenstein, else one will not be thinking in his spirit, which always proceeds from the positing of ingenious problems and opens up new vistas. Such 'going beyond Wittgenstein' I perceive particularly in the demand to isolate the factors of the language-game.

2. One must not proceed according to Wittgenstein's instructions, nor according to his metaphilosophy, but should orient oneself rather to the pattern set by him. It is only if one succeeds in discovering interesting problem situations and approaches which lead to philosophical problems being clarified and mastered that one will gain philosophically valuable results, and not if one contents oneself with the

ascertainment of speech usage and with the linguistic-semantic interpretation of linguistic forms of expression.

3. Philosophical problems must not be dismissed as mere effects of one's being bewitched by language – or more precisely: by an eccentric use of language –, and one must not delude oneself with the hope that through a return to ordinary language the philosophical problems will really be made to disappear; rather, one has to find adequate language-games and structural theories for them in which they can be treated and explained. True, there exist metaphysical pseudoproblems – which can be brought to light by showing that they are not based on any genuine problem-situations –, but philosophical research must not be sterilized by antiphilosophical general clauses such as are constituted by Wittgenstein's criticized theses.

6. Concluding remark

I have played the philosophizing Wittgenstein off against the metaphilosopher Wittgenstein with his tendency toward ordinary language philosophy in order to break a lance for philosophy, which strikes me as being as much endangered by the natural-usage argument as by the thesis that philosophical problems arise only from distortions of such natural usage."

Appendix (written in 1995)

As Wittgenstein's language-game theory sees it, the normal language is, as it were, an open set of language-games. It is not a rationally and strictly uniformed system, but only a totality brought about through a loose basic grammatical structure and loose terminological relationships. The concept apparatuses of the individual language-game can be defined exactly through reconstruction. However, ordinary language as a whole is not a system that has been logically and conceptually ordered in a strict and conflict-free fashion.

If this opinion is correct, then this will have major consequences for the postulates of Ordinary Language Philosophy. The normal language itself cannot be an independent yardstick of philosophical thinking; the demand that nothing in normal language should be changed would – if taken seriously as a basis for philosophical analysis – render it impossible to build up clear and systematic theories, to reap the fruits of depth-grammatical analyses, and to derive profit from the language-game theory.

It is an evident consequence of the language-game conception that the normal language does not constitute a uniform conceptual system ordered as a totality. It therefore does not furnish an adequate basis for scientific (rationalized) investigations.

Von Wright is probably also aware that the tying of the philosophical construct to the language of the community, as Wittgenstein demands it, is not valid totally and unconditionally. (I believe this thesis of Wittgenstein's is hardly tenable if one accepts the fruitful thesis of depth-grammatical analysis, for it is only in the form in which it shows itself, i.e. in its superficial character, that the language of the community could reject reconstructions, but not if the outward form in which the language appears is replaced by the language's "real" structure, i.e. the critically constructed depth-structure.) Von Wright clearly sees that Wittgenstein's language-games do not always – in my opinion: actually do never – move only within the linguistic sphere, but frequently also comprise relationships with situations of substance.

Here we find an essential difference between my view and Wittgenstein's – and this difference applies also to von Wright's conception. What is constitutive is not the language-game (regardless of whether it also comprises relationships of substance or not), but the problem situation, from which it is necessary to proceed primarily. Here, however, language – expressibility – always plays a part as well, but a secondary one (and one which may usually be given different shapes). Put succinctly: what is essential is the problem situation, with language only being a means of presentation and communication here. Philosophy's task is analysis of substance, not of language.

The investigation, as I see things, does not proeceed from the language, but from problems of substance. This difference is a serious one, and it reveals itself also in the totally different approaches used by von Wright and in my outlook respectively.

The manner in which the system of deontic operators was constituted may serve as an example. Only in a linguistic perspective can the Ought and May operators be assumed to be relevant in the same way and to be mutually definable without limitation. If, on the other hand, norms are looked at from the point of view of their action-determining function, then the fundamental function of the Ought (a commanding or a forbidding one) in comparison with the May will become clearly apparent. On the basis of the relationships of substance it is a simple matter to realize that Permission (May) cannot be the suitable primitive concept for deontics, since a purely permissive system can have no regulating function, for regulation means the exclusion of behavior possibilities. Furthermore, in looking at things from the side of substance one will note that the definition of the norm-content can only be obtained through satisfaction functions which assign Ought contents to factual states of affairs. Since permissions can be neither satisfied, nor violated, there is no analogous way of determining the content of permissive sentences by means of a relationship with fact-describing descriptive sentences.

To von Wright, deontic logic is an offspring of modal logic. This I deem to be a consequence of the approach that proceeds from the language. If, in contrast, one regards norms as specific action determinants, then their selective function will become predominant (as is the case with all practical sentences). The construction of logical systems of practical reasoning rests on dichotomous semantics and therefore must be concerned first and foremost with Jörgensen's dilemma. Thus one will gradually get onto the path toward a genuine logic of norms.

Of two kinds of Ought and finally of a technical Ought one will speak particularly when taking primarily lingustic forms of expression as one's material for consideration. In an analytically corrective and reconstructive intention one will insist strictly on the clarifying separation of Ought sentences from sentences about Ought (or about norm systems). Then, a technical Ought will not have to be regarded as a type of Ought, but as a presentation form, with a linguistic shape of its own, of causal relationships.

Practical inference is looked at by von Wright from another perspective than I do because he regards the justification process of the action as a behavior-producing factor. Actions cannot be explained by causal rules. To this end, the "Why?", i.e. the reasons (motives) must be resorted to. And the realized action indicates the result of this process. I believe, in contrast, that the active, behavior-producing moment is present in the agent, presenting itself in his inclinations, intentions, goals or whatever one wants to call it. The deliberation and selection process is not the source of his action (does not produce his behavior), but is only the factor which determines the direction and/or the concrete content of the action. Therefore, I prefer to work, not with the practical inference as action conclusion, but with the theory of action determination through information. This strikes me as more adequate for two reasons: (I) because the respective perspectives – on the one hand; action deliberation, and on the other hand: interpretative explanation of actions – should be distinguished from one another, and (II) because in this way the problem of conscious vs. semiconscious and unconscious determination processes can be left out of consideration.

I have several reasons for not taking consciousness of the action determination as a characteristic feature of willing and of the teleological determination of the action. Already from our inner experience we know that the degree of our becoming conscious of determination in our action varies, without the action as an observable process thereby changing in great measure. In motive interpretation it often can hardly be ascertained just in how far there is question of conscious processes or of purpose-determined, automatic action. Structurally, collective action appears analogous to the action of the individual human being, although in the action of collectives there is no question of any acts of consciousness by the collective.

(Though *Nicolai Hartmann's* well-known contrasting of purpose-oriented action and expediency bases itself in essence on purpose-determined acting resting on acts of consciousness, I do not regard this delimitation as an adequate stipulation.[5] I regard the formal-finalistic view as far more favorable, since it is able to recognize the epistemological distinction of action analysis – into deliberation and interpretation –, and since it presents a structural theory of the "selection of means". In Hartmann's book, the argumentation mechanism of teleological reflection is only mentioned and given a name, but not analytically described. For all its valuable philosophical merits, Hartmann's book does not discuss the structure of teleological thinking – the argumentation of the choice of means – in any way.)

Admittedly, the psychological task of explaining just when (and in what function) teleological processes become part of our consciousness continues to exist. However, this, in my opinion, is not a task of formal action theory, but a problem of psychology.

In various works, particularly in "Norm and Action" (1963) and in "Freedom and Determination" (1980), von Wright has presented important analyses of human action. On the whole it can be said that he performed these analyses in the mirror of language, even though frequently paying attention to relationships of substance and obtaining results that often could be and have been used for a structural presentation. Undoubtedly, much can be learned from these considerations.

Since von Wright's analysis of the concepts that are connected with human action is oriented to a high degree to the normal language, important relationships have, to be sure, been clarified, but the systematic questions as to what concepts are required for an adequate build-up of action theory – and whether other ones, although customary in linguistic practice actually are not necessary for the the-

[5]N. Hartmann, Teleologisches Denken (Teleological Thinking), de Gruyter, Berlin 1951.

ory – cannot be answered (cf. my remarks on the ordinary language on p.304 et seq., which indicate that the concepts of language do not constitute an ordered system, but may rather belong to different language-games.)

If action is not only considered from the point of view of the argumentation structure, but as a real phenomenon, the still open questions pertain particularly to the relationships between the personal action determinants of the individual agent, and to the determining social relations. The theory of institutions, closely connected with the action theory, tries to find clarifying answers here.

Von Wright's greatness lies, in my eyes, in two things: 1. his perspicacity in recognizing essential problems, and 2. his unique ability to propose, again and again, new ingenious constructions for the clarification or solution of the questions posed. I know no other thinker of our age who is gifted with so mobile a mind as von Wright is.

Index of Proper Names

Index of Subjects

THEORY AND DECISION LIBRARY

SERIES A: PHILOSOPHY AND METHODOLOGY OF THE SOCIAL SCIENCES

Editors: W. Leinfellner (*Vienna*) and G. Eberlein (*Munich*)

1. G. Zecha and P. Weingartner (eds.): *Conscience: An Interdisciplinary View*. Salzburg Colloquium on Ethics in the Sciences and Humanities (1984). 1987 ISBN 90-277-2452-0
2. R.W. Scholz: *Cognitive Strategies in Stochastic Thinking*. 1987 ISBN 90-277-2454-7
3. H. Nurmi: *Comparing Voting Systems*. 1987 ISBN 90-277-2600-0
4. M. Schmid and F.M. Wuketits (eds.): *Evolutionary Theory in Social Science*. 1987 ISBN 90-277-2612-4
5. C.L. Sheng: *A New Approach to Utilitarianism*. A Unified Utilitarian Theory and Its Application to Distributive Justice. 1991 ISBN 0-7923-1301-1
6. F. Forman: *The Metaphysics of Liberty*. 1989 ISBN 0-7923-0080-7
7. G. Bernard: *Principia Economica*. 1989 ISBN 0-7923-0186-2
8. J.W. Sutherland: *Towards a Strategic Management and Decision Technology*. Modern Approaches to Organizational Planning and Positioning. 1989 ISBN 0-7923-0245-1
9. C. Vlek and G. Cvetkovich (eds.): *Social Decision Methodology for Technological Projects*. 1989 ISBN 0-7923-0371-7
10. P. Hoyningen-Huene and F.M. Wuketits (eds.): *Reductionism and Systems Theory in the Life Sciences*. Some Problems and Perspectives. 1989 ISBN 0-7923-0375-X
11. K.G. Grunert and F. Ölander (eds.): *Understanding Economic Behaviour*. 1989 ISBN 0-7923-0482-9
12. G. Antonides: *The Lifetime of a Durable Good*. An Economic Psychological Approach. 1990 ISBN 0-7923-0574-4
13. G.M. von Furstenberg (ed.): *Acting under Uncertainty*. Multidisciplinary Conceptions. 1990 ISBN 0-7923-9063-6
14. R.L. Dukes: *Worlds Apart*. Collective Action in Simulated Agrarian and Industrial Societies. 1990 ISBN 0-7923-0620-1
15. S.O. Funtowicz and J.R. Ravetz: *Uncertainty and Quality in Science for Policy*. 1990 ISBN 0-7923-0799-2
16. J. Götschl (ed.): *Erwin Schrödinger's World View*. The Dynamics of Knowledge and Reality. 1992 ISBN 0-7923-1694-0
17. R. von Schomberg (ed.): *Science, Politics and Morality*. Scientific Uncertainty and Decision Making. 1993 ISBN 0-7923-1997-4
18. J. Baron: *Morality and Rational Choice*. 1993 ISBN 0-7923-2276-2
19. M. Allais and O. Hagen (eds.): *Cardinalism*. A Fundamental Approach. 1994 ISBN 0-7923-2398-X
20. E. Carlson: *Consequentialism Reconsidered*. 1995 ISBN 0-7923-3547-3
21. J. Götschl (ed.): *Revolutionary Changes in Understanding Man and Society*. 1995 ISBN 0-7923-3627-5
22. A. Camacho: *Division of Labor, Variability, Coordination, and the Theory of Firms and Markets*. 1996 ISBN 0-7923-3832-4

23. R. Hegselmann, U. Mueller and K.G. Troitzsch (eds.): *Modelling and Simulation in the Social Sciences from the Philosophy of Science Point of View*. 1996
ISBN 0-7923-4125-2
24. J. Nida-Rümelin: *Economic Rationality and Practical Reason*. 1997
ISBN 0-7923-4493-6
25. G. Barbiroli: *The Dynamics of Technology*. A Methodological Framework for Techno-Economic Analyses. 1997 ISBN 0-7923-4756-0
26. O. Weinberger: *Alternative Action Theory*. Simultaneously a Critique of Georg Henrik von Wright's Practical Philosophy. 1998 ISBN 0-7923-5184-3

KLUWER ACADEMIC PUBLISHERS – DORDRECHT / BOSTON / LONDON

Printed by Printforce, the Netherlands